W9-DHH-241

Words and Things

*An Examination of,
and an Attack on,
Linguistic Philosophy*

BY

Ernest Gellner

WITH A FOREWORD BY

Bertrand Russell

ROUTLEDGE & KEGAN PAUL
LONDON, BOSTON AND HENLEY

First published by Victor Gollancz Ltd in October 1959
This revised edition published in 1979
by Routledge & Kegan Paul Ltd
39 Store Street, London WC1E 7DD,
Broadway House, Newtown Road,
Henley-on-Thames, Oxon RG9 1EN and
9 Park Street,
Boston, Mass. 02108, USA

Printed in Great Britain by
Lowe & Brydone Printers Ltd,
Thetford, Norfolk

British Library Cataloguing in Publication Data
Gellner, Ernest
Words and things. – Revised ed.
1. Philosophy, English – 20th century
I. Title
192   B1615   79–40276
ISBN 0 7100 0260 2
ISBN 0 7100 0285 8 Pbk

The later Wittgenstein ... seems to have grown tired of serious thinking and to have invented a doctrine which would make such an activity unnecessary. I do not for one moment believe that the doctrine which has these lazy consequences is true ...

The desire to understand the world is, they think, an outdated folly.

Bertrand Russell

ACKNOWLEDGEMENTS

I AM GREATLY indebted to Mrs. E. Llewellyn for secretarial assistance, to Donald Aldridge for designing the diagram, to Charles Taylor and Arnold Kaufman for reading the book at various stages and making valuable suggestions, and to Norman Birnbaum, Dennis Duerden and Norman Hotopf for reading parts of it and making critical or encouraging comments. The responsibility for the views expressed is of course mine only.

My philosophical debts are obvious or indicated in the text. But I should also express my thanks to the members of the Social Anthropology Department at the L.S.E., who taught me how, without prejudice to its validity, one should see a set of related ideas and practices as a system of mutually supporting, and sometimes conflicting parts, and interpret it in terms of the services it performs and the conditions it requires in the social context of which it is a part.

But my greatest individual debt, and a very considerable one indeed, is to John Hajnal, whose painstaking notes and patient discussions have helped me to be less confused than would otherwise be the case.

CONTENTS

Chapter VII: *Assessment*

Chapter VIII: *Implications*

Chapter IX: *Sociology*

FOREWORD

by

BERTRAND RUSSELL

Mr. GELLNER'S BOOK *Words and Things* deserves the gratitude of all who cannot accept the linguistic philosophy now in vogue at Oxford. It is difficult to guess how much immediate effect the book is likely to have; the power of fashion is great, and even the most cogent arguments fail to convince if they are not in line with the trend of current opinion. But, whatever may be the first reaction to Mr. Gellner's arguments, it seems highly probable—to me, at least—that they will gradually be accorded their due weight.

The first part of his book consists of a careful analysis of the arguments upon which linguistic philosophers rely. He sets forth what he calls "The Four Pillars" of the theory of language which forms the basis of the philosophy in question. The first of these four pillars he calls "the argument from the Paradigm Case". This consists in reasoning from the actual use of words to answers to philosophical problems, or from a conflict in actual uses to the falsehood of a philosophical theory. Mr. Gellner quotes as an example of this argument what some, at least, of the linguistic philosophers regard as a solution of the free-will problem. When a man marries without external compulsion, we may say, "he did it of his own free will". There is, therefore, a linguistically correct use of the words "free will", and therefore there is free will. No one can deny that this is an easy way to solve age-old problems. The second of the four pillars consists in inferring values from the actual use of words. The third, which is called "the Contrast Theory of meaning", maintains that a term only has meaning if there is something that it does not cover. The fourth, which is called "Polymorphism", maintains that, since words have many uses, general assertions about the uses of words are impossible. All these four pillars assume that common speech is sacrosanct, and that it is impious to suppose it capable of improvement. This fundamental dogma, it is not thought necessary to establish.

While the first portion of Mr. Gellner's book is admirably done and very necessary for the support of his general contentions, I have found the later chapters even more interesting. In these later chapters he examines the motivation of the advocates of the new philosophy and the effects which it is likely to have if it remains prevalent. What he has to say in these later chapters will, I fear, be resented, though, in my opinion, unjustly. Linguistic philosophy, he says, "has an inverted vision which treats genuine thought as a disease and dead thought as a paradigm of health". It excludes almost everything that is of genuine interest, and prescribes either ineffable mysticism or dreary exegesis of the nuances of usage. It is attractive because it has renounced science and power, and because it is suitable for "gentlemen" in a society which has become democratic. With a reference to Veblen's theory of conspicuous waste, he accuses it of "conspicuous triviality". It holds, he says, that the best kind of thought is pedantic and dull, and that ideas are to be eschewed because they are generally products of carelessness and confusion. This criticism is summed up in an epigram: "A cleric who loses his faith abandons his calling, a philosopher who loses *his* redefines his subject."

Behind all the minute argumentation of the linguistic philosophers, there is a curious kind of arid mysticism. In Wittgenstein's *Tractatus*, the mysticism still had a certain substantiality, but with time it has grown continually more dim and dusty. Nevertheless, it remains an essential ingredient. Wittgenstein maintained that there are things of which one cannot speak. This view, which is an essential part of all mysticism, Mr. Gellner parodies and rejects in the final sentence of his book: "That which one would insinuate, thereof one must speak."

For my own part, I find myself in very close agreement with Mr. Gellner's doctrines as set forth in this book. The outlook which underlies the linguistic philosophy is one which has recurred at intervals throughout the history of philosophy and theology. Its most logical and complete form was advocated by those who adopted the Abecedarian heresy. These heretics maintained that all human knowledge is evil, and, since it is based upon the alphabet, it is a mistake to learn even the ABC. Carlstadt, originally an ally of Luther, after adopting this heresy, "forsook all study of Holy Scripture and looked for Divine truth at the mouths of those who, by all ordinary men, were accounted the most ignorant of mankind"*. In milder forms, similar doctrines have been not uncommon. Pascal's dictum "the heart has its reasons which reason does not know" leads easily to such views. So does Rousseau's adulation of the "Noble Savage". Tolstoy's admiration of the peasants, and his preference for *Uncle Tom's Cabin* to more sophisticated literature, belong to the same way of feeling. The Oxford Abecedarians do not reject *all* human learning, but only such as is not required for a First in Greats—i.e., such as has been discovered since the time of Erasmus. This, surely, is a somewhat arbitrary limit. I cannot see why we should not condemn everything discovered since the time of Homer or the time of Adam and Eve. It is only by means of a mystic illumination that science is shown to be unnecessary for a philosopher, and one would suppose that the insight thus derived might just as well be more sweeping.

When I was a boy, I had a clock with a pendulum which could be lifted off. I found that the clock went very much faster without the pendulum. If the main purpose of a clock is to go, the clock was the better for losing its pendulum. True, it could no longer tell the time, but that did not matter if one could teach oneself to be indifferent to the passage of time. The linguistic philosophy, which cares only about language, and not about the world, is like the boy who preferred the clock without the pendulum because, although it no longer told the time, it went more easily than before and at a more exhilarating pace.

* *Dictionary of Sects, Heresies, Ecclesiastical Parties and Schools of Religious Thought,* edited by the Rev. John Henry Blunt, D.D.

THE SALTMINES OF SALZBURG

or

WITTGENSTEINIANISM RECONSIDERED IN HISTORICAL CONTEXT

"In the saltmines of Salzburg, they throw a bare winter branch into the worked-out depths of the mine. Two or three months later it is brought out covered with brilliant crystallisations: the tiniest twigs no bigger than a titmouse's claw, are decked with myriad diamonds, dazzling and ever-changing; the original branch is unrecognisable.

I use the word *crystallisation* to describe how, with everything that occurs, the mind discovers new perfections in the beloved." (Stendhal, *On Love*.)

But it is not so in love alone. Things come to pass in this manner in *belief* as well. Faith is a form of love. The world is rich in interconnected systems of ideas. Many of them clearly possess considerable merits. But generally speaking, we can take them or leave them. Not all of them fascinate and dominate us. Mostly they hang in our cupboard like suits, to be taken out on appropriate occasions, cleaned if necessary and then put away again.

But not all of them. Some systems of ideas are exceptional. Some of them we love. Some undergo a Stendhalian crystal-lisation. It is this which marks off what is properly called ideology. It is pointless to use this term to cover any system of ideas whatever. An ideology is a system of ideas with a power-ful sex appeal. In fact, Stendhal did call his study of love *un livre d'idéologie*, though not with exactly the same point in mind. He apologises:

"I apologise to the philosophers for using the word *ideology*: it was certainly not my intention to usurp a title which by right belongs to another. If ideology is a detailed description of ideas and all the parts of which they are composed, the present work is a description . . . (of) *love* . . . I do not know the Greek word meaning discourse on feelings, as ideology means discourse on ideas.''

It isn't so much that we need one word for an account of ideas and another for an account of sentiments, but rather we need one word for the clusters of ideas which engender powerful sentiments (and perhaps the other way round).

Now there can be no shadow of doubt but that the later ideas of Ludwig Wittgenstein did undergo crystallisation. Those who were entranced by them, at the time of their first impact, were not savouring them as but one set of ideas amongst others, due to take its place in the long procession of human thoughts. No: this was all-embracing, this was a final fulfilment, or a new dawn, or indeed both at once. "Once the crystallisation has begun, one revels in each new beauty that one discovers in the beloved.''

Now just what was the branch or twig thrown into these saltmines of Salzburg? And just what was the mechanism which produced such enchantment? What cravings were satisfied by it?

THE TASKS

Modern thought does not live in a vacuum. It faces certain pervasive problems. The serious ones amongst them are not in the least invented by and within the professional guild of thinkers. They arise independently, and inescapably impose themselves on our attention. Two such problems have persistently haunted modern thought:

(1) the problem of validation;

(2) the problem of enchantment.

Over and above this, there is also a problem which is merely internal to the thinkers' guild:

(3) the issue of its own professionalisation.

The twig which Ludwig Wittgenstein threw into the saltmines of Salzburg some time during or around the 1930s, re-emerged a little later covered with glittering diamonds, or so it seemed. Why so? The central part of the answer is perfectly clear. With one and the same simple idea, Wittgenstein solved, or so it appeared, *each* of these three problems.

VALIDATION

The problem of validation is absolutely central, and is beset by a number of profound difficulties. In fact, the number and awkwardness of these difficulties has increased under modern conditions. One difficulty is that of regress. Where and how can you stop in the chain of justifications? Either you are willing to give reasons for your premisses—in which case they are *ipso facto* not final, and the argument goes on—or you are not willing to give reasons—in which case you are being dogmatic and arbitrary.

Liberalism and individualism have aggravated the problem. It is widely felt that every individual should take responsibility for the norms and standards which govern his activities. It seems somewhat shameful for him to pass the buck. So if he relies on some putative external proof or authority, he is guilty of *mauvaise foi* or of abdicating his free choice or whatever. If, on the other hand, no such proof is available or he makes no use of it, is he not guilty of caprice? You cannot win.

There are obvious features of our social and intellectual climate which underscore this problem. If a society has a homogeneous world picture, underwritten by both political and clerical authority, answers to terminal questions are built into that very picture. For a variety of familiar reasons, there is no such picture now and, in liberal states, no one enforces it.

Around the beginning of this century, a new strategy for dealing with the problem of the regress of validation became fashionable. If you cannot beat them, disqualify them! If you cannot prove rival views to be *false*, then say that they are *meaningless!* This is validation of one view by means of the exclusion of possible rivals from eligibility as candidates, in virtue of their claims having "no meaning".

THE MEANING PLOY

Laymen are often puzzled that philosophers should be so hung up about *meaning*. The meaning-gimmick of modern thought is a big part of the answer. Bitter experience has shown that you cannot, without circularity or regress, show your own picture to be *true*, and its rivals to be *false*. But if the rival contentions cannot be shown (without circularity) to be false, perhaps they can be *devoid of meaning* instead? Why on earth had we not thought of this before? Why, this must obviously be the solution that had so long eluded us! Hurrah!

The idea that *meaninglessness* might provide the solution to the problem of validation and regress was not just a passing fancy plucked out of the air. As a loose way of denigrating rival viewpoints it is of course very old. For instance, Friedrich Engels used it in a letter to J. Bloch:

> "the ultimately determining element in history is the production and reproduction of real life. More then this neither Marx nor I even asserted. Hence if someone twists this into saying that the economic element is the only determining one, he transforms that proposition into a meaningless, abstract, senseless phrase. . ."

Clearly here "meaningless" and "senseless" are just ways of saying "not true". But about the turn of the century, developments occurred which fed the hope that one might turn something which had once been but a stylish form of abuse, into the very base and foundations of our vision of the world. The so-called Absolute Idealists had anticipated this idea. One further and important source of encouragement for this egregious hope came from the work in the foundations of mathematics. Logic had acquired a new notation with a rigorously prescribed syntax. It was found that some expressions, though they satisfy the rules of this notation, nevertheless generate contradictions. If you can get your mind around the concept-twister known as Russell's paradox, ask yourself: is the class-of-all-classes-which-are-not-members-of-themselves, itself a member of itself? If it is, then it isn't; but if it isn't, then it is. This problem rocked the foundations of mathematics in Russell's opinion. The question *could* be formulated within the existing rules of the logical notation (designed to provide mathematics with its foundation) and thus it "had meaning". Yet either answer—Yes or No—implied its opposite. Such contradictions are not to be tolerated.

The solution proposed was to exclude the kinds of expression which are responsible for these difficulties as *meaningless*, as violating the limits of meaning, even although they had not violated any of the initial rules of notation or "grammar". Meaning evidently has its limits of which the mind knows nothing, at least until properly instructed.

This gave "meaninglessness", once just a classy piece of abuse, a good technical, mathematical, scientific standing and role. It lurked where we did not suspect it, ready to snare us into unsuspected absurdity. We had to be vigilant and exclude whatever permitted "meaninglessness". And if this worked here, could it perhaps also work in other awkward spheres. . . ?

That *meaning* is the basic starting point of twentieth-century philosophy is asserted for instance, by Professor Michael Dummett in his much acclaimed *Frege. Philosophy of Language* (London, Duckworth, 1973, p. xv):

> "the centre of gravity of philosophy has altered. . . The most far-reaching part of Descartes' revolution was to make epistemology the most basic sector of the whole philosophy . . . Descartes' perspective continued to be that which dominated philosophy until this century, when it was overthrown by Wittgenstein who in the *Tractatus* reinstated philosophic logic as the foundation of philosophy. . ."

But, "The *Tractatus* is a pure essay in the theory of meaning. . ." (p. 679). And in the very final sentence of the book: ". . . the revolution which made the theory of meaning the foundation of philosophy. . ." One may have doubts about this second revolution. If *meaning* is a notion which can be used to exclude rival doctrines, and if it also blesses that which it does cover— and *both* these ideas were clearly held by Wittgenstein—then it does really look terribly like a crypto-epistemology, a camouflaged normative doctrine about what we may know and hence—what we *are*.

Meaning-preoccupation functions as a crypto-epistemology twice over. It proscribes rival views. But also, by instructing thinkers to concentrate on what we "mean", it implies that *truth* is not their business, and hence that they cannot hold our views to account, and hence that they must leave everything "as it is". Thus it can damn dissident views; and it can bless our inherited or favoured set of ideas, which otherwise may seem to be in dire peril, by excluding their critique from philosophy, and thus providing them with a kind of clearance.

THE EMPIRICIST CONFLUENCE

There is also another idea of meaninglessness. A language is a set of noises or marks, or the rules governing these, and the functions they perform. It is intuitively plausible to suppose that language only performs the job of reporting on reality if it interacts with reality, if it somehow varies concomittantly with it. If reality is *this way*, then one says one thing; if it is *another* way, one says another. But if there is some bit of language, some part of that system of noises and marks, which insensitively remains constant *whatever* things are like, well then is it doing any job at all. . . ? Does it have any real *meaning?* As Wittgenstein once put it: "If a sign is *not necessary* then it is meaningless. That is the meaning of Occam's razor." (*Tractatus*, 3.328.) Signs which do no work are not earning their keep. Their job is to mirror the world. Those signs which make no contribution towards this end are redundant parasites. This idea underlies certain theories of language and of mind, and obviously it has a certain inherent plausibility.

This is where Wittgenstein's youthful work, the famous *Tractatus Logico-Philosophicus*, comes in. In it, Wittgenstein in effect *combined* those two ideas. The new technical "meaninglessness" hinged on proscribing certain kinds of self-reference, which were held to be responsible for those paradoxes or contradictions. The *Tractatus* drew a tight severe circle around what language may do, around what "may be said", a circle which, at the same time, also corresponded roughly to the old philosophical idea that language is only doing its job if it interacts with reality, if it "reflects facts".

Reality was conceived in a very granular way, and this was taken for granted. Language would do no more than reflect and collate these grains. But the *reason* given for this old restriction was the new interdict on self-reference, borrowed from or inspired by the experience with formal notations, where self-reference had led to trouble. There, self-reference had been banned, declared "meaningless", so as to obviate certain paradoxes, such as Russell's, which were seen as consequences of it. The diagnosis of the habit of transcending the limits of meaning, of going out of linguistic bounds of philosophy, was that it attempted to say something about the relationship of language to reality within that language itself, and thus to be self-referential. Language or thought, as Keynes once put it, was trying to catch its own tail. So the two kinds of "meaninglessness" converged. The proscription of anything which "lacked meaning" however allowed but one vision, which thus became the unique residual legatee of truth. So a unique vision was vindicated, vindicated exclusively and, in the author's estimation, with finality.

WITTGENSTEIN WHEN HE WAS YOUNG

Note that the *Tractatus* (in which this outlook was presented), though a very highly poetical work, was never really rewarded with a Stendhalian crystallisation, except perhaps in its author's eyes. He, at the time when he wrote it, found its conclusions beyond doubt or challenge, and was not inhibited by any modesty from saying so. Others, notably one of its earliest readers, Bertrand Russell, were not at all of the same view. But in any case, the *Tractatus* never succeeded in assembling a community of shared-crystal-gazers, in the way in which Wittgenstein's later work did.

Yet, as a work of poetry, it will live. It deserves to stand on the shelf next to the poetic works of T. S. Eliot. It has the same pessimism, portentousness, pretentiousness, and fringe mysticism. But above all, it belongs to the same period and employs the very same stylistic devices. Eliot had taken themes, allusions, symbols which had, by the then stale conventions of Victorian or Georgian lyricism, been conspicuously un-poetic, and welded them into a literary unity with poetic and "deep" elements. These thereby acquired or regained a freshness and impact which, on their own, they could no longer command. And precisely this mix, the same reinforcement of the mystico-poetic by the prosaic elements dredged from the daily life of an industrial and scientific age, is also found in Wittgenstein's *Tractatus*.

But really the philosopher did it better and more effectively than the poet. Eliot's borrowings from ordinary unpoetic speech, however accurately observed and skilfully deployed in the texture of a poem, always retained the air of being dredged up from a world which was not the poet's own, probably with a gloved hand if not with pincers, and the result was a kind of *collage*. Now Wittgenstein's poetry was different. Far from being a collage, it claimed logical continuity for all the elements it employed. His reinforcement-borrowings were from technical logic and mathematics, not common speech, and they were welded with the deep and cultural stuff into what purported to be an absolute and indissoluble unity. All the propositions in the *Tractatus* were *numbered*. This conveyed that they were part of one indissoluble system. There were only (very significantly) *seven* of them with cardinal numbers, and the others, in between, had to make do with decimals, on the library-catalogue principle, which indicated their place in the system and hierarchy of importance. In the original German, the last and culminating tantalising-mystical proposition can, as is well known, be sung to the tune of Good King Wenceslas. *Wovon man nicht sprechen kann, darüber muss man schweigen.*

Consider some examples of the deep stuff:

The sense of the world must lie outside the world, . . . all happening and being-so is accidental.

Ethics and aesthetics are one.

Of the will as the subject of the ethical we cannot speak.

The world of the happy is quite another than that of the unhappy.

Death is not an event in life.

The solution of the riddle of life in space and time lies *outside* space and time.

The solution of the problem of life is seen in the vanishing of this problem.

But there are also the prosaic-technical and ultra-modern elements:

We must not say, "The complex sign 'aRb' says '*a* stands in relation *R* to *b*' ", but we must say, "that '*a*' stands in a certain relation to '*b*' says that *aRb*".

If we change a constituent part of a proposition into a variable, there is a class of propositions which are all the values of the resulting variable propositions.

No doubt all this also means something, but the heart of the matter is that the two kinds of element in this poem are claimed to be parts of a single continuous, seamless unity. (They even all have, literally, the very same status, in as far as they are all disavowed by the author himself as meaningless at the end.) Now any humanist intellectual can make observations such as that the world of the happy is different from that of the unhappy, etc., etc. He can do it as part of an essay, TV programme, or dinner-table conversation. Some do it better and some worse, and Wittgenstein's efforts in this genre do not rise above what is customary in purple passages of novels.

Likewise, there were and are other men competent in technical logic, with views on the questions treated in some of the earlier parts of the *Tractatus*. Here again his work, though highly distinguished, is not unique. What was quite unique was the *joint* presentation of both these elements, as one unity, dramatically defying the boundary of what later came to be called the Two Cultures.

And yet, despite this remarkable performance, no crystallisation took place. The work had and deserved a certain *éclat*, but that was all.

But note that it would (if accepted) solve the problem of validation. A tight and severe circle is drawn around the legitimate kind of discourse, thereby outlawing all rivals, and this settles the problem of choosing between rival visions, by proscribing all but one—a really dramatic use of the new *meaning-ploy* in philosophy, as described. At the same time, a remarkably permissive *carte blanche* is also issued to mankind in the later, mystical parts of the *Tractatus*—to indulge its religious or other leanings, provided only they are not expressed in words. But only that which was spoken, articulated, was treated so severely and restrictively. If you found other means of communication, that was allright. The Cambridge philosopher Frank Ramsey observed with irony, apropos of Wittgenstein's remarkable double standards for the spoken and the intimated, that if you could not say something you could not say it, and you couldn't whistle it either. Wittgenstein evidently thought otherwise.

But all the same, no crystallisation took place on that occasion. As Stendhal would no doubt agree, there is one big difference between the saltmines of Salzburg and the birth of a *Schwaermerei*: the fate of a twig in Salzburg can perhaps be predicted, but intellectual/emotional crystallisations cannot. They occur mysteriously and as mysteriously fail to occur. It did not befall the *Tractatus*. The twig, attractive though it was, remained but a twig. But his second try proved more successful. Then the magic did work, and with a vengeance.

WITTGENSTEIN WHEN HE WAS OLD

His second position was both a continuation and an inversion of the original one. What it was, and how both continuity and inversion were achieved, can perhaps best be seen if one considers how both positions handled the two great problems of Validation and Enchantment. His early position satisfied both needs, but in an uncomfortably tight, constraining manner. Science and mathematics were re-validated, so to speak, in as far as they met the requirements of his formal, notation-inspired model; so were common-sense assertions, but only in as far as they were abbreviated or coded versions of the former; and so was mystical awareness, but only as long as it remained mute and dumb. It is an impoverished world, and not one which many would wish to inhabit. For instance, the exciting areas within which historical or scientific facts inspire, support or contradict our basic human self-image—in other words a great part of the intellectual history of mankind—was not merely not catered for, but explicitly proscribed by the vision of the *Tractatus*. "The Darwinian theory has no more to do with philosophy than has any other hypothesis of natural science" (*Tractatus*, 4.1122).

This is quite false. Darwinism *is* philosophically relevant. It contradicts one world-enchanting thesis—namely, the idea that the world is the custom-made, purpose-endowed creation of a God. It also happens to suggest other and rival meaningful visions. The choice between such options is philosophy.

Things were different in his "later philosophy", expounded in *Philosophical Investigations* and other posthumously published works, though the exclusion of the content of science and history from philosophy persisted. He continued to provide validation by means of that characteristically twentieth-century philosophical gimmick, the circumscription of meaning. But the theory of meaning itself which was to delimit the zone of that which had meaning was now dramatically inverted. The rules were no longer to be supplied by the requirements of the foundations of mathematics, or the principles of a universal notation: now the rules were given by nothing more or less than *actual linguistic custom*. Validation was still achieved—but it was now much broader and more permissive. Language was its own master; it was not subservient to formal logic or notation; it served many purposes; and the norms and practices it observed in so doing legitimated themselves, and neither required nor allowed any other kind of validation.

Let us see how sympathetic observers characterised this.

"That there can be no . . . superior tribunal has also been one theme of contemporary analytical philosophy in Britain, beginning in the late 1930s and gaining strength since the war. Philosophy as a kind of anthropology of knowledge and belief is a conception revived in the later work of Wittgenstein. His suggestion was that we should turn our attention to the justifications of belief, and of claims to knowledge, which are customarily accepted, and not look for a rationally satisfying justification altogether outside our established habits of thought: such a justification could never in principle be found. The proper work of philosophy is purely descriptive, to set out the linguistic facts that reveal our habits of thought. . ." (Professor S. Hampshire, in *David Hume: a Symposium*, ed. D. F. Pears, London, Macmillan, 1963, p. 5.)

Or again

"[what] Wittgenstein calls 'forms of life'. Human speech and activity, sanity and community, rest upon nothing more, but nothing less, than this. It is a vision as simple as it is difficult." (Professor S. Cavell, *Must we mean what we say?*, Cambridge University Press, 1976, p. 52.)

Difficult to understand it is not. We can see perfectly well how, *were it true*, it would solve our problem of validating what we do. Cultures, "forms of life", are self-justifying. So the problem of validation is solved. But the cultures which provide the solution also contain that ample richness which gives our life its fulness. So, the very same move which so easily solved the problem of validation, also generously solved the problem of Enchantment.

ENCHANTMENT

The problem of Enchantment is largely a speciality of modern post-Cartesian man. Curiously enough, philosophers do not discuss it under this name, and indeed do not have any name for it at all. The less perceptive ones amongst them, who only recognise what is officially on the curriculum under its own name, and have little sense for the latent questions which can pervade a debate, may well deny that they are preoccupied with it at all. But in fact, most if not all modern philosophies are obsessed with it. Sociologists by contrast are rather familiar with it under more than one name. The name used here comes of course from Max Weber, who discussed the obverse—Disenchantment.

The problem is simple. Modern man is (*a*) numerous, (*b*) habituated to and greedy for comfort and affluence. He can only be maintained in the style to which he wishes to be accustomed at the price of abstract science, powerful technology and large-scale organisation. These jointly presuppose, in turn, a certain way of organising both our concepts and our institutions: they require regular, orderly explanatory schemata and conduct. These in their turn destroy warmth, idiosyncrasy, individualism, magic, enchantment. These lost traits of course survived in our speech from the past, but the confidence had gone out of them. They are to a real enchantment as filling Xmas stockings is to a real faith-pervaded world.

The "late-Wittgenstein" theory of language, and of the authority it conferred on all its customs and norms, simply in virtue of being part of a natural language, changed all this with a single stroke—and it was the very same stroke which had also solved the problem of validating the norms of our life. It saved our rich old *Lebenswelt* whose practices and perceptions are built into our language, as well as validating our principles. At long last we could embrace both our principles and our mistress, and yet fear neither pox nor gallows. If ordinary speech, and the entire corpus of custom of which it is part, are a self-justifying system which neither permits nor requires external validation—well then, we need never fear the erosion of our customary ideas and of the identity articulated in terms of them. Disenchantment thus proves a hollow and groundless fear. Our idiom is shown to have a firm, secure grasp on reality; and the reality in terms of which we live is shown to be sound and true. The sickening sense of living in a dream, powerlessly, is exorcised.

To do so much, and to do it with such an economy of means! This twig, extracted from the saltmine, shone with an eye-dazzling brilliance.

WHAT ARE WE DOING?

As if all this weren't achievement enough, it also at the same time solved the little internal problem facing the thinkers' guild, concerning its own professional status and role. This is not of universal significance, like the other two problems, but it is not without interest or indeed amusement-value.

Philosophical thought in free modern societies operates under terms of reference which are difficult if not downright absurd. Once upon a time, it was not so. When there was a recognised final Authority and intellectual court of appeal, the professional thinker could perform a useful function and he could do so with dignity—especially if the authoritative truths were available in a Holy Writ, and literacy which gave access to it was a specialist accomplishment which he did not share with all and sundry. Surrogate final sources of truth have since been sought—the Inner Light of Reason, Experience, History, Nature—but unfortunately these ladies do not speak with a clear, single or unambiguous voice.

The questions are still there, but the answers have gone. There are various further well-known features of our scene which aggravate the situation. Universal literacy and egalitarian liberalism deprive the thinker of any right to claim special insights. Substantive knowledge of nature is on skids—it is now recognised that the findings of science are transient, and thus the most prestigious form of knowledge is also at the same time highly unstable and thereby, so to speak, sets a bad example for all those who understandably seek reliable and permanent solutions. The sheer quantity, specialisation and technicality of a great deal of knowledge makes synoptic visions difficult or impossible. Yet general questions will not go away.

Is there any point in institutionalising a specialised profession dealing with them? There is no very obvious answer to this. If one simply abolished the profession, the handling of these questions would re-appear in other fields and as parts of leisure activities. In considerable measure this happens anyway, and it is arguable that valuable contributions to philosophy have of late come mainly or exclusively from outside the profession (from linguistics, logic, the history of science, the social sciences). On the other hand, it is equally arguable that the existence of a guild, professionally obliged to maintain some measure of familiarity with the history of human thought and with the main opening moves and strategies in it, does somewhat raise the level of debate.

I am not at all clear or confident about this matter and it is reasonable to suspect that this uncertainty is well grounded, for the solution adopted from country to country varies wildly. What counts as "a philosopher" differs far more from country to country, or even within them, than is the case for any other "subject". Societies or cultures which do not differ radically in other respects, display extreme differences at this point, which would seem to suggest that the shared intellectual or social situation of our time does not of itself impose any single solution on us.

The local constraints operating in the milieu in which the Wittgensteinian twig crystallised were very distinctive, and relate intimately to the professionalisation-of-thought problem. The British educational system and its tertiary sector are sharply stratified in terms of social prestige, and the most prestigious universities are at one and the same time serious centres of learning and finishing schools. Their distinctiveness and attraction hinge on this conflation. In no subject, however, is this double role, this double set of constraints or requirements, more visible and operative than in philosophy. The terminal, ultimate, and humanly relevant nature of the questions treated not only produces the difficult terms of reference sketched out above: it also and at the same time makes the subject continuous with what educated or thoughtful people discuss without pedantry when they meet in relaxed conversation, say at a dinner table. There is an overlap (and rightly so) between the nature of the musings of a Hamlet, the general, strategic issues facing a scientist, and the conversational accomplishments of a cultivated person. And indeed, one would not wish this to be otherwise.

But here once again, the Wittgensteinian solution is quite perfect. Philosophy is equated with the guardianship of conceptual table manners. It is actual linguistic custom which is authoritative and thus defines the bounds of sense, which takes care of the problem of validation. By validating the *content* of our existing intellectual customs, a solution for the problem of enchantment is equally and simultaneously provided. The *method* permits and encourages philosophy-as-bavardage, whilst the *conclusions* leave room for any cherished obscurantism.

How so? The idea that "meaning" is a circumscribed island is retained; and so is the associated use of this delimitation as a *norm* of how we may rightly speak and think. But it is now a different and *much* more spacious island—namely that of our actual, customary speech. Previously the vernacular had been but a messy, inferior, folk edition of a Goodspeak, which in turn was scientifically, logically, and mathematically prescribed by the needs of a fact-mirroring, contradiction- and redundancy-avoiding Occamist notation. Now it was the other way round. Ordinary speech was normative, because it was functional within our 'form of life' (culture), and because this very functionality ('use') actually *defined* meaning. Thus rival views were still excluded as devoid of meaning. But the retained views were now much richer and enchantment-guaranteeing. The earlier misguided pursuit of a universal notation, aspiring to transcend all concrete, socially incarnate functions of language, and sitting in judgment on them, was said to be the very root and source of all philosophic errors, and indeed of all past philosophy.

All this also solved the problem of the professional role of the paid thinker. He attends to the uses of speech, and finally, and above all, cures the temptation to diverge from the existing verbal custom.

The Wittgensteinian solution was all the more attractive in that it called on pre-existing locally traditional skills of linguistic sensitivity, and thereby ensured them an outlet and worthy employment. There were other attractions. The solution provided for a handling of philosophical questions which implied no dogmatic authority, no access to supernatural realms, no deep cognitive inequality. Those, to our modern minds, seem archaic, uncivilised devices for ensuring assent. The naturalism, secularism, egalitarianism of the age were not offended. And yet perfect validation was attained; so was re-Enchantment; and so was secure professionalisation. Can one conceivably wonder at the success of this philosophy?

BETWEEN NATURALISM AND MYSTICISM

Modern thought faces the twin problems of validation and enchantment: the need on the one hand to justify the basic premisses of the options we have collectively chosen or will choose, in our cognitive, political, economic and other styles, and, on the other, to save our picture of the world and of ourselves from that icy disenchantment which threatens to engulf us. These two often conflicting tasks are faced against the background of two different thought styles, which may loosely be called naturalism-secularism on the one hand, and romanticism-mysticism on the other. Other names are available and in use, and nothing hinges on the names as such.

What it amounts to is this. On the one hand, there is an inevitable and progressively increasing elimination of appeals to the supernatural, the transcendent or the idiosyncratic. Time was when the supernatural put its seal on the crucial parts of the natural and social world, ratifying political authority, confirming the great *rites de passage*, giving answers to the terminal questions, and so forth. As it gradually disappears both from nature and society, it also comes eventually to be eliminated from knowledge: no special, unsymmetrical, exclusive claims are to be entertained. All claims to knowledge are subjected to the same kinds of test and to the same humiliating, holiness-precluding doubt and scrutiny. This equally applies to types of explanation, which are also subjected to corresponding kinds of requirements of intelligibility and symmetry.

It is the pressure of such naturalism or secularism which makes the problem of validation so difficult. Natural explanations make manipulation *easy*, and make awe *difficult*. Their very naturalness, transience, human and earthy roots preclude reverence. By contrast, validations which really clinch matters, by appealing to something outside and above, are hard to believe; and those which can be believed, only validate (at best) in a lukewarm, and often a conditional, un-authoritative manner.

That very naturalism, which makes validation so difficult, at the same time also constitutes the problem of disenchantment. In a way, it *is* disenchantment. Another (pejorative) name for it is "reductionism". But *reduction* is the inescapable fate of intellectual life, the price of our cognitive advance. To explain something is always a matter of showing it to be really something else, where the something else is more general, and behaves in the same orderly manner wherever it happens to be found—and this *ipso facto* excludes idiosyncrasy, uniqueness, individuality, warmth, and any special and reassuring relationship to the knower.

Wittgenstein's early philosophy was already directed at a simultaneous solution of both these problems. The early part in effect told us, under the guise of a story about "meaning", what actual valid cognition was really like, and just how very narrow its limits were. It allegedly consisted of mirrors-simulacra of atoms of reality, and the cumulation of such little mirrors. The final parts of the book told us what remained to be said—or rather, what was *not* to be said—about What Was Left, those mystical realms of ultimate human concern.

But what a pathetically unsatisfactory effort that had been! No wonder it never caught on. It is not just that, as an account of scientific knowledge, the mirror-plus-cumulation theory is grossly inadequate. This is a so to speak technical inadequacy which would not have dimished the appeal of the theory, had it been otherwise attractive. Simply as an ideological commodity, as a satisfaction of the needs of validation and of enchantment, it was a rather poor specimen, unlikely to give widespread satisfaction and to receive popular acclaim.

What it offered was dreadfully narrow. At one end, the area which was re-validated was so very severely circumscribed that it resembled the stringent cognitive puritanism of the most severe of radical empiricists, and not surprisingly the doctrine was often confused with theirs. At the other end, the re-enchantment, conferment of meaning-of-life, was also in its own way terribly austere. The mystical was to be strictly mute and also quite devoid of any specific incarnation in nature or history: no natural or historic fact was to be specially sacred. ("All propositions are of equal value." *Tractatus*, 6.4.) The mystical was everywhere and nowhere, symmetrically, in a rather pantheist way.

Men generally find it very difficult to deprive themselves of graven images, of special incarnations of the divine, as the unavailing zeal of iconoclasts demonstrates; and the functional equivalent of graven images in modern secular faiths are very special events (*the* Revolution, past or to come, natural selection, national liberation, or whatever) *inside* the world. But within this austerely symmetrical vision there was no room for anything of the kind. There was to be nothing sacred in nature or in history. The sacred was to be invisible and acknowledged only in silence—though the author of this view granted himself a special dispensation to speak, explaining why *others* must remain silent.

Yet, despite this unsatisfactoriness, the theory was a good trial run and harbinger for that later version of his position which, notoriously, was to be so very generously blessed with crystallisation. That later theory retained both the validation-by-theory-of-meaning, and that simultaneous double gratification of the validity-requirement and enchantment-requirement; and, as described, the theory of meaning in question was *even more* naturalistic. Meaning is now defined and bounded by custom, it really *is* linguistic custom, nothing else, and what is there more natural and mundane than human custom? Even the cogency of mathematics, an old problem or ideal for philosophy, was to be explained in terms of human custom, convention and decision*. But this theory of meaning was also more pliable and permissive than the old one. It does not narrowly circumscribe legitimate cognition; nor does it banish the mystical, the sense-of-life-activities, to an eternal if pregnant silence. Henceforth, the mystical could be as voluble and garrulous as it wished. Nor was it debarred from indulging in those highly specific incarnations which seem so dear to the human heart.

THE TRUE CENTRE

This is the essence of the matter. An admirer of Wittgenstein, in the final culminating summary of the end chapter significantly entitled "The True Centre", has noted this, in slightly different language:

> "it is only half of the truth to say that his resistance to science produced his later . . . philosophy. There was also his linguistic naturalism, which played an equally important role. The two tendencies, one of them anti-positivistic and the other in a more subtle way positivistic, are not dia-

* See, for instance, Professor Michael Dummett, "Reckonings—Wittgenstein on Mathematics", in *Encounter*, March 1978.

metrically opposed to each other. . . . Each of the two forces without the other would have produced results of much less interest. The linguistic naturalism by itself would have been a dreary kind of philosophy done under a low and leaden sky. The resistance to science by itself might have led to almost any kind of nonsense. But together they produced something truly great." (David Pears: *Wittgenstein*, London, Fontana/Collins, 1971, pp. 183, 184.)

This needs a little translation: anti-science or anti-positivism corresponds to what I have described as the tendency towards enchantment or mysticism. But leaving aside the final evaluation, the summary is very perceptive, astonishingly so given that the author seems to have but a limited grasp of what his statement really implies.

Distinguished fellow-members of the linguistic movement such as Gilbert Ryle, or J. L. Austin, of course shared and emulated Wittgenstein's linguistic naturalism and the method based on it. They did not share the other crucial element in his philosophical and personal make-up, namely his mysticism ("resistance to science"). The very idea of secret indulgence in mysticism by Gilbert Ryle or J. L. Austin will produce a smile on the sternest face. So, in these thinkers, the linguistic naturalism operated on its own. By the iron laws of logic, what follows is, in Mr Pears' own words, "a dreary kind of philosophy done under a low and leaden sky".

The two tendencies, the linguistic naturalism and the permissive mysticism ("anti-positivistic . . . resistance to science . . .") are not merely not diametrically opposed, they are strictly complementary and require each other in the production of Wittgenstein's particular brew. The linguistic naturalism, the reduction of the basis of our thought to linguistic etiquette, ensures that there is no appeal whatever to Extraneous Authority for the manner in which we speak and think. Naturalism, this-worldliness, is thus pushed to its final limit. But at the very same time, and for that very reason (language and custom being their own masters, beholden and accountable to no Outside norm), the diversified content of language and custom is indiscriminately endorsed. Thus the transcendent, if and when required, slips back ambiguously, in virtue of being the object of natural practices, customs, modes of speech. Ironically, it was just because the theory of language contained in the *Tractatus* was covertly not quite naturalistic, but rather prescriptive, that it could endeavour to draw a tight line around cognition proper. But now, a self-justifying corpus of linguistic custom revalidates whatever you wish, and yet also re-enchants the world. "Philosophy leaves everything as it is."

SATISFACTION GUARANTEED

Thus the two fundamental—and, alas, opposed—requirements of modern thought seem to be satisfied simultaneously and by the very same move! But there is more to it than that. It is not just that the problems of validation *and* of enchantment are given a unique and seemingly final answer, and one which satisfies the most demanding exigencies of naturalism, whilst yet also bestowing on us the richest, most colourful and fully enchanted world. The achievement of the Wittgensteinian belief system is even greater than this.

The formula made it possible to mix the two elements *in any desired proportion*. The philosophy is in effect a Do-It-Yourself ideological kit, a *carte blanche* for the construction of any desired world, in which the proportions of naturalism and mysticism can be precisely what your particular taste requires. Once again, Stendhal foresaw it all:

> "Once the crystallisation has begun, one revels in each new beauty that one discovers in the beloved.
>
> But what is beauty? It is a new capacity for giving one pleasure.
>
> Everyone's pleasures are different, and often contradictory: that is why what is beauty for one person is ugliness for another. . .
>
> The crystallisation formed in each man's head must be the same *colour* as that man's pleasures."

Enchantment may generically be the same for us all, but the specific content of what we cherish varies a great deal. The philosophy under discussion does not merely guarantee Enchantment for All, but also supplies an easy-to-follow recipe for providing that particular combination of delights, that specific brew of naturalism and mysticism, which corresponds to any one of an endless variety of possible individual tastes. You simply pick the contents of those particular kinds of discourse, "forms of life", "language games", which you happen to favour—be that form of life religion, art, or anything else. The validity of the content is thus ensured; as language-in-general (which includes this particular language game) is viewed naturalistically, as de facto custom, *and* is validated by the claim that language is the measure of all things (there being no other measure), the position is at the same time protected from the most stringent, positivistic, reductionist critique. Not just protected: it is itself the most ultimate, most uncompromising form of such a critique! An erstwhile practitioner, Professor Alastair MacIntyre, looks back on this method of re-enchantment, as favoured by himself in the field of religion:

> "[The] central contention, alike my own [at the time] has been that religion is a specific form of life with its own criteria, its own methods of settling its own questions." (*Metaphysical Beliefs*, by S. Toulmin, R. W. Hepburn, A. MacIntyre, preface by A. MacIntyre to 1970 edition, p. x; SCM Press, 1970.)

As the author later noted the position was its own *reductio ad absurdum*.

RE-ENCHANTMENT AND PROFESSIONALISATION

We have seen how this ideological product satisfied the two great requirements of modern thought, leaving aside for a moment that little parochial matter of the philosophers' need for professional standing. But there is a connection. The problem of disenchantment is also the problem of the adequacy of ordinary thought, of common sense. In a happy condition such as that which preceded modern "disenchantment", men could feel at home in the world because their ordinary, intuitive conceptualisation of the world seemed adequate to them. When this is so—and only when this is so—one has a kind of intellectual citizenship, a conceptual *droit de cité*.

If the ideas and notions which I instinctively use visibly have a grip on things and are recognised as having it by others, I may truly feel at home in my world. If, on the other hand, reality is only seized by some set of notions which I do not fully command, which I might only learn with difficulty and use without confidence, whilst my own vernacular is inadequate, then I inevitably feel, and indeed I *am*, a second-class citizen. This is one of the most crucial aspects of "disenchantment"; the loss of confidence in one's own natural idiom. A sense of such conceptual *dépaysement* is of course greatly encouraged by a variety of obvious features of the modern world, notably the technicality and specialisation of truly powerful forms of knowledge, and their great distance from that which is intuitively obvious, and by contrast, the ephemeral, fashion-ridden, waffly quality of enchantment-granting styles of thought.

Wittgenstein's early philosophy was a little ambiguous, not to say ambivalent, on this point; but his later, crystallised philosophy was perfectly clear. If it was true, then it restored confidence and solidity to all our ordinary conceptualisations, and it did so with one mighty sweep.

But if our ordinary thought is so satisfactory and self-sufficient, why do we need specialised philosophic thinkers at all? It is at this point that the celebrated "therapeutic" theory of philosophy enters the argument. This is of course the obverse of the "diagnostic" theory aimed at pre-Wittgensteinian thought: previous philosophy is seen as a deviation from the self-sustaining, self-authenticating common sense built into ordinary speech—deviations which allegedly had been inspired by wrong, over-simplified and non-naturalistic models of how language works. Philosophical questions ("puzzles") are simply symptoms of the malfunctioning of language. When running smoothly, language makes no unwelcome noise: and just as unusual noises are danger-signs in a machine, so "odd" questions indicate that some concept is out-of-its-place and needs adjustment. The point of the therapeutic/diagnostic theory is of course that it simultaneously provides professional philosophy with a definite task, yet refrains from claiming any special positive information or special cognitive channels, either of which would be offensive to the spirit of the age.

This of course helps to explain that curious *mélange* of frivolity and scholasticism which gave this school of thought its characteristic aroma. The former is clearly appropriate for a movement whose great underlying discovery is that ordinary language neither requires nor allows any correction, that philosophy is the handmaiden, not of theology, but of common sense. At the same time, however, the tortuousness of the investigations allegedly required to lead people back to actual working of language, the machinery that needs to be set up for this, all that painstaking detail, provide the profession with the arcana without which it could hardly justify its existence and its prestige.

It is thus that the trade secrets of philosophy all at once revalidate our concepts, re-enchant our world, *and* warrant a trade. . . Any craft must of course have its mysteries, and in the case of an intellectual/proselytising one, these often internally split the practitioners into monks and monsignors. Without monks in the wilderness, the worldly clientele might not be impressed and inclined to suppose that the Order has anything very special or different to offer them—for it knows its monsignors a little too well; but without the monsignors in the salon, arid monks might not have those prestigious connections with centres of power which demonstrate that the movement is indeed blessed. Movements need both PROs and mystery. The Founder had a genius for publicity combined with seeming to flee it—rather like T. E. Lawrence. (Elie Kedourie drew my attention to the similarity between the two men.)

Thus the curious and characteristic fusion of frivolity and scholasticism had its social base in the playboy/pedant coalition. Sir Isaiah Berlin reminisces about this (*Essays on J. L. Austin*, Oxford University Press, 1973, p. 16), when describing the meetings of the group around J. L. Austin, a most important sub-segment of the movement:

> "We were excessively self-centred. The only persons whom we wished to convince were our own admired colleagues . . . I suspect that those who have never been under the spell of this kind of illusion . . . have not known true intellectual happiness."

Others have found intellectual happiness in the blinding flash of discovery, the emergence of a new unsuspected connection, the appearance of order in previous chaos; but *chacun à son goût*. In the case of this movement, the matter is further complicated by the fact that some of the best monsignors in the business fondly consider themselves to be monks. Moreover, as the flowering of the movement coincided more or less with the increased impact of mass media, the more lighthearted wing was provided with a direction for new development, a line of escape when faith declined: from language games to panel games, as you might say.

All this is an old story—indeed by now a stale one. But if this doctrine is false, what is the truth?

The problem of validity simply cannot be solved by invoking the norms built into our ordinary speech or our conceptual custom, for the simple reason that our custom is but one of many, and has in any case undergone rapid change and will continue to do so: the problem is precisely to choose *one* set, or *one* direction of change, amongst many possible ones. We cannot use the notion of *meaning* as our ladder to heaven. We cannot assign to it the responsibility for selecting our options. We cannot pass the buck in that direction. . . .

If we do—and no one tried harder than Wittgenstein—two possibilities arise: *either*, "meaning" is interpreted as covering anything that is recognised in a given speech-and-cultural community; *or*, it is defined more narrowly. The former option is the one Wittgenstein took in his later life, and leads to the absurd re-endorsement of every and any culture, and to a total misdescription of our problem situation, in which we must choose between cultural alternatives, not fall back on them as solution; whilst the second alternative simply passes the buck to whatever stricter and more selective criterion of "meaning" we happen to favour—whilst *seeming* to deduce the conclusion from that notion of meaning, wrongly treated as given.

Such slender plausibility as this view may even have had—and it has very very little—it owes, ironically, to the very fact that three centuries of philosophic work have already sifted out and in some measure codified a new common sense, rooted, not in custom, but in extraneous, independent criteria. Wittgenstein's "solution" is simply a misdescription of the problem. The solution can only absolutise one particular set of conceptual habits, selected by taking an arbitrary cross-section of a society at a given point in time, and ignoring other times and places.

The solution quite literally consists of pretending that history does not exist. But the incredibly radical intellectual and social changes of the past three centuries have *not* left everything "as it is". Philosophy is the attempt to understand, codify and evaluate these changes. It is of course true that the notions of daily life are functional—they work, more or less, in the context of daily life. If their here-and-now functional adequacy constitutes validity, they are, in that sense, valid. But in fact they have a mass of far-reaching assumptions built in, whose validity is in no way automatically established or sustained by the practical viability of the life styles within which they occur.

The connected problem of enchantment similarly cannot be solved in this manner. The two problems are connected because it is precisely the establishment of an impersonal, symmetrical world, subject to general explanations, which makes "disenchantment" acute. The problem of the validity of science and its vision is largely the problem of establishing reasons for *accepting* that impersonal picture; whereas the problem of enchantment is getting out of it once again, of finding limits to it which would enable us to retain a little humanity, and *escape* impersonality. The Wittgenstein crystallisation provided just this—but in an appallingly cheap, facile, and invalid way.

This solution may indeed apply in areas such as gastronomy, clothes, and table-manners. Linguistic philosophy, having equated the rules of thought with conceptual table-manners, made logic into a species of etiquette. The equation does not hold, but within the area such as sartorial or gastronomic conventions, in which there is indeed nothing beyond custom, and its loose and somewhat circular connection with our taste, this kind of solution may be acceptable. Indeed it may there be the only one available to us. But questions concerning how we are to think and to know, how our productive and political life is to be organised, simply are not touched by trite considerations of that kind. The meaning-ploy in philosophy— the idea that a vision could be validated by excluding rivals as "meaningless", by giving it access to meaning *en exclusivité*— led naturally to the late-Wittgensteinian position by being combined with a naturalistic-functional theory of meaning: whatever is used by a cultural/linguistic community, has meaning for its members. Meaning is use.

But their ploy then becomes totally unselective and constitutes its own *reductio ad absurdum*. It endorses anything that "has a use".

A *selective* use of the ploy may still be possible. But then, of course, the burden of the discussion would have to shift to the principle of selection. Within this movement, no such discussions occurred, and there is no logical room for them.

A DEMONSTRATION?

All this is obvious, but it is implicitly denied by the Wittgensteinian vision. But it isn't denied *squarely*, in which case there might be some intellectual benefit to be drawn from examining its case. When I say that its negation is obvious, I do not mean, of course, that it is beyond challenge, and ought not to be discussed. If someone can think of good or even plausible reasons for challenging it, it would be interesting to examine the force of the considerations which can be raised against it.

But Wittgensteinianism does not really challenge this rival view, it simply bypasses it. The need to examine our concepts, our linguistic habits, is initially justified either by an appeal to alleged conceptual hygiene, or by the view, which Wittgenstein endorsed, that his and the logico-platonistic theories of meaning are the only two possible philosophies:

> "he once told me that he really thought that in the *Tractatus* he had provided a perfected account of a view that is the *only* alternative to the viewpoint of his later work." (Norman Malcolm: *Ludwig Wittgenstein, A Memoir*, Oxford University Press, 1958, p. 69, Emphasis in the original.)

On this claim, if the normative Platonism of the *Tractatus* is rejected, his later views do indeed become the only possible ones, by simple elimination. *Des deux choses une* . . . So the solution of the two great problems, of validation and enchantment, is not even urged or argued explicitly. It is pervasive but implicit. It is simply built into the *procedural rules* of the game. Philosophical problems are conceptual. Conceptual issues are about our linguistic custom. Ergo, when we examine that custom in sufficient detail, the problem must disappear. Language is what *we* do; we make the rules; there's no one to tell us any better. The fascinating underlying picture is really this—the world itself cannot be problematical. The trouble must lie in our way of speaking about it, or rather, our mistaken ideas *about* our way of speaking about it. It is truly curious that Wittgenstein, who put forward this vision of, in effect, *an unproblematical world*, should also have accused Russell and Moore of "problemlessness".

But in fact, the world *is* problematical. In fact, it is *very* difficult to know just which world we are in—for instance, is it an intelligible, at least partially controllable but icy one, or on the contrary an unmanipulable but humanly cosy one? (This, in effect, is the debate between "scientism" and romanticism.) But those who were under the spell of the crystallised vision did not let this bother them. The fact that the method does not even really "dissolve" these problems merely shows that they belong to some other subject or field, for which a new name can be invented. So, in the end, this philosophy says nothing at all.

It is an essential part of crystallisation that it produces an aura of uniqueness which then surrounds the object of love. In the case of belief-systems, this means that in the first flush of intoxication, the system of ideas appears totally discontinuous from all others, and not at all co-ordinate with them. They cannot threaten or rival it, they are simply not on the same plane. Other systems are only seen in its terms, and they highlight its glory. And so it was Wittgensteinianism heralded the end of previous philosophy. An intelligent participant/observer looks back with admirable candour and a little sheepishly:

"Foreseeably near were the total dissolution of ancient problems and the final extinction both . . . of . . . metaphysical doctrines . . . and of . . . traditional empiricism . . . The means of both dissolution and revelation was a refined . . . and . . . realistic awareness of the meanings of words. The method . . . inspired a kind of hope which was not, at the time, absurd. It was possible to speculate how long it would take to "finish off" traditional philosophy. . ." (Sir Peter Strawson, "The Post-linguistic Thaw," *Times Literary Supplement*, September 9, 1960.)

It always was and will be absurd to suppose that the problem of validation, of choice between cognitive and social styles, could be solved by examining the way in which the question allegedly arose from our use of the terms involved (or our misunderstanding of that use). Our terms embody one set of choices, express one culture, amongst many possible ones. They could only contain a solution if that culture were somehow absolutised, and uniquely right. The problem is, precisely, to see whether the choice can be justified. It does not justify itself. The linguistic "meaning" method is a covert and absurd way of pretending that it does.

DEFENCE BY RE-DEFINITION

With crystallisation gone, we must once again see this beauty as one amongst her rivals, and then alas she no longer shines. Yet, at the time when she seemed unique, in fact the others also existed. The other problems facing thought, notably that of validation, were still there, and unsolved. Wittgenstein did not solve it: he merely claimed that it could not arise.

If it persisted in seeming to exist, there was always a second line of defence: if it did exist, it was no part of philosophy, but of something else. This alternative was there in small print, though it increased in size over time. If you read the small print with the large, you eventually saw that all possibilities were covered and nothing was being said at all. It was like his own erstwhile theory of logic—true, but only in the sense of saying nothing. The appeal of the doctrine lay in seeming to solve important questions or rather showing that they did not arise at all. The real message, which provided the psychic pay-off, lay in the definition, which in effect said that the world was unproblematic—because philosophy was about our understanding of our *concepts*, not about reality. Yet this pseudo-definition, this crypto-theory, would not itself be discussed. . .

People still exist who appear to accept this implicit definition. For instance, Mr. P. M. S. Hacker writes (*Law, Morality and Society*, ed. Hacker and Raz, Oxford, University Press, 1977, p. 2), "The family of philosophic styles commonly referred to as 'linguistic' or 'analytic' . . . has often been condemned . . . [but there is] . . . a brilliant refutation of such nonsense."

Now we know. On page five Hacker goes on in effect to

restate the Wittgensteinian theory or crypto-definition of philosophy: ". . . the oddity of the traditional answers is, after all, characteristic of every branch of philosophy. Reflect for a moment on the oddity of the answers which philosophers have given. . ." And he then proceeds to explain along the characteristic lines why this alleged oddity arises, and how it is to be avoided.

The view that philosophic doctrines are "odd" and that this is "characteristic of every branch of philosophy" is the obverse of the absolutisation of a given cultural vision and the idea that misunderstanding concepts leads us to see problems where there are none. Understand the real working of your language and the problem will dissolve! But this could only be so if the *residue* left after such understanding had been attained, i.e. our customary vision, was inherently unproblematic.

But traditional answers are not generally or necessarily "odd" at all. Many of them have indeed become implausible, owing to the radically transformed authority-structure of our social and intellectual world. "Law", for instance, to take Hacker's example, is not difficult to define in a society which believes it to be divinely ordained and both warranted and identified theologically. The difficulty arises because the background beliefs making this definition acceptable, and the social conditions sustaining those beliefs, are being eroded. The difficulty does *not* arise, as Hacker suggests because we fail to understand the distinctiveness or complexity of categorial concepts, etc. Some concepts may indeed be odd, but that is not the trouble. Problems arise through the difficulty of validating cultural options. This difficulty is inherent in the nature of things, but the awareness of it becomes more acute under some social conditions—notably our own.

The idea that philosophical questions arise from a misunderstanding of language and can be dissolved by seeing how our language really works could at the very best by a hypothesis, an idea amongst others, possibly true, possibly false. So presented, it can easily be shown to be false. There are many ways of conceptualising reality. Some of these possibilities are actualised in history. The problem of choice *between* such options has become particularly acute in recent centuries. The fact that these options are built into a given language does *not* validate any one of them or offer any solution.

But in fact, the idea worked not as a theory but as a definition. Even that doesn't fully describe the situation. Under conditions of crystallisation, it was a kind of *sacred* definition, which didn't merely define philosophy logically (that was so only when it found itself under attack), it emotionally defined the world and also the rules of legitimate discourse.

But, though a "mere" definition, it was not a harmless one. Definitions are not innocuous. The redefinition of "philosophy" as that which fitted Wittgenstein's theory, the claim that it is a by-product of misunderstanding of language, whilst other problems consequently *had* to be something else, had two consequences: it trivialised philosophy, and it irrationalised the discussion of those other issues, by carelessly bequeathing them to anyone who cared to claim them—or to the local conceptual custom, whatever it happened to be.

All theories no doubt contain a protective penumbra of criticism-evading ploys. But Wittgenstein asymptotically approached the limit at which the evading ploys *were* the philosophy itself—in the end there was evasion without any theory. He actually claimed not to have any positive theory, merely to cure the errors of others. But there was of course a meta-theory, concerning the nature of the errors and their cures, and it is in effect contained in this definition of philosophy, and is far from criticism-resistant.

THE POISONING OF WELLS

An admirer of Wittgenstein, Mr. B. McGuiness, writing at a time when criticising Wittgenstein was unthinkable, said

> "Newman had to meet the following argument: 'Dr. Newman teaches that truth is no virtue; his denials that he teaches this are not to be credited, since they come from a man who teaches that truth is no virtue.' He described this as an attempt to poison the wells." (Letter dated November 11th, in *The Times* November 1959.)

This was aimed against Wittgenstein's critic. But ironically Wittgenstein, early and late, *never* philosophised in any way other than by well-poisoning. He always knew *in advance* of the discussion that his opponents were conceptually diseased and thus that their views were to be discounted. In the *Tractatus* (6.53) this is stated as follows:

"The right method in philosophy would be this. To say nothing except what can be said, i.e. the propositions of natural science, i.e. something that has nothing to do with philosophy; and then always, when someone else wished to say something metaphysical, to demonstrate to him that he has given no meaning to certain signs in his propositions . . . it would be the only strictly correct method."

In *Philosophical Investigations* (paragraphs 116-133) this well-poisoning, the *a priori* discounting of anyone who dares to disagree, returns: "The results of philosophy are the uncovering of one or another piece of plain nonsense and of bumps that the understanding has got by running its head up against the limits of language." All dissenters speak nonsense. If this is established in advance of all debate, what can you do?

But under pressure, this "idea" became a definition. Consider the testimony of the late Conrad Hal Waddington:

"I came to know [Wittgenstein] when he came to a lecture I gave . . . about some rather general topic on the philosophy of science . . . Wittgenstein . . . emerged to state that I had not been talking philosophy at all, but had talked science. . . . I firmly told him that what I had been talking was philosophy in the sense that it was classified as such by the University Librarian and that books on this topic were available on the library shelves labelled as Philosophy. We had a rather stimulating discussion, much to the horror of most of the members of the Club, who were not used to anybody standing up to Wittgenstein. . ." (Alan Robertson, F.R.S.: *Conrad Hal Waddington, F.R.S. 1905–1975.* Biographical Memoirs of Fellows of The Royal Society, vol. 23, December 1977.)

Sir Karl Popper had virtually the same experience, on a more famous occasion:

"Early in . . . 1946–47 I received an invitation from . . . the Moral Sciences Club in Cambridge to read a paper about "some philosophical puzzle". It was of course clear that this was Wittgenstein's formulation, and that behind was

Wittgenstein's philosophical thesis that there are no genuine problems in philosophy, only linguistic puzzles. . . I decided to speak on 'Are there philosophical Problems?' "

After some trouble because of Popper's challenge to the terms of the invitation

"Wittgenstein jumped up again, interrupting me, and spoke at length about puzzles and the nonexistence of philosophical problems. . . I interrupted him, giving him a list I had prepared of philosophical problems. . . These Wittgenstein dismissed as being logical. . . [Another one offered] he dismissed as mathematical. . . I then mentioned moral problems. . . Wittgenstein in a rage, threw the poker down and stormed out of the room, banging the door behind him." (Karl Popper, *Unended Quest*, London, Fontana 1976, pp. 123, 124.)

It was all done by a trite definition. But the aura which surrounded it made it seem much more. This was the displacement effect: there was nothing to back up the re-definition, and it shrivelled to nothing more than a definition when it came under attack. But amongst the faithful, in whom horror was aroused by an attempt to criticise, it was much more; it was seen in crystallised form, as quite changing the world, and yet beyond doubt. In *Words and Things*, I sketched out the effect his ideas and example had on the practice of the faithful. As the sketches have been challenged, perhaps I may quote the testimony of Professor W. Kneale, FBA, much-admired historian of logic, a man noted for his moderation, and personal friend of many of the older members of the movement. He wrote (*The Hibbert Journal*, Oct. 1960, vol. LIX, 1960/61, p. 197),

"members of the general educated public . . . have heard of a Revolution in Philosophy . . . If such persons ask for an opinion about the correctness of Mr Gellner's story, it must be admitted that there are individuals and coteries who hold the views he describes and behave in a way which justifies his irritation."

At the same time as philosophy was redefined to suit these practices, those other things which had normally been called philosophy were handed over, in a vague way, to establish custom, or whatever: "Philosophy may in no way interfere with the actual use of language. . . For it cannot give it any foundation either. It leaves everything as it is" (*Philosophical Investigations*, para. 124). It isn't quite true however that Wittgensteinian philosophy "leaves everything as it is". It leaves everything somewhat tarnished with irrationalism. "The actual use of language" includes the norms governing moral, political, religious discourse, which are in this weird and devious way made self-justifying.

Under conditions of crystallisation, this key principle operated simultaneously as an hypothesis and as a definition (it becomes the latter when it is under attack). But let us look at it, de-crystallised, as the bizarre hypothesis which it is. What on earth would the world look like, were it true?

IDEAS IN HISTORY

It is part of the perfectly sensible conventional wisdom of the Oxbridge tradition that when facing a statement, we should ask ourselves just what it means and whether it is true.

I warmly endorse this, but would supplement it, in the case of philosophical ideas, by a third question: what would human history look like, if this idea were valid? It is instructive to apply this query to Wittgensteinianism. The answer is something as follows: Before Wittgenstein, for many many centuries, men tormented themselves with doubts, endeavoured to convert each other, sometimes with violent and brutal means, concerning the general ideas about the world they lived in. After Wittgenstein, the intellectual life of mankind, and hence much of its socio-political life, changed drastically. In the happy A.W. era, once his insights became well-diffused, there were no further crusades, ideological wars, heresy-hunts, inner torments and struggles. No, no: mankind realised that there were two kinds of question, philosophy proper, arising from language, and the others, which had once caused turbulence in our hearts and societies, but which were now seen neither to have nor to need any extra-linguistic backing. . . All crises of faith, all ideological conflict, were henceforth a matter of the past! It is perhaps significant that Bertrand Russell, a genuinely open-minded man who was ever willing to change his mind on most questions and often did so, had a sustained, unwavering, total, and wholly justified contempt for the "later thought" of Wittgenstein.

The final dissolution of human philosophic perplexity was held to be imminent: "There really were people who saying that the whole of philosophy would be over in 50 years. What they thought was that the major problems would be dissolved. . ." (Bernard Williams, *The Listener*, 9th March 1978). Mr Bryan Magee had the impression: "In the new dawn of linguistic philosophy people were inclined to think that the fundamental problems of philosophy would be solved in about 20 years. . ." (*The Listener*, 9th March 1978. Republished in *Men of Ideas*, ed. B. Magee, BBC Publications, 1978). Magee's friends in the movement were evidently more impatient or optimistic than Bernard Williams', in a ratio of twenty to fifty years—but what are thirty years between friends?

But the really important thing to note is this: the expectation of a final dissolution of philosophic problems was not just a matter of over-valuing a given method. It *necessarily* followed from the view that these problems are shadows cast by our own speech. Understand language by observing it with care, and the shadows will cease to haunt you. The obverse of this is—our given cultural visions are unproblematic. Mankind had been tormented by mere shadows, and they are now exorcised. . .

It is all bizarre and absurd. Yet this was the real psychic pay-off of the vision, the implication of the inherently trite definition which solved the problems of validation and of enchantment, and which thereby gave the position its glamour, its crystallisation. It *totally* misrepresented our real situation, which involves choosing our forms of life, as best we can, and *not* treating them as ultimate. The idea that, once malfunctioning concepts are put right, the world itself is quite unproblematic —or the parallel notion which supports it, that the conceptual custom of a culture is a sufficient base for our decisions— presupposed a complacency so profound as to be almost impressive. At the same time, this "idea", though pervasive and operative, wasn't often spelt out in anything like such candid words, for within the vision it was part of the unquestioned background, and to discuss it within philosophy would have been an error about the very nature of the subject.

One may distinguish between philosophy A—defined roughly as the set of problems conventionally recognised as philosophical —and philosophy B—the class of problems satisfying Wittgenstein's definition of the subject, i.e. problems generated by the misunderstanding of how language works. In fact, of course, A and B are not remotely identical. They have at best a small overlap, consisting precisely of the problems which intrigued Wittgenstein in his youth, and which arise from the misguided pursuit of a parallelism between a notation, thought, and reality.

Linguistic philosophy then lives in a kind of triangle, made up of three propositions:
  (i) Philosophy A is linguistically generated.
  (ii) Philosophy B is linguistically generated.
  (iii) Reality is unproblematical (alternative reading: common sense is sound).

Proposition (ii) is trivially true. (i) is false. (iii) genuinely does follow from (i): *if* all deep problems about things arose from the misunderstanding of how language works, then the removal of such misunderstanding would leave reality unproblematical. Robust common sense (which of course would have to have a unique vision) would then rightfully inherit the earth.

The movement depended for its plausibility on a systematic confusion of (i) and (ii). The trivial truth of (ii) made it impervious to all attacks. The logical potency of (i), the fact that it really could generate (iii) as a consequence, made it into a vision with a powerful appeal, at least for some. This was virtually all there was to it—plus a little work in areas in which the linguo-genetic thesis seemed to possess some plausibility (e.g. the mind–body problem). But such work had largely the role of the conjuror's patter. It distracted attention from the shuttle-cocking between (i) and (ii). The mechanism was of course not fully conscious. It worked to perfection none the less, or perhaps all the better for it.

And yet, bizarre and absurd though it was, it *was* a vision, of a kind. As such, it was probably preferable to the evasive, watered-down versions which persist after de-crystallisation. The twig never sparkled for me, but it was less sad to see it sparkling for others than to see them cling to a rotting twig without crystals.

WHAT IS LEFT?

Of the famous immediate successors, J. L. Austin, the Brian Clough of philosophy, tried to persuade listeners (and for a time succeeded) by sheer confidence rather than argument that the problem of validity did not arise; that when our cultural stock of ideas was challenged by for instance empiricist scepticism, there was no case to answer. As A. J. Ayer observed (*Symposium on J. L. Austin*, ed. K. J. Fann, 1969) "It is . . . a tribute to his wit and strength of personality that he was able to persuade so many philosophers that he had succeeded". It is customary to distinguish his position from Wittgenstein's, but it rather resembles it in offering no real solutions, but instead, promisory notes of unspecified solutions to come, some day. Most characteristically, he once said that, "roughly speaking", his method illuminated *all* philosophical problems. *Precisely* speaking it illuminated none. By contrast, Gilbert Ryle does deserve respect for actually trying to make the method work in a definite field, in the mind-body problem, and thereby demonstrating pretty conclusively that it did not. His solution was a form of behaviourism. He was inclined to deny this strenuously, though the manner in which his position differed from behaviourism remains a well-guarded secret.

The crystallisation has now faded. The moment when the twig was pulled out of the mine now seems long ago. The salt crystals have faded, the sparkle has gone, and a sad rotting twig is appearing under the salt. Yet it was part of the erstwhile crystallisation that this vision could appear to some as the one and only, the sole possible object of intellectual adoration. Such is love. The circle was complete: meaning must be clarified first, otherwise your thought will be faulty. But meaning is to be understood naturalistically. The full consummation of this natural vision of language is to see it as a diversified set of human customs; the only questions sanctioned are such as are within the compass of the solutions found within that custom. But the custom also contains invocations of non-natural elements. So they too are in order. And so, once again, naturalism and mysticism, between the two of them, filled out the world.

Once crystallisation is gone, once seen not as *the* vision beautiful, but merely as one vision amongst others, it loses not merely compulsiveness, but also any plausibility. It is not, as Wittgenstein taught, that we must see philosophical terms alongside their everyday usage, in order to be brought back to the proper understanding of them. Exactly the opposite is true: we must see this doctrine itself as one philosophical doctrine amongst others. And then it is seen to be false.

Froxfield, 1978

CHAPTER I

OF LINGUISTIC PHILOSOPHY

I. INTRODUCTORY

LINGUISTIC PHILOSOPHY IS a certain cluster of views about the world, language and philosophy. This cluster has a considerable measure of unity and inner coherence. It merits treatment as "a philosophy", that is, a distinctive outlook, a way of looking at things, with its associated style of reasoning and of setting about solving problems, of recognising problems and solutions. This philosophy underlies the views and practices of what has become the dominant school of philosophy in British Universities, and particularly in Oxford, since the war. Before the war it was upheld by an influential *avant-garde*. Its main origin is to be found in the later views of Ludwig Wittgenstein.

For a variety of reasons inherent in that philosophy, it seems to me unlikely that an adequate account of it can be expected from those who subscribe to it. For this philosophy need only be stated clearly for certain disastrous defects in it to become apparent.

Those who are committed to it and subscribe to it have no incentive to bring out its defects. In fact, the philosophy contains a number of features which militate against a clear statement of the general position. These features include the notions that certain important things are unsayable, or that truth must be communicated in a kind of oblique way, and that it can only be done in an extremely piecemeal and detailed manner if it is not to be misleading. The founder of the movement was obsessed by the inevitability of being misunderstood. These views may be held in good faith and have some merit, but their consequence is that the uninitiated have great difficulty in ascertaining just what the key ideas of the movement are, and a clear statement which would highlight their weaknesses is avoided.

The accounts of the philosophy which are available tend to be either esoteric, or piecemeal and fragmentary, or historical, in that they attempt to convey the key ideas by showing how they emerged from previous trends of thought.* Each of these ways seems to me unsatisfactory. Instead, I shall begin by a comparatively simple account of the position as a whole, explicit rather than oblique, and presenting the ideas themselves rather than their applications or their origins.

The fact that I present both a logical and a sociological account of the views of this movement may give rise to a misunderstanding: it may be thought that the sociological analysis is intended to be a refutation—a refutation by means of ascription of motives and effects. Nothing of the kind is intended. On the contrary: in as far as this book argues that those ideas are false, this is *argued*; it is not merely inferred from the existence of a social context.

At the heart of the ideas of this movement, there is a claim or a hope that awareness of language, or of some hitherto neglected features of it, will completely transform our outlook, or has already done so.† It was claimed that fundamental questions which had hitherto seemed too hard and elusive for the human mind would at least receive answers, or that the questions themselves would be convincingly shown to have been misguided and would cease to haunt us.

Whether or not the new vision has, will or should transform the outlook of mankind, it certainly has radically and dramatically transformed the mores and procedures of one professional guild, namely, teachers of philosophy. Even if the ambitious claims and promises of the movement were not a matter of living memory, this change in procedures would show how seriously the participants took the new vision.

Whatever their merit, these ideas are an interesting culmination of a long philosophic tradition of self-consciousness and of criticism—of the attitude that we must understand our tools before we use them; of the idea that there are things which are beyond the scope of these tools, and that only ill can come of attempting them. A certain novelty in the outlook under discussion is that the tool in question is envisaged as *language*— rather than, as used to be the case, *mind*. It is interesting to see

* Since I wrote the first draft of this book, Mr. D. Pole's excellent *The Later Philosophy of Wittgenstein* (London 1958) has appeared, which is not open to these objections.

† Cf. the very title of a recent book, *The Revolution in Philosophy*, edited by Professor G. Ryle. London 1956.

what this linguistic form of self-knowledge has attained, what revelations it brings and what policies, or self-denials, it ordains.

A revolutionary change has occurred in philosophic practice —revolutionary not merely *vis-à-vis* the recent past, but *vis-à-vis* all past thought—and it is interesting to examine the reasons which can be given, and were given, for this innovation, *and* to note alternative justifications when they occur.

2. FIRST APPROACHES

A rough first approximation of the central ideas of Linguistic Philosophy is this:

Philosophic problems are intimately connected with language and somehow emanate from it. They "arise from" the use of words: and especially "from the *ordinary* use of words", or from deviations from it.

The fact *that* language exists, plus some facts *about* language, are central for philosophy: they are the condition of solving or "dissolving" those fundamental problems which men have called "philosophy". Ordinary language, as actually employed, rather than some general features of language which might best be conveyed by a simplified model language, is what is relevant. The diversity of ordinary language is essential for the understanding of it and of philosophic problems.

(Old) philosophy is somehow the pathology of language: philosophical problems arise from a misunderstanding of language; philosophical theories are misuses of language.

In as far as this is true, it follows that the philosophical (in the old sense) view is always wrong or at least misleading, and that the *un*philosophical view which can also be called "Common Sense" is right. Common sense is either identical with, or at least closely related to, what is asserted or implied in the common use of language, briefly referred to as "Usage".

What follows further is that the proper job of the philosopher is to be the diagnostician and therapist of a certain type of error, namely error arising from misunderstanding of language. He has no positive function. Positive views can be left to common sense or some other source.

These ideas can be summed up roughly either as ideas about philosophy, or about language, or about the world, or about mind.

3. A THEORY OF PHILOSOPHY

The theory of philosophy runs: past philosophy has been mainly abuse of language, future good philosophy will be the diagnosis and elimination of such abuse. (It is admitted that some past philosophers did good work without understanding what they were doing.)

This lends itself to various conceptions of the good work left for philosophers to do in the future:

Euthanasia of philosophy. Or *autopsy*. Or endlessly protracted *prophylaxis*. Or others still, including *l'art pour l'art*.

These possibilities must be explained more fully:

Linguistic Philosophy can conceive of its own activities as the euthanasia of philosophy. There is, in its view, no room on the map of knowledge for the kind of special insights that past philosophy claimed, or indeed for the kind of special, strange questions with which it was preoccupied. But those alleged questions and putative insights are not to be simply outlawed, but gently, so to speak *comprehendingly*, eliminated. Only such understanding, "therapeutic" elimination is truly effective, and as a by-product of it we get some understanding of how we use language. Simple proscription was ineffective.

The question arises whether there is not a danger that, the euthanasia being completed, the linguistic philosopher may find himself out of a job. This disagreeable possibility is countered in a number of ways: Linguistic Philosophy is conceived not merely as a therapy or euthanasia, but also as prophylaxis, and as a prophylaxis against a necessarily ever-present danger. The disease it wards off is inherent in language: all language-users will ever be tempted to misinterpret the various uses of their language in terms of each other. . . . This is the Night Watchman theory of philosophy: it has no positive contribution of its own to make, but must ever be on guard against possible abuses that would interfere with, confuse, genuine knowledge.

Even more sophisticated theories guaranteeing continued employment of linguistic philosophers exist: what one might call the Dialectical Theory envisages illness and therapy feeding on each other, each cure itself calling for another cure, perhaps in a pendulum-like pattern.

Finally, there is the idea that usage may be investigated for its own sake, even if no problems are illuminated on the way.

Naturally, once this is allowed as a legitimate exercise, Linguistic Philosophy is safe (from criticism, anyway, if not from extinction by boredom). The promise of therapeutic effects constituted *some* check on its claims (even if not a sharp one, for no deadline was set for the therapeutic efficacy, which might always be just round the corner); without it, *no* checks on its claims are left at all, for it has then dropped its claims.

There are also watered-down versions which fuse these ideas with less novel and controversial ones. Linguistic Philosophy has a watering-down mechanism built into its ideas and practices, so that every characterisation could be qualified by pointing out that some linguistic philosophers have chosen ready-made evasions. This makes all criticism complex in formulation, but not less effective, for in general the following fork holds: either the linguistic philosopher holds the strong variant, in which case he is saying something interesting, but open to criticism, or he is holding the watered-down version, in which case he is beyond the reach of criticism, but saying something which is too feeble to be controversial.

Evasiveness is implicit in the ideas and in the practice of Linguistic Philosophy.* This kind of evasiveness is not uncommon among philosophies. The remarkable thing about Linguistic Philosophy is the thoroughness with which it is built into its key ideas and the way it is essentially connected with them, as will emerge.

4. A THEORY OF THE WORLD AND OF LANGUAGE

As a theory about the world, Linguistic Philosophy runs like this: The world is what it is, and not another thing. Everything in the world is what it is, and not another thing. (These statements are not as tautological as they seem, as will emerge.) *Inside* the world, there are men, and men use language. Language is a set of events, activities, dispositions. It has its uses. The uses of expressions have to do with human purposes in the world in which men find themselves, with the contexts in which those purposes operate. Language is an activity, a form of life. (Goethe's Faust pondered on whether "in the beginning there

---

* I should like, however, to express my respect for those philosophers who nevertheless display admirable forthrightness in debate, such as Professors Ryle and Urmson, or Messrs. R. Hare and A. MacIntyre.

was the *word*", or the *deed*. Linguistic Philosophy has solved that dilemma for him: the word *is* a deed.)

The general purposes of language are, for instance, the communication of information, the issuing of orders, the assessment of characters, the assessment of aesthetic satisfactoriness, the assessment of probabilities, preaching, edifying, justifying authority, etc., etc. To each of these purposes and activities there correspond some expressions, some linguistic acts. (Of course, an expression may serve a number of them, or many kinds of expression may serve one purpose.)

But what sense could there be in asking, as old-fashioned philosophy did, whether the world has such general properties as being made up of facts or containing universals, values, beauty, relations, what not? The world is what it is: general terms of this kind, corresponding to kinds of uses of language, can never be misapplied, unless perhaps by one ignorant of the language. The force of "the world is what it is" is really: general, "categorial" terms (Beauty, Rightness, Fact, Inference, Abstractness, etc.) are not misapplied. It does not make sense to speculate what the world would be like without them, for the world neither contains them—nor fails to contain them. They are kinds of uses of language. Metaphorically speaking, categories like Beauty, etc., are shadows which the uses of language cast on the world.

This leads us back to the diagnosis of (past) philosophy: it was the attempt to do *about* these concepts what we can only do *with* them; to do with categories as a whole what is only legitimate inside each of them: to ask questions *about* them.

What Linguistic Philosophy says about language, positively, has already been sketched in describing the place of language *in* the world. There remains to sketch roughly the negative theory of language—what language is not—and to give some specific doctrines about meaning.

What language is *not*: It is not something opposed to, *vis-à-vis*, the world, mirroring it. It is from the rejection of this doctrine, amongst others, that Linguistic Philosophy sprang. The Mirror theory of meaning, the idea that when a term or an expression means something there must *be* something somewhere, has led in the past, it is claimed, to all kinds of Mysterious-Universe theories, and to the Mysterious-Mind theories. It is these theories that are being opposed, and their denial gives a non-vacuous sense to saying that the world is what it is. Or, what it seems.

It is important to note how the view of the world and the view of language support each other. One can argue either way: *Because* the world is just what it seems (and as it seems to an unimaginative man at about mid-morning), therefore, naturally, language is but a set of activities in it. What else could it be?

But equally well one can argue: *Because* language is found on examination to be but a set of tools for mundane—or at any rate, intramundane—purposes therefore the world is only what it seems. For old philosophy argued from features of language to strange realms: from adjectives to Universals, from substantives to Substances, from hypothetical expressions to a Realm of Possibilities, etc., etc. But once one sees all kinds of expressions as *tools*, one also sees all such inferences to strange entities or realms to be misguided. Hence, the world is as it seems, before we started to philosophise. (Let us not ask when *that* was.) For "tools" are, *ex hypothesi, used in* the ordinary world.

There is really only one idea here. But it *seems* to be two or many, and the multiplicity of its manifestations all seem to lend each other support.

5. A THEORY OF MIND

Linguistic Philosophy is also a theory of mind. Or one might say it "implies" a theory of mind. But whilst indeed the characteristic doctrine of mind is a corollary and application of the central doctrine, it is equally possible to reach that central doctrine as a corollary or implication of the theory of mind.

The most famous statement of that theory is to be found in Professor Gilbert Ryle's *The Concept of Mind*. The doctrine is, roughly, that the human mind is *not* an entity or process or class of events or receptacle radically distinct from corporeal events or things, but on the contrary that, very generally speaking, mind is the way we do things. This may be called Behaviourism, and indeed it is, but it differs from other forms of Behaviourism in important ways: it maintains that its discoveries are simply the making explicit of what is in fact contained in our concepts, in our ways of using words which refer to thought, etc. So the account claims not really to be denying

the existence of something, but merely to give a correct
interpretation of what its existence amounts to, of how the
expressions referring to it are related to others (notably those referring to bodies and their behaviour). So Ryle's Behaviourism
is intended to be an explication, which leaves everything as
it is, excluding only philosophical misinterpretations of the
situation.

This Behaviourism, if valid, would have very important consequences—it would show the unreality of the puzzle about how
we can know what other people think, and the even more important one about how mind and body can interact. The
"dissolution" of these two problems was indeed claimed.

For the allegedly mistaken traditional philosophy of mind
supposed the existence of two sets of odd entities: what I call
"cold" entities, such as propositions, universals, etc., envisaged
as "objects" of thought, and what I call "warm" entities, such
as inner sensations and states.

The linguo-philosophical approach reduces *both* these kinds
to aspects of doing. By eliminating or playing-down the warm
entities it destroys the doctrine of a private world composed of
them: from this the other aspect of Linguistic Philosophy follows, namely the naturalistic view of language (it cannot then
refer to the private world, or to a Platonic world of the cold
entities, and so it must be an activity, a "know-how", *in* the
public world).

The existence of "cold" mental entities (abstractions such as
Ideas, Concepts, Universals, Propositions) is denied outright.
This is well in keeping with the nominalistic temper of the age,
and does not constitute a distinctive feature of Linguistic Philosophy, at any rate not in opposition to its immediate philosophical predecessors.

The denial of "warm" entities, such as "sense-data", intro-
spectible states and so forth is a more difficult and controversial
matter. Most people who reflect on the matter are convinced
that they experience these entities, and it is difficult to convince
them that they do not. Moreover, recent philosophies have
often operated with these notions, and the supposition of their
existence in no way offends the spirit of the age.

In its more sensible and moderated formulation, the Linguistic
Philosophy of mind does not deny the existence of warm mental
entities. It merely argues that they are irrelevant, in as far as

their presence is not essential to the use—and hence, the meaning—of those expressions which were once held to designate them. For instance, an angry man may or may not be experiencing an inner feeling of anger: what is essential to his anger is only that he be disposed to *act* in an angry way.

It must be noted how this philosophy of mind depends on the theory of language: if the meaning of terms is their *use*, as tools in the public world, then, naturally, the use of the tool can only be specified in terms of what is necessary to its employment. (If inner states may sometimes be absent and yet a "mental" term be applicable, then those states are not necessary for its use and cannot be a part of its meaning.)

Given the "use" or "tool" theory of language, the philosophy of mind necessarily follows. If words are *tools used in the public world*, then their meaning cannot, naturally, depend on something in a private or a transcendent realm. (And the denial of these realms is precisely what that philosophy of mind is concerned to achieve.) But this theory of language is the very basis of one main method of argument used: the examining of the employment of "mental words". In the light of this it is concluded, not surprisingly, that a behaviourist theory of mind is valid . . .

So, in a sense, all the protracted and detailed argument is redundant. The conclusion could have been demonstrated briefly, had the tacit presupposition of the method been made an explicit premiss.

Nevertheless, let us not be ungrateful for the detailed elaboration. The Linguistic Philosophy of mind is amongst the more genuinely interesting and illuminating contributions of the movement, even if it does not succeed, as was claimed, in solving the (very important) mind–body interaction problem, nor the (largely academic) problem of the knowledge of other minds, and although it makes itself rather ridiculous in its attempts to solve the related problem of determinism.

But whilst the philosophy of mind is deducible from the philosophy of language, the reverse also holds. The main difficulty of the "use" or "tool-in-the-world" theory of mind is that it appears to reduce communication to a kind of blind ritual. It seems plausible enough to apply it to situations in which we behave "mechanically"; a man who orders his habitual menu in his usual restaurant does not "mean" anything—he does what he does, and his use of language can most plausibly be described as a *doing*-in-the-world. (He might as well have just nodded to the head-waiter.) But when the same theory is applied to, say, a man composing a poem or solving a difficult problem, it becomes far less plausible: there appears to be no pre-established system of rules or habits within which such a man's verbal or symbolic activity is a "move".

When facing this difficulty, the "use" theory of language invokes the activity theory of mind: it is then claimed that of course the original and creative use of words or symbols still is not evidence for one of the old, "mirror" theories of language— it merely shows, as the theory of mind insists, that thinking is a kind of *activity*.*

There is no breaking out of this circle. But the various moves within it are treated by Linguistic Philosophers as independent confirmations of the circle as a whole.

Be it stressed: Linguistic Philosophy is not a theory of the world *and* of language *and* of philosophy *and* of mind. These four are but aspects of each other; they mutually entail or insinuate each other. The doctrine can be conveyed in many ways: in terms of any one of the above or in terms of the specific ideas about meaning: or, most characteristically, in terms of none of these but by application, by exemplification.

---

* The circle does not even end here. In the case of original and creative thought, it is difficult to see how the new and creative step fits in with the preceding stages: for what distinguishes the creative act is that it succeeded in doing something *new*, i.e. something not prescribed in the pre-existing language game. But if so, is the new step not arbitrary? How can it be the solution or completion of a previous question or problem?

Here the theory of language is invoked again. One of its tenets, as will emerge later, is that connections, series, are not simple, but manifold and "open", and chosen, not given. Choosing is a kind of *doing*. Something is *done*, nothing is mirrored.

CHAPTER II

OF LANGUAGE

I. THE THEORY OF LANGUAGE EXPANDED

LINGUISTIC PHILOSOPHY IS, amongst other things, a theory of language. In essence, it consists of seeing language naturalistically. Language is a natural thing, an *activity* undertaken by concrete men in concrete contexts. As already indicated, the force of this view is best appreciated if one stresses what this view *denies*.

This view denies that language is, in fact or in principle or in some hidden way, a mirror of reality, a mirror such that, from the nature of the basic constituents of *language*, one could infer the basic constituents of *reality*. Some view of this kind was tacitly assumed, it is said, by much of past philosophy: if linguistic philosophers are right, this was *the* crucial error of past philosophers, and the fact that the human mind is given to this type of error is the basis of all or most (past, mistaken) philosophy, whilst the essence of good (linguistic) philosophy is the elimination of the manifold errors springing from that key mistake.

It has often been said that man in the past saw nature, and God, in his own image. It now also appears that he saw things in the image of his own language. So the overcoming of logomorphism supplements the overcoming of anthropomorphism.

The new view also denies that language *could* be such a mirror of reality and hence clue to its basic constituents. This view asserts not merely that natural languages *are* simply sets of activities of a certain kind in which men engage with concrete ends in mind and in concrete circumstances; it also asserts that language is inescapably, essentially, a class of doings of this kind. No fundamental logical skeleton underlies the manifold doings of concrete speakers. No logically constructed language could replace actual kinds of speech and claim some kind of priority.

This type of view of language, or attitude towards its philosophic significance, is communicated by linguistic philosophers in a number of ways, of which one of the most interesting and characteristic is through the notion of "language games" and its exemplifications.

2. LANGUAGE GAMES

The word *game* is a pejorative sound, suggesting triviality, unimportance, arbitrariness. ("It is *just* a game.") This is *not* intended by linguistic philosophers.

What is intended is that any assertion only has meaning, a role, in a certain kind of context. This context can be artificially invented, as when the exclamation "Bingo!" has a certain role in an invented game; then we have a "game" in the literal, ordinary sense. Alternatively, however, we may take part in games we have not invented, games which, as traditions or forms of life, have persisted over a long time and which all the players learn but none has deliberately built. Of these games, the language we ordinarily speak is the most important.

Wittgenstein * sketched a number of "language games", simpler versions of language, games using words, resembling actual language in various ways, though none of them getting near it in its complexity and richness. The point of this was to bring out the similarity between the simple rules of the invented games and the complex ones of actual language, and above all the general similarity that a context of rules *was* presupposed, that an assertion was in a sense a "move" in a game (in an activity with rules). What are the important features of games?

(1) The rules governing moves in the game, the use of the tokens in it, *are* that game and cannot be contradicted, for if you do, you no longer play *that* particular game. Rules can be explained (they generally are) with the help of paradigm examples of the use of the token in question. To do something incompatible with that Paradigm Case is *not to play that game*.

(2) The rules can be seen as a kind of norm, prescribing what the tokens should do, or what should be done with them.

The rules need not be strict, of course; they may allow some latitude and not disqualify him who fails to live up to them. But one cannot question their norms. Within rugby, it makes no sense to ask whether scoring tries is a good thing. Rugby is defined in terms of this being so.

* *Philosophical Investigations.* Oxford 1953.

(3) A genuine move must have a possible alternative, "an antithesis". (This isn't strictly true of either games or languages. There are situations in chess when there is no alternative, there may perhaps be sentences which it makes sense to assert but not to deny.) But this seems true of games as a whole, even if not of all moves within them. A game without alternatives is not a game but a ritual, a charade. (Actually, some things that children call games are just like this.) When a game which is meant to have alternatives is somehow made to have none, we call it a farce. We feel this way about predetermined ("cooked") trials or elections.

(4) Most if not all games, and presumably all games of reasonable complexity, require tokens of radically different kinds: one might say, tokens of different categories. Substituting one of these tokens for one of a different category leads to a particularly grave kind of nonsense, graver than simple violation of rules. For instance, it would be very bad in chess to confuse the board, or the squares on the board, with the pieces. Past philosophers were confused people who, it was to be shown, not merely asked whether we can play chess without the Queen —a new kind of chess-without-queen is easy to invent—but who have asked whether the board can move as the Queen can, whether the *square*—and not a piece—can move backwards, etc.

3. THE FOUR PILLARS

The four implications of the notion of a "language game" which I have specifically drawn out in the preceding section are in fact doctrines about language that have played an important part in the practice of Linguistic Philosophy.

They are veritably the Four Pillars of Linguistic Philosophy. It has been maintained that one can use them without fully committing oneself to them. I believe and I shall try to show that, on the contrary, to use them at all is to be committed to their generalised application. In an open or camouflaged way, as doctrines or as presuppositions or procedural rules, they underlie most or all of Linguistic Philosophy.

Let us define them in slightly more detail.

(1) *The Argument from the Paradigm Case* (which I shall sometimes refer to simply as the APC).

This is the argument from the actual use of words to the

answer to philosophical problems, or from a conflict between the actual use of words to the falsity of a philosophical theory. (For instance, the "proof" of the existence of material objects from the fact that material-object-words are employed in our language, or the "disproof" of the theory that we never know what others feel, from the fact that we customarily employ language which conveys that indeed we do.)

(2) The habit of inferring the answer to normative, evaluative problems from the actual use of words. This has been called the *generalised version of the Naturalistic Fallacy.*

(3) *The Contrast theory of meaning,* to the effect that any term to be meaningful must allow at least for the possibility of something *not* being covered by it.

(4) The doctrine I shall call *Polymorphism.* This doctrine stresses that there is very great variety in the kinds of use that words have, and that with regard to any given word, there can be great variety in its particular use. From this correct insistence on the variety of uses, both between and within concepts, it is concluded, incorrectly, that general assertions about the use of words are impossible.

These four mistakes or half-truths are closely linked. Indeed the first three are merely different aspects of each other. The fourth is independent but nevertheless closely linked with the preceding set.

Though fallacious, or employed fallaciously, these ideas have great plausibility, especially when presented in certain oblique ways which obscure both their outlines and their defectiveness. This is how, in fact, they have often been presented by those who advocate Linguistic Philosophy. By going over these mistakes in some detail we shall simultaneously be describing the reasons which have led to the adoption of these arguments, and expounding their fallaciousness. Exposition and refutation are one.

4. THE ARGUMENT FROM PARADIGM CASES

(1) The Argument from the Paradigm Case is absolutely essential to Linguistic Philosophy: * it pervades it and it is

* Cf. "Use and Meaning", *The Cambridge Journal*, September 1951 (written before the APC came to be known by this name); J. W. N. Watkins, "Farewell to the Paradigm-Case Argument", *Analysis*, December 1957, and also a series of further articles in *Analysis*, triggered off by Watkins.

presupposed without qualification, denials notwithstanding. It seems, superficially, a powerful argument.

Suppose someone says, foolishly, "There are no tables: tables do not exist." One might say: such a man is either demented or is using words in some new way, in senses which make it a plausible statement. There is no other possibility, linguistic philosophers suggest.

The argument from the Paradigm Case is this: stress that, after all, words mean what they normally mean (unless and until redefined). Their meaning is their use. We often have occasion to use the word "table". It means whatever it is used to refer to, and, as we often do use it, that to which it refers to *is* a "table". Therefore, tables exist.

The argument may also be applied to more controversial cases. (*In a sense*, no one wishes to deny the existence of tables. Philosophers who have denied the reality of material objects were trying to convey some idea which, whether sensible or not, is *not* in conflict with the indisputable fact that we normally speak as though furniture existed.) For instance, it may be used to establish the—most controversial—reality of free will. What do expressions such as "of one's own free will" mean? Why, let us look at their paradigmatic use. Should we not use it of a smiling bridegroom marrying the girl of his choice? Well then, *that* is the kind of thing the expression means. What else could it mean? Ergo, free will is vindicated. This proof is breathtakingly brief. All the worry about how to square human responsibility with what is known of nature, of human physiology, with what appears to be the case in psychology, with what may be the case about the march of history . . . all that was, it appears, quite unnecessary. The Argument from Smiling Bridegrooms solves it all.*

The APC has a variant in terms of how we learn to understand words. (The original formulation is in terms of how a word can mean anything—irrespective of the psychological question of how we come to learn its meaning.) We must have learnt to understand such terms as we do understand, by hearing them in suitable contexts: those contexts give it meaning, for what other meaning could a term acquire? Hence a theory which explicates the meaning of a given term, and at the same

* Cf. Professor A. G. N. Flew, *Essays in Conceptual Analysis*, London 1956, p. 19.

time wishes to deny the occurrence of those very contexts which gave it meaning, *must* be false.*

Note that we have here an *argument* which confirms what common sense supposes it knows without argument, namely that there are tables. Linguistic Philosophy is the buttressing up of common sense by an argument based on a theory of meaning, namely that "the meaning of an expression is its use". It is the refusal to grant what one could call philosophic licence: the refusal to conduct philosophic discussion in a different tone, with different rules, from those of ordinary discussions. It refuses to leave common sense with hat and umbrella at the door when entering into a philosophical debate. On the contrary, it makes a cult of it. It differs, however, from what might be called a pure philosophy of Common Sense, which simply insists on Common Sense without justifying it, by having a reason —the theory of meaning just outlined.

One might call this approach the *Dr. Johnson-plus*. Dr. Johnson "refuted" Berkeley by kicking a stone. Linguistic Philosophy does precisely that ("solving" problems by kicking stones, reminding us of smiling bridegrooms, etc.), *plus* a theory of meaning, and a theory of philosophy. The theory of meaning

* The APC is generally presupposed and insinuated rather than stated. It is presupposed by being used as a tacit premiss, as a guarantee of an inference from an usage to a conclusion, and is insinuated by stressing that such an inference is incontrovertible. Consider for instance Professor J. L. Austin's " Other Minds" (*Logic and Language II*, ed. Flew, Oxford, 1953, p. 123) described, rightly in a sense, as "classic" by Professor A. G. N. Flew (*Essays in Conceptual Analysis*, London 1956, p. 2).

Austin himself gives us what he calls the gist of what [he] has been trying to bring out". This consists of saying that if there is a conflict between a commonsensical way of speaking (that we sometimes know when someone else is angry) and a theory, the latter must give way.

Similarly, for instance, Mr. B. F. McGuinness sums up his paper to the Aristotelian Society (*Proceedings*, 1956/57, p. 320) by saying "it is necessary for the reader to fix his mind most firmly upon the truth that while it is a *fact* [italics his.—E. G.] that we sometimes know with absolute certainty what others want, it is a mere *theory* that . . ." (and then, a philosophic theory follows).

How do Professor Austin and Mr. McGuinness *know* what they claim to know with such totally decisive certainty? *Only* by presupposing the theory that, as paradigmatic uses give meaning to expressions, a customarily used expression (such as "knowing what someone feels") cannot be generally wrong, for it would then lack a Paradigm Case. Just this is the theory under discussion.

says that acts such as kicking a stone are what gives terms like "stone" meaning,* and the theory of philosophy maintains that the checking of philosophic theories against the meaning of the terms employed in them—the meaning being established in Dr. Johnson's way—is *the* way of testing them.

This theory of meaning has a certain plausibility, both inherently (what, other than our use and the context of that use, *could* endow words with meaning?), and as a corollary of certain important ideas in Linguistic Philosophy, notably the denial of the possibility of a fundamental language.

What really gives this theory its appeal is the combination of tough, hard-headed, Dr. Johnson-esque common sense, the firm refusal to allow oneself to be talked into anything uncommonsensical, with the great refinement and sophistication of the theory of meaning which underwrites this refusal—an exclusive sophistication which claims to see right through fallacies and naïvetés that most past philosophers have taken for granted. So, one is simultaneously on the side of healthy ordinary common sense, *and* one up on the intellectuals, outdoing them in their own sophistication! No wonder that a doctrine which offers so much has been enthusiastically acclaimed.

Whilst, from one viewpoint, immensely plausible, it is also immensely silly. I shall try to bring out both the plausibility and the ultimate silliness.

It has the same plausibility as the language game model of language, the activity theory of language. The reason why, disclaimers notwithstanding, the APC pervades Linguistic Philosophy is that it is really only a reformulation of the "Game" model. After all, words *are* given meaning by their use. In a given and determinate language, what sense could there be in denying that a word is rightly applied in those very cases which are a standard of its right application? The Argument from Paradigm Cases does not even say that a word is always rightly used, but merely that it is rightly used in the Paradigm

* Strictly speaking, it is only the *paradigmatic* stone, or perhaps the paradigmatic kick, that is allowed to count: it is conceded that there may be derivative, metaphorical, etc., uses of terms which are not clues to their central meaning. This distinction of course enables the linguistic philosopher, given some ingenuity, to pass off any account of the real meaning or use of an expression, discounting those that do not fit his case as "derivative", etc. This ploy has been wittily exposed by Mr. P. L. Heath, *Philosophical Quarterly*, 1952.

Case of its employment: and surely we should be prepared to grant this. Indeed, it is a contradiction to deny it. Words mean what a given language, its rules, its custom say they mean, neither more nor less. To deny that a word means what it is customarily said to mean shows either ignorance of the language or a desire for reform of it. But philosophic theses which often went contrary to the paradigm use of the word claimed to be more than neologisms. They claimed to be *corrections* of the rules for the use of these words. But this surely is absurd!—it is claimed.

This argument is plausible even when stated alone. Moreover it fits in with all the other new views of language and philosophy which are on the scene. Yet the argument is silly, and its silliness can be explained briefly with the help of the simplest of semantic distinctions, namely that between connotation and denotation. The argument confuses the two. The fact that there are standard cases for the application of the term such as "miracle" in a given society in no way proves that such terms have a *legitimate* use.* They do certainly "have a use" but this in no way proves that the terms are justified. The term may in fact have no empirical application though members of a society think it has, or alternatively the term may even be incapable of having application, being internally inconsistent. The fact that a term has a use, a range of uses, or a paradigm use only shows that the users, apart from attributing to it some sense, also suppose that this sense so to speak finds the object to which it refers, in other words its denotation. *It in no way establishes that they are right in this supposition.* The meaning of the term of "one's own free will" is not defined in terms of smiling bridegrooms, but on the contrary the behaviour of smiling bridegrooms is interpreted in such a way as to make those terms applicable. The interpretation may be mistaken.

The terms which are crucial for philosophy and philosophic issues are what may be called "categories", for instance Beauty, Rightness, material objects, logical relations, probability. Roughly speaking, a category is a term which indicates or embraces a whole species of human discourse. Philosophic theories are very frequently about the nature or the very existence of a whole category. If the argument from the Paradigm Case were applicable to *them*, it would indeed be a powerful tool. This is

* J. W. N. Watkins, *Analysis*, December 1957.

just where its application was tried. (Its non-applicability *within* categories is after all fairly obvious: everyone knows that individual things which have expressions referring to them, and are supposed to exist, often turn out not to exist at all, to have been misinterpreted, to be in fact something else under suitable guise. The APC does not apply to them. Neither the existence of black swans, nor the non-existence of unicorns can be established by the APC.)

The claim that the argument from Paradigm Cases is applicable to categories can be urged along the following lines. A man who denies a whole category denies a whole species of human discourse. He is deluded into thinking he is making a move within a language game, when in fact he is only denying, absurdly, the existence or viability of the language game as a whole.

But basic language games are indispensable, it is claimed. We cannot do without talk about material objects, about the suitability of actions, or the attractiveness of visual prospects. In other words, to deny material objects, rightness or beauty looks like making a genuine claim, but is in fact a pointless attempt to abolish a whole species of use of language. If the attempt succeeded, it is argued, we should only have to invent new words to do the work previously done by the abolished category. Categories are like God: if they did not exist we should have to invent them.

Various conclusive objections exist against this suggestion. First, it is impossible in practice and perhaps in theory to distinguish sharply between categorial and non-categorial terms. Even if it *were* true that it is pointless to deny or speculate about the nature of terms which really *are* categorial, and which designate a whole and indispensable species of use of language, yet few terms, if any, have an unambiguously "categorial" status. It is far from clear generally whether in asserting or denying the existence of something we are making a move *within* a language game or denying a language game as a whole. We are very frequently doing *both*. Somebody who denies the existence of witches is making a perfectly legitimate move within the broader game of asserting or denying what kind of species of beings exist: and at the same time also he is recommending the abolition of a whole genre of speech, witch-language. The fact that he is also doing the latter in no way by itself invalidates the possibility that he is right in making the former claim. If the former claim is valid then the recommendation of the abolition of that language game, witch-language, is indeed a good recommendation.

Secondly, it is by no means obvious, though linguistic philosophers have supposed it so, that there is never any point in recommending the abolition of a whole category. The use of teleological language has probably diminished, and it is not self-evident that it would be impossible to abolish the use of it altogether. Whether this is a good or a practicable thing or not can in no way be settled by appeal to the fact that we have used that kind of language hitherto. This constitutes some evidence, but is by no means conclusive.

Thirdly, there is no non-question-begging way of delimiting a "category" or a "language game". The limits of such games are not something *given*. To ascribe these limits, which are *not* "given" by actual language, is either to have found, or prejudged, the answer to a philosophic problem.

The argument from Paradigm Cases is essential, fundamental and pervasive in Linguistic Philosophy. It has pervaded its procedures, and before that the procedures of the Common Sense philosophy of G. E. Moore, long before it was named in 1953. Since it has been named and also criticised some linguistic philosophers have attempted to disclaim it, or to use it with qualification or with discrimination. In view of this attempt to drop the now unwanted ballast, or some of it, certain observations about the role of the APC are essential.

The APC is essential to Linguistic Philosophy because it is merely the explicit formulation of the procedural rule underlying the use of the notion of language games, and of the appeal to use and usages in the solving of philosophical arguments. The whole idea of language games is used to convey that words mean what they mean in the given context of the language game currently employed; hence that there is no other meaning they could have, to which one could appeal, and in terms of which one could contradict the use implicit in that particular game. And although one can reform current usage this, they hold, is philosophically irrelevant! * This, even more than

* Cf. for instance A. Quinton in *The Nature of Metaphysics*, ed. D. F. Pears, p. 148. London 1957.

Professor Flew's admission of its past pervasiveness,* shows the impossibility of jettisoning it without jettisoning the method and outlook as a whole.

Furthermore it is not an argument which can be used with discrimination; if it is sometimes irrelevant or insufficient, then it can never be sufficient. If some additional arguments are required to establish that in this or that particular case the paradigm use is correct, then those arguments are sufficient, and the Argument from Paradigm Cases need not be invoked. So it is either insufficient or redundant.

5. FROM FACT TO NORM

(2) The argument from actual to valid use, or the "Generalised Naturalistic Fallacy".

The famous "Naturalistic Fallacy" is in essence the fallacious inference from what *is* to what *ought* to be. The name was given by G. E. Moore to the mistake occurring in a whole class of ethical theories, namely those which *equate* the meaning of "good" with some determinate characteristic (or set of characteristics), thereby making it impossible to ask or discuss, whether that characteristic, or set of them, is good. (For if they are what "good" *means*, there can be no sense in asking whether they are good: both the question and the answer to it should be trivial. But, Moore argued, questions about whether X is good are *not* trivial, however general a feature X might be. Therefore, X cannot be the *meaning* of "good".)

The *special* application of the Naturalistic Fallacy is this demonstration that key *ethical* terms cannot be defined in terms of non-ethical ones. The *general* application of it is to *any* evaluative concept, whether connected with moral evaluation or not. No normative issue, no question of validity, can be decided by a mere definition.

Linguistic Philosophy consists essentially of a systematic and dogmatic violation of this rule. It consists of "solving" philosophical problems by examining the actual nature of some concept, or the actual rules governing some kind of discourse, and then treating these *de facto* rules of language, its tacit definitions, as *de jure*, as valid answers. That this has in fact been happening in Linguistic Philosophy was noticed by an exponent of it,

* *Essays in Conceptual Analysis*, p. 18.

Professor Flew; * and that it is a fallacy was previously noticed, even within the movement, by Professor Urmson.†

Neither Urmson nor Flew, however, noticed that this concession—the admission that arguing from *de facto* usage to solutions of normative problems—*cannot* be restricted to some small class of problems, leaving the linguistic method intact. They both supposed, and to all appearances still do, that this concession is only relevant to a small sub-class of issues, namely those which raise problems of value. And again, as in the case of the APC, if the argument from usage to norm is *sometimes* invalid, then the additional arguments proving usage in *particular* cases to be valid are sufficient on their own. They then leave the argument from usage to norm either insufficient or redundant. But virtually *all* philosophical problems are in this sense problems of value: only philologists are concerned with just how, in fact, a word is used. A question becomes philosophical when it is about the valid use of a term. This is what philosophy has always meant, and the only thing it sensibly can mean, and *this is precisely why past philosophers were not tempted to be philologists or lexicographers* (even of the "higher" variety).

Note however that the general form of the naturalistic fallacy, like the APC, can be immensely appealing. How could we challenge the norms implicit in a language we speak, without in fact merely introducing another language? The very notion of a language game, the activity-theory and the context-theory of language impel one—or seem to—to agree that no meaning can be attached to a criticism of the norms built into a given language and its concepts, whilst one is speaking that language. One cannot "stand outside"; or, if one does, one is speaking another language, playing another game.

Yet this is precisely what philosophy is and should be: The

* ". . . almost everyone who has used them [Arguments from Paradigm Cases.—E. G.], certainly the present writer, must plead guilty to having from time to time failed to see this" [that they "will not . . . establish any matter of value, moral or otherwise"]. Observation of linguo-philosophic discussions confirms Professor Flew's concession, but it is difficult to see what one could make of his hint that there were also occasions when he and others did not fail to see this. If it were even *sometimes* seen, the APC would *never* be used—for the mere possibility of such occasions robs it of its relevance.

† J. O. Urmson, "Some Questions Concerning Validity", in *Essays in Conceptual Analysis*, p. 120.

asking, not of specific questions within a category, but of questions about categories as a whole, about the viability, possibility, desirability, of whole species of thinking. Linguistic Philosophy, starting from the *game* model of language, attempts to maintain that this is impossible. (At any rate it does this in its early dogmatic stage. In its later, watered-down stage, it merely maintains that whilst possible, it is extra-philosophical. This amounts to an inconvenient and arbitrary redefinition of "philosophy", maintaining within it a trivial exercise and consigning the important re-consideration of basic concepts to some as yet unknown field of thought.)

The fallacy is the same one as underlies the APC: the idea that one cannot ask questions about categories as wholes, about whole species of human thought or discourse, and that these categories are "given", both in the sense of being unchallengeable and in the sense of being objectively delimited. And hence that usage is authoritative, or anyway there is no court of appeal in terms of which it could be judged. Again, when the fallacy is shown to be indefensible as a *theory*, it is turned into a *definition* of philosophy: it is trivialised by simply and arbitrarily excluding the evaluation of kinds of thought from what is to be called "philosophy".

The main comment to be made upon Urmson's and Flew's concession is that the normative problems admitted to be irrelevant to the linguistic method are virtually co-extensive with philosophy. Thus *nothing* survives the concession.

Few things illustrate the silliness of Linguistic Philosophy more conclusively than the fact that there was even the need or occasion for Urmson's article to be written. Its conclusion, that usage cannot settle normative issues about how we *should* think, is something so obvious that it has never in the past been doubted. On the contrary, it was taken for granted, and just this was the reason why pre-linguistic philosophers did not appeal to usage. Urmson's point in the article in question is perfectly true (though he failed to see the full implications of it). What is ironic is that, but for the existence of Linguistic Philosophy, there would be no one to whom it could be addressed, no one who would not consider that point so self-evidently true as not to require statement. In view of this it is either naïve or misleading to claim, by re-publishing the article in a series whose aim is to communicate the ideas of the movement to the world, that this discovery is to be credited to that movement! On the contrary, the denial of this point was at the *basis* of the movement, and its doctrines collapse when this insight is re-admitted.

6. THE CONTRAST THEORY OF MEANING

(3) The Contrast Theory of Meaning is a fallacy closely similar and related to the preceding two.

The argument runs: terms derive their meaning from the fact that there are or could be things which fall under them *and that there are others which do not.* "Apple" has meaning because some things are apples and others are not. "Unicorn" has meaning because something *could* satisfy the conditions for being a unicorn (though it so happens that nothing does), and there are conditions (in fact satisfied by everything) which warrant the non-application of the characteristic of unicornity.

The argument runs as follows: a term and its denial between them exhaust the universe, or at least a universe of discourse. The demarcation line between a term and its denial may perhaps shift as we change the meaning of the term, as often we do. But: there is one kind of shift of meaning which is both disastrous and characteristically philosophical, and that is to make the criteria for what falls under a concept either *so* severe, or *so* loose, that either *nothing* at all *can*, or everything *must*, fall under it.

The term then loses any contrast; it is then used "without antithesis". People who commit the fallacy of using a term "without antithesis" do it, it appears, from the essentially philosophical desire to say something wholly all-embracing, not realising that this ambition is incompatible with saying anything at all.

Once again, the old-fashioned philosopher is accused of recommending an impractical reform, which if adopted will only call for the invention of a new word, to do the work done by another one before. Antitheses, like God, have to be invented when they are lacking. When a term is used so that everything must fall under it, or that nothing can, it ceases to discriminate and hence to convey anything at all. Those who commit the fallacy often do not realise, it is said, as they excessively tighten or loosen the criteria of the use of a term, that in their pursuit of a pure or powerful sense for the word in question, they have overstepped the limits which alone can make the term serve a useful purpose. But the very generality and necessity of philosophic theories, based on a prior tacit misuse of some term along these lines, show what has really happened. . . . The first thing is to show how an antithesis is lacking, and then to exhibit the deficiency in the implicit re-definition of the term which has led to this.

The positive picture of language behind this argument is that the role of language is to separate, not to unify.* One might well object that this doctrine itself does not appear to have a contrast, that the Contrast Theory itself would require, presumably, that language should sometimes be used to unify and sometimes to separate. (The Contrast Theory when made explicit leads to a neat paradox; on its own grounds, a language should sometimes be usable without contrast, so that "contrast" may have a contrast.)

The Contrast Theory of meaning, though statable and usable independently, is really but an aspect or inverse of the Argument from the Paradigm Case. For the Contrast Theory in effect says that a meaningful term must have cases where it does *not* apply, where the APC said that it must have cases where it *does* apply. The Contrast Theory insists that every term must have Paradigm Cases of its own absence, Paradigm Cases of non-applicability: it is the APC in reverse. It follows from the APC itself: not everything can be the Paradigm Case of a concept else one could hardly call it a paradigm; not everything can be a case of it, and the cases *not* falling under a concept must also have *their* paradigm.

Like the APC, the Contrast Theory has a certain appeal. It is easy to get oneself into the state of mind of seeming to see that it *must* be true, and this state of mind is induced by working out the implications of a seemingly sensible model of language, the "game" model.

An important thing to note first of all is that, as in the case of the APC, it does not make sense to use the Contrast Theory

---

* This suggestive formulation was used by Professor J. L. Austin in a Seminar conducted by him, when by means of the Contrast Theory he refuted phenomenalism on the grounds that sense-data are a contrast-less notion. I am quoting from memory but there was little doubt about the general trend of the argument, nor about the fact that this was a central, not a peripheral point.

selectively. If sometimes inapplicable, then the reason which makes it relevant or not, and not the theory itself, is what matters.

There is a further danger here: the APC, the Contrast Theory, and the generalised Naturalistic Fallacy *all* share (and for similar reasons) the characteristic of being insufficient on their own and redundant when supported by other considerations. But their insufficiency on their own may be camouflaged by bringing them in jointly, each or two of them in turn, creating the illusion that they support each other and provide each other with the required additional evidence. But these three arguments are, each on their own, deficient in a way so similar that their joint use presents no stronger case than each of them would on its own. Their joint presentations cannot count as independent evidence for any one of them.

How can one bring out the falsehood of the Contrast Theory? *

Its very formulation presupposes that one can distinguish between assertions within a given contrast, *within* a given polarity, and the specification of that polarity itself; in other words, between language games and moves within them. But this is not so. Take a very broad class of uses of language such as moral, evaluative language: It might be argued against moral nihilism, the doctrine that *no* moral statements are true, that it pointlessly abolishes the contrast between valid and invalid moral judgments. But the nihilist may well reply that the drawing of moral distinctions is only a matter of subordinate distinctions, *within* a wider class of meaningful assertions, and that he is saying that within this *wider* contrast, one of the classes is to be rejected (because, for instance, it is arbitrary). In brief, he may maintain that moral utterance is not a self-contained language-system but a move within a wider game, and that he is pointing out that it is a *bad* move.

The Contrast Theory cannot refute him: for it is vacuous: it cannot tell us *which* contrasts are legitimate, which are necessary, which can be dispensed with. Linguistic philosophers prejudge this question in favour of customarily employed contrasts, and mistakenly suppose that the conclusions which they thus smuggle in are warranted by the quite distinct and vacuous

* Cf. C. K. Grant, "Polar Concepts and Metaphysical Arguments" *Aristotelian Society Proceedings*, 1955/56.

contention that *when* contrasts are necessary, they cannot be dispensed with.

On more specific planes the irrelevance of the Contrast Theory is even more apparent. The argument has incidentally a very long history going back well before Linguistic Philosophy. Santayana once parodied it somewhere by saying that very poor Spanish peasants, who eat nothing but lentils, and in whose diet consequently lentils have no contrast, therefore eat nothing at all. This fails to follow, not merely because other components of diet are conceivable, but also because eating is contrastable with drinking. Eating-language is not a language game, eating is not a category. Other, more serious uses of the argument from contrast commit the same or similar mistake.

The model underlying the attraction of the Contrast Theory suggests that language falls neatly into games, systems of alternatives or contrasts that are fully determinate. In fact, contrasts often overlay presuppositions which are worth bringing out, and sometimes worth denying: the contrast between good and bad witches is worth ignoring for the sake of denying that either kind exists. Far from thought generally moving within a tacitly determinate system of contrasts, it often happens that by refining a concept which at the time is contrast-less, a new contrast, a new concept is brought into being. This picture of the progress of thought, associated with Hegelianism, seems to me far truer, and certainly more illuminating with regard to *important* ideas, than the picture associated with the Wittgensteinian approach, of thought consisting of moves within *pre-existing* games, and none of them allowing an abrogation of its contrast. The job of philosophy is perhaps to unravel presuppositions of old contrasts, or discover contrasts where hitherto none had been perceived: and not to inhibit thought by insisting on well-established ones.

7. GENERAL COMMENTS ON THE THREE FALLACIES

The three fallacies analysed and outlined have a great deal in common. Their plausibility is rooted in a common model of language. They are each of them invoked as charters of the most characteristic linguistic procedure, namely the so-called dissolution of philosophic problems by appeals to the actual use of words. Not only their specious plausibility but also their fallaciousness is extremely similar. The error springs in each case from the failure to realise that thought is not bound and enslaved by any of the language games it employs, but on the contrary that a most important kind of thinking consists of reassessing our terms, reassessing the norms built into them and reassessing the contrasts associated with them. Philosophy is generally thinking of this kind—but not only philosophy. One of the things linguistic philosophers fail to notice is that this kind of thinking—which they consider to belong to the pathology of language—is most characteristic of any kind of intellectual advance. Discoveries are very seldom, if ever, moves within a pre-established language game, but tend to be the establishment or discovery of a new kind of more satisfactory, more suggestive, more perceptive or profound language, a discovery or construction which generally follows on criticisms of previously existing ones. Such criticisms invariably violate, and in the nature of things have to violate, the three kinds of fallacious principles outlined. If these principles come to be generally respected, the result would be inhibition of all interesting thought. (The false claim that they are not generalised, or that it is possible to use them without generalising them, has been discussed.)

These three pillars of Linguistic Philosophy are joined by a fourth which I shall call *Polymorphism*. This one, though related in an interesting way to the preceding three, is not merely another reformulation of them, and has some interesting features of its own.

8. THE CULT OF THE FOX

(4) Modern philosophy began with Descartes' requirement of clear and distinct ideas. Linguistic Philosophy has reversed this. It insists on unclear and indistinct ideas.

This is not a wholly absurd requirement. It is based on an interesting theory, namely, that our ideas, the rules governing our uses of words, are in fact indistinct, complex, with jagged or cloudy edges: and that our Cartesian attempts to make them neat, precise and homogeneous, or, worse still, to interpret our old concepts as if they already were so, lead us to confusion and to intellectual "cramps". Our concepts, being the verbal activities of complex organisms in a complex social and natural environment, are bound to be untidy. To unify and simplify them is to travesty them. Past philosophy is such travesty.

The doctrine of Polymorphism is in some ways the most striking and characteristic feature of Linguistic Philosophy. For some purposes it might also be called idiographism or Heracliteanism. The idea is an immense stress on complexity, on variegation, on the shadowy borderlines and transitions of concepts, on the *sui generis* nature of linguistic forms and of philosophic problems. By contrast, generality is treated with utmost reserve, if not with contempt.* The idea is not so much that generalisations must be checked against instances, but that generalisations *as such* are suspect, or even ex officio damned. A general model of language or of a kind of discourse is alleged to be mistaken, not because it happens to be a bad model, but because it *is* a general model. Generality *per se* is treated, either as an index of falsehood, or at least as harmful in philosophy. Linguistic philosophers would presumably not deny the validity of the ideal of generality in the sciences (though Ryle did so for psychology: cf. *The Concept of Mind* p. 323), but their special view of philosophy differentiates it precisely by this fact, that in it generality is to be at least distrusted and probably avoided in principle.†

The underlying idea is that language as employed is extremely manifold and complex, which in a sense is true: furthermore, that philosophic questions and/or mistakes always, or predominantly, or characteristically, arise from the misinterpretation of manifold linguistic reality, mistaken by seeing it as exemplifying unique and simple models. This diagnosis is complementary to that of the APC, etc. The APC and Contrast Theories show up the falsity of a philosophic theory through its conflict with usage, and demonstrate the truth of the commonsense view through its agreement with usage. Polymorphism then explains the temptation which produced the mistaken, philosophic view—the pursuit of simplicity and generality in accounting for our use of a word or concept. The correct procedure to adopt is to reverse this, to observe linguistic complexity in its full richness: not to generalise but to demolish general models.

* P. L. Heath discusses it in *The Philosophical Quarterly*, January 1956, p. 66, "Wittgenstein's object, we are reminded, was to make an end of the customary traffic in philosophical generalities . . ."

† Cf. S. Toulmin, *Universities Quarterly*, August 1957, p. 345.

I distinguish two kinds of Polymorphism. I shall call them Internal and External (to concepts). Linguistic philosophers have not themselves explicitly made this distinction.

The *internal* complexity of concepts is something like this: Many philosophers, even though they are nominalists and do not suppose that a concept refers to a unique *thing*, nevertheless suppose that concepts do or should refer to a class of things delimited by a definite criterion. This criterion is then the connotation of that concept; the things satisfying that criterion, if any, are its denotation. (Of course, the same *word* may have a number of separate criteria of applicability, defining distinct classes; these classes are conceptually distinct. When a *word* has a number of meanings—e.g. "racket" means something to do with tennis, but also something to do with nefarious activities—we are dealing with two concepts which happen in a given language to be conveyed by the same word. This is simply a case of homonym.)

But the traditional assumption was that a concept, if clear, has one criterion (which may of course contain a number of conditions in conjunction or even as alternatives), and that if on the other hand there is multiplicity of sets of criteria, we are dealing with homonyms. There was no third possibility.

Just this assumption is what is denied by the discovery of the internal complexity of concepts. This denial is a kind of doubly strong assertion of nominalism: not only is the meaning of terms not some unique thing, essence or form, but there isn't even necessarily a unique criterion of the applicability of any one concept. If this is so, the temptation to logical realism, to the belief in entities as correlates of abstract words, is doubly undermined.

One favourite example of this is the word "game" itself.

The argument runs: There is no single criterion or even set of criteria which fit all the things that are customarily described as games. Yet this is not the case of a mere homonym, of accidentally using the same word for a number of disparate things. Games do in some ways have something in common: when new activities emerge it is on the whole possible to decide non-arbitrarily whether or not the term "game" applies to them or not. The "polymorphous" diagnosis offered of this situation by Linguistic Philosophy runs as follows: a term may very well apply to a whole class of objects A, B, C, etc., in a way such that

A does have something in common with B, and B with C, but not necessarily A with C. There may, as it is put, be a "family likeness", such as occurs when every member of a family is recognisably one of it and yet no two members need necessarily have any features in common.

A more important case for which polymorphousness is claimed is the concept of "thinking". It is claimed that one of the roots of the notion that thinking is some kind of mysterious process is the pre-conception that terms in general, and hence "thinking" in particular, must refer to *a* delimitable thing or process—this pre-conception preventing one from realising that "thought" is displayed in a large variety of ways.*

The *external* polymorphousness of concepts denies the assumptions that all *kinds* of words or concepts are used in similar *ways*. It is suggested that this assumption was widespread if tacit in traditional philosophy, and that a large number of philosophic errors can be attributed to it. For instance, both the famous Ontological Proof of the existence of God and the dark theorising of some contemporary Existentialists are claimed to spring from a fallacious assumption that "being", "to exist" functions in a manner analogous to terms like "singing" or "to bark". Professor Ryle has popularised the expression "category mistake" as the name for views based on a confusion of one kind of use with another.

The positive theory underlying the denial of similarity in kind of various verbal expressions is this: words are used in many diverse ways and for quite diverse purposes. Language uses are legion. The communication of facts is but one of them. There are, for instance, the making of suggestions, the issuing of orders, the expression of feeling, the making of a legally or ritually significant verbal act, the assessment of chances, the appraisal of beauty, etc., etc. Traditional philosophy, it is claimed, just as it mistakenly assumed that concepts were internally homogeneous, also assumed that they were all similar in kind. If it didn't claim that they were all of one kind, it at least believed that they were all of one of a small number of kinds, easily discernible in type, and isolable.

A particularly striking instance of mistake based on an over-simple view of how language works is said to be the theory that there are universals, essences, "intentional objects", objective

* Cf. Professor Gilbert Ryle's *British Academy Lecture*, 1958.

values, etc. This mistake is diagnosed as springing from the tacit assumption that all meaningful terms are *names*. The entities in question were then supposed to be the *bearers* of those names.

The rejection of a unique, fundamental or pre-eminent or basic language is one important aspect of Linguistic Philosophy, and the doctrine of Polymorphism is one of the main weapons by means of which the idea is attacked. The idea of a perfect or fundamental language is alleged to be closely connected with the belief that the philosopher is capable of making counter-commonsensical revelations about the world: for if there were such a fundamental underlying skeleton of our thought or speech, then the specification by the philosopher of its concepts or terms would at the same time be the indication of what "the world is really like".* Conversely, if the philosopher were capable of telling us what the world is really like as distinct from what it appears to be, then the words he would use in describing that fundamental reality would also be the fundamental language. So, the linguo-philosophical rejection of a basic language and the insistence on sticking to the common-sense view of things—and the impossibility of philosophically correcting common sense—are mutually dependent, and both depend on the insistence on the essential, inescapable manifoldness of the uses of language.

Types of expression are *not* reducible to other kinds. "Everything is what it is and not another thing." "There is an indefinite number of kinds of expression." "Every proposition has its own logic."

How is this variegation brought out? By examining, carefully and minutely, all the manifold actual uses of some expression, or of the whole group of expressions connected with some topic or problem. This examination, by bringing home to us the complexity and the actual, real context and purpose of the use of the terms, will, it is claimed, dissolve the problem.

For one thing, having seen the full use of the relevant terms, how *could* there be a problem left? Secondly, by *rubbing in* the full complexity, it frees us from the temptation to seek a "reduction" of one kind of expression to another, by exhibiting the impossibility and irrelevance of such an attempt.

* Cf. Professor J. N. Findlay, *Philosophy and Phenomenological Research*, 1948, p. 222.

Of course, the exhibiting of *all* the relevant uses may not be enough. The sufferer from the philosophic complaint may still, despite having seen all the uses and their contexts and function and whole context and function, be driven somehow by an urge to formulate questions or ideas which violate those very functions and contexts. The explanation, Linguistic Philosophy maintains, is that tacitly, in a kind of logical or conceptual unconscious, he is wedded to some inapplicable or over-simple model of how words work or how that particular kind of expression works, some un-polymorphic idea, and he persists in seeing it in that light. For instance, it is very natural to be wedded to the model of knowledge as a kind of *contact* (between a mind and a thing known). The puzzlements which result when this model is applied to, for instance, knowledge of the past, is well known. Or take the model of all inference as deductive reasoning: notoriously, if applied to inductive inferences it leads to the conclusion that inferences to the future are never justifiable.

The linguistic philosopher thus has to go not merely through the virtually indefinite set of actual uses of the cluster of terms relevant to the problem, he may also have to go through an endless set of other types of expression to find the model which is misleading the sufferer. . . . When he has done so, the problem is dissolved—or is supposed to be. The idea that all philosophical problems are "dissoluble" in this way has two merits: it follows from the naturalistic picture of the world and the functional picture of language—for what philosophical problems other than those so dissoluble *could* there be? And secondly, it is unfalsifiable: one does not know how long one will have to go through both positive instances of use and possible misleading models, and so the fact that some problems have as yet not been dissolved in no way proves that there is no way of dissolving them.

There was once a film about the Thousand and One Nights in which a comedian tried to find a magic formula to make the carpet fly by endlessly going through possible formulae at random. Linguistic philosophers similarly go through an endless process trying to find the set of formulae that will, in Wittgenstein's phrase, "let the fly out of the bottle". Some of them perhaps believe they have a nose for hitting the formula without having to look too long.

Some general observations are worth making about Polymorphism. There is an old theory of theology and metaphysics
which asserts that these alleged disciplines, because they concern themselves with objects which cannot be experienced or
cannot be conceptualised in a normal way, must speak of them
in an "analogical" way. Linguistic philosophers, inspired by
the polymorphic view of language, have also seen ordinary,
non-transcendental philosophy as essentially analogical. They
see the old philosophy, which tries to say something, as the mis-
application of analogies, seeing one type of use of language as
another—with meaningless doctrines, unanswerable problems
and so forth as a result. For instance, there are: the mistaken
interpretation of thinking as a kind of inner *process*, or of abstract words as names (producing the theory of Universals),
or of moral evaluation as the ascription of a characteristic, and
so forth. As indicated, linguistic philosophers see their own task
as the undermining of such analogies, and the curing or control-
ling of the temptation to indulge in them.

One might put this as follows: Past philosophy assumed one
language and many or problematic "worlds" or realms. Linguistic Philosophy has many language uses in one unproblematic world. It claims to be neutral about what that one world is
like (pretending merely to investigate and describe the "languages" in it), but in fact insinuates a certain vision of it.

The implications of this outlook are fairly obvious. It underwrites a reluctance to reduce old concepts in the interests of
neatness or logical consistency or progress, or to innovate under
the inspiration of the same considerations. It equally underwrites the insistence on carefulness and minute observation in
philosophy. It also, of course, provides a prop for the linguo-
philosophical theory of mind and thinking, as a multitude of
variegated things and not as one kind of thing.

9. EVERYTHING IS UNLIKE EVERYTHING ELSE

There is an undeniable element of truth in Polymorphism,
both logically and empirically. As a matter of simple fact it is
true that languages are complicated and consist of a variety of
activities. It is also, perhaps, a necessary truth that any language
that does anything worth while has to contain elements or tools
of radically different types, and so *cannot* be internally entirely

homogeneous and simple. Nevertheless, the exaggerated use of Polymorphism * by Linguistic Philosophy is disastrous and unjustifiable. Its weaknesses are similar to those of the three fallacies outlined previously with which it is closely associated. It is an attempt to undermine and paralyse one of the most important kinds of thinking, and one of the main agents of progress, namely intellectual advance through consistency and unification, through the attainment of coherence, the elimination of exceptions, arbitrarinesses, and unnecessary idiosyncracies. It in effect tends to underwrite all current concepts, however useless, anachronistic, inconsistent. For linguistic philosophers conceive their philosophical thought to be the undermining of general models and of models *as such*, as models— only the actual ungeneral *description* of an usage is philosophically "aseptic", and commendable.

In addition to the defects it shares with the preceding three fallacies, it has some interesting ones of its own: the idea that we can grasp linguistic functions in their full idiosyncrasy, without generalising, presupposes two most questionable things: (1) the possibility of an idiographic science, and (2) the possibility of conceptual neutrality.

By idiographic science I mean a study which claims to know individual things "in their full individuality", so to speak, and without the intermediary of general terms or concepts. The idea of such a science is similar to what used to be called "knowledge by acquaintance", that is to say knowledge by direct contact with an individual thing, a kind of knowledge which does not need abstractions to mediate between it and the thing known.

Linguistic philosophers do not openly subscribe to the theory of either idiographic science or of "knowledge by acquaintance". On the contrary, their ideas spring in part from the rejection of a theory of knowledge which assumed that knowledge by acquaintance must be at the base of all knowledge. But: their ideas on how they themselves can and do handle the objects of their own investigations and knowledge, namely concepts or forms of language or uses of expressions, presupposes precisely this idea of knowing-by-contact, by "showing" or "exhibiting": they implicitly claim to know or describe an individual thing, a use of language, *without* having to employ some general concept.

* The "57 Varieties" way of doing philosophy, as it has been wittily described by Professor S. Körner.

This idea is presupposed by the claim to neutrality which is so often made on behalf of Linguistic Philosophy, and also by the related claim to being free of positive doctrine (the claim that it is only a rectification of confusions about language, and the display and account of the actual uses of our words). These claims could only be true if it *were* indeed possible simply to "show" a concept, to exhibit the use of a group of words: but in facts such activities presuppose the validity of those concepts, classifications and so on which are inevitably employed in describing them, even if this is only done tacitly. Linguistic philosophers delude themselves that none such are employed, by two means: (1) By claiming merely to *exhibit* the uses of words, so to speak, without comment. This is one of their illusions concerning the nature of their own practice. Philosophy, they say, is an activity and not a doctrine. But, even when they succeed in living up to this theory and merely "display how a word is used"—which is not always the case—all that happens is that some general idea, some "puzzlement-terminating" insight is *insinuated*, by means of the manner in which the usages are exhibited, by the problem to which they are alleged to be relevant, and so on. (2) In "describing" usages, the concepts they employ are in fact simply the whole of the current ordinary language, as applicable to the description of verbal behaviour and its contexts. This ordinariness is somehow supposed to make them neutral or non-question-begging. But this is simply to *prejudge* the validity or applicability of this ordinary language —or the part of it one cares to use—whereas this was just what the method was supposed to establish. Here, as elsewhere, the circle is complete, and granted we play the game according to the rules linguistic philosophers recommend, there is no breaking out of it.

It is amusing to watch a dilemma which they face at this point: either the linguistic method consists merely of the description of usages—in which case, *why* indulge in it? Is it not trivial?—or, something else emerges in consequence of the interminable examinations of how we use words—in which case, could not that something be articulated, assessed, evaluated? Linguistic philosophers choose the former alternative when someone else attempts to elicit what their elusive insight is: they protest and raise empty hands to the skies, declaring that, *qua* philosophers, they hold no views and are not committed to any.

If, on the other hand, they are charged with trivial word-collecting, they claim that it is a "quaint" * travesty to suppose that *only* usage-collecting is involved; some deep insights are apparently induced by those practices.

This dilemma corresponds to the ambivalence within Linguistic Philosophy, or rather its inherent ambiguity between being a dogmatic naturalism and a mysticism, an ambiguity which will be explored later. In essence, it is a naturalism propagated *as* a mystical revelation.

10. THE BEST OF ALL POSSIBLE LANGUAGES
Or, Polymorphism and Functionalism

It is worth noting that the great stress on variety of role does not necessarily or generally lead the linguistic philosopher to an image of language as a kind of fragmented, chaotic aggregate. The stress is not merely on diversification, but on diversification of *role*, of function. There is a strong suggestion that language is a neatly integrated whole with which it is undesirable or unnecessary to tinker.† "Every sentence is in order as it is."

Linguistic philosophers would not always claim in so many words that any natural language is perfect, but there is a strong presumption in favour of treating any particular usage as not

---

* Cf. Mr. R. F. Holland, in *The Universities Quarterly*, November 1957, p. 81.

† An apparent exception to this is this statement by Professor Austin: "It seems to be too readily assumed that . . . each (concept) will fit into place in some single, interlocking, consistent schemes . . . all historical probability is against this. . . ." Presidential Address to the Aristotelian Society, *Proceedings*, 1956/57, p. 29.

In the same paper (p. 11), however, Austin makes up for this supposition that language may not be a harmonious whole, by also arguing that there is a presumption in favour of belief that, even if not harmonious, it is otherwise well-adjusted to its ends. Though not integrated, it nevertheless does not call for much change. This argument in favour of ordinary language, based on the survival-worthiness it has displayed by surviving, is not, whatever its other demerits, really compatible with the *main* argument in its favour used by Linguistic Philosophy, namely that it is in order because there cannot be a perfect, logical language in terms of which it could be judged to be imperfect. The two arguments really cancel each other out: if there is no way of saying that a thing is imperfect, it cannot then also display its nearness to perfection by its capacity to survive! Despite this inconsistency, the two arguments are found together; indeed, they are not always clearly distinguished.

requiring improvement, as beyond criticism. In any case, there is a very heavy onus of proof on the innovator.

The belief that natural language can be expected to have good reasons for what it does is expressed, for instance, by G. Warnock ". . . language does not develop in a random or inexplicable fashion . . . it is *at the very least* [italics mine—E.G.] unlikely that it should contain either much more, or much less, than [its] purposes require. . . . It is at the same time very *un*likely that any invented . . . terminology will be an improvement" (*English Philosophy Since 1900*, p. 150).

Professor J. L. Austin puts the point as follows: ". . . ordinary language . . . embodies . . . the inherited experience and acumen of many generations of men". (Presidential Address to the Aristotelian Society, *Proceedings*, 1956/57, p. 11.)

The reasons for this apotheosis of the accidents of actual language may be of different kinds: either, as above, the usual type of reason for venerating tradition—our elders had some sense, and a kind of natural selection must have operated, and underwrites the usages that have survived till our time. (The objections one can, decisively, oppose to this are: what survives in one set of conditions may be far from ideal for a radically new environment, and the environment of man—technologically, socially, intellectually—has changed and is changing so radically and fast that past survival creates but a feeble presumption of fitness—and indeed, can sometimes be an index of unfitness. Past usages are often based on currently rejected presuppositions. Arguments relevant against the APC are also relevant here.)

The second reason for viewing language as well adjusted is this: it may be admitted that reform is often called for, but it may be maintained that such reform is "extra-philosophical": philosophy is concerned with understanding our concepts, and pragmatic, empirical, technical, ethical or other considerations which inspire reform are outside it. This argument is simply based on a definition of "philosophy" which happens to be both arbitrary and unworkable, though it is a definition inherent in the whole outlook of Linguistic Philosophy. It is arbitrary, for if there is such a thing as fundamental conceptual, linguistic reform, then it, and the evaluations of reasons for it, *is* philosophy: it is something far more important and interesting than either "therapeutic" or *l'art pour l'art* observation of the use of words.

The new definition is also unworkable, for the reform and the observation of use are inseparable. Interesting observation of use generally springs from practical needs and goes with the possibility of reform. Philosophy does not spring, as Wittgenstein thought, from our being blinded by grammar, but from the need to reorder our concepts.

The third reason, or rather sense, for deeming natural language perfect, the sense which is most important in Linguistic Philosophy, is simply the denial of the existence or possibility of an absolute, basic or perfect language, a way of speaking possessing some kind of logical priority, in terms of which other ways of speaking could then be better or worse. In as far as there is no such logical-linguistic absolute, all other languages are indeed "perfect"—though only in the left-handed sense that there is no yardstick in terms of which they could be measured. Wittgenstein in his youth conceived Philosophy as the specification of such a language, and in his age he saw it as the specification or insinuation * of why such a language was impossible, and for this reason deified actual language. (It is perfect because there is no norm of perfection. . . .) The denial of such an absolute language norm made him treat all actual language as in order, and hence in *that* sense perfect. But the sense of "perfection" unfortunately vacillates between the rather left-handed "perfection" which a thing has simply in virtue of there being no norm in terms of which it could be *im*perfect, and the more full-blooded sense of "functional adjustment". There is evidence for *both* interpretations: but it is the first of the two senses which is essential for the movement and constitutes its original contribution.

Thus there is a confusion between the various justifications of idolatry of ordinary language: (1) it is its own standard (there can be no other) and so there *can* be no "improvements", (2) ordinary language has stood the test of time, (3) innovations are possible but extra-philosophical, and also (4) innovations are only called for in technical subjects, not in ordinary language.

Now in the left-handed sense (1), the "perfection" of actual, natural language may indeed be the case. But even if we grant

* He switches to insinuation of it when he remembers that to specify even a negative thesis about all language—that *no* proper logical language is its substrate—is to say something outside any specific language-system or game: and hence that it is something which, on his own views, cannot be said.

this, it in no way follows that there are not many other criteria, other than those implicit in the notion of an absolute, perfect language, which may not be applied to actual ways of speaking.

It follows even less from the denial of a perfect logical language that the application of other criteria to natural languages is "outside philosophy". Unfortunately, the valid, thin sense in which Wittgenstein is right—directed primarily at his own earlier views—is not separated sharply enough by him and his followers from the other, invalid senses: from the attempt to exclude—arbitrarily—evaluation of concepts from philosophy; or from the substantive doctrine that specific natural languages are well-integrated if complex wholes and that one should never tinker with them, or only if the case for innovation is overwhelmingly strong.

What may be called a Linguistic Functionalism—the doctrine to the effect that all parts of language have a useful role to play and perform it efficiently, so that it is very difficult to improve on natural speech either in detail or in principle—tends to be associated with the more central view of language held by Linguistic Philosophy. Such associated views and the central one support each other, if only because they sound very similar if formulated briefly.

CHAPTER III

OF PHILOSOPHY

I. ACTIVITY NOT DOCTRINE

THE BASIC OUTLOOK of Linguistic Philosophy can be communicated, as shown, either, by indicating its view of the world, philosophy or language—or by specifying some particular doctrine concerning language and the way words mean things—or, most characteristically, it can be insinuated without any general formulation at all, from the treatment of specific cases.

Such piecemeal investigations, which do not avow the general premisses which inspire and guide them, have the consequence that these general principles, not being avowed and indeed being disclaimed, cannot easily be criticised. This is not simply a trick, though its effects are the same as if it were.

This piecemeal procedure is suggested by "Polymorphism", and by the other aspect of the theory of language. In turn, this procedure is the basis for the view that (traditional) philosophy, with its habit of formulating explicit doctrines, is the pathology of language. Hence sane philosophy is merely the removal of confusions and errors arguing from the failure to see the truth of Polymorphism and hence it brings no positive or general truths. Thus everything dovetails neatly with everything else.

Apart from the ideals of clarification, of removal of confusion, this way of proceeding has a definite set of slogans, images and doctrines to provide it with a rationale; namely, that philosophy is an *activity*, and the earlier idea that some things are *ineffable*. These two notions are intimately linked: philosophy is an activity as opposed to being a doctrine. It cannot be a doctrine because it cannot have anything to say. It cannot have anything to *say* either because there is nothing left for it to say, or because it "cannot be said", is "ineffable". So it must be an *activity*. But what the activity conveys must again be either ineffable or nothing at all. But though it cannot be said, it can perhaps be "shown" (by an activity which doesn't actually articulate it), or made clear, or somehow conveyed.

The idea that philosophy is an *activity*—as opposed to a doctrine—has a strong general appeal quite apart from dovetailing with the other ideas of Linguistic Philosophy: it provides an answer to the puzzling question of how philosophy is possible at all, how a subject can exist which neither gathers information nor calculates: how philosophers who do not claim special faculties can nevertheless have something to contribute.

It fits in more particularly with the doctrine of language, which leaves no room for philosophical propositions, and it fits in well with the doctrine of the world, which leaves no room for general and absolute characteristics such as would be of concern to the philosopher.

Thus, negatively, the doctrine of activity fits in very well. It avoids the need for statement, and it has the incidental advantage that statements that are not made cannot, *a fortiori*, be open to criticism. As Professor J. O. Urmson describes the situation:

> "It is notorious that many philosophers claim that they are adherents of no philosophical doctrines whatsoever, and even regard adherence to a philosophical doctrine as a sign of a fundamental misunderstanding of the nature of philosophy . . . there seems to be nobody left under the age of eighty who is prepared to confess himself a rationalist, or empiricist, a neutral monist, a materialist, a logical atomist, a pragmatist, a realist, an idealist. . . ." (*The Philosophical Quarterly*, July 1957, p. 267.)

But, one may rightly object that an activity cannot be a random activity. It must have a starting point, a terminating point, and rules of procedure. These rules or criteria are, and presuppose, something that *can* be said! Linguistic philosophers however in general abstain from making them explicit, and the doctrine of ineffability provides them with a justification.

It must be said that there is not now an explicitly held and formulated Ineffability Doctrine in the movement though the phrase "what cannot be said" *is* encountered. (Indeed the trouble with it is that there is almost nothing that is explicitly formulated—not even this idea that there is nothing to formulate.) As an explicit doctrine, it belongs to the views of Wittgenstein's youth, worked out in the *Tractatus*. But the habit of talking of "what cannot be said", what "transcends language", etc. has survived into Linguistic Philosophy proper, and is essential to it.

It is essential to it because what does define linguistic philosophers and what they do have in common, is the conviction that there cannot be specifically philosophical propositions (unless, trivially, we allow them to count reports on how we use words as "philosophical propositions"). Hence philosophy, if it exists at all—and linguistic philosophers have a professional interest in this being so—must be an activity, the way one goes about investigating how we speak.

This specifically philosophical *activity* must however be distinguished by something. Either it conveys some ineffable insights (and then we have an Ineffability Doctrine), or it is by nature therapeutic, removing "mental cramps", or it is just a case of *l'art pour l'art*. Each of these alternatives has its disadvantages. The first, being a doctrine, is liable to be criticised by opponents. The second, being an implicit promise of a cure from philosophic questioning, is liable to disappoint by nonfulfilment. The third is plain trivial.

2. THE IMPERTURBABLE UNIVERSE

What triggers off this activity? In other words, what is made to count as a philosophical problem? The characteristic answers are given in terms like these: perplexity, cramp, puzzlement, paradox. In the case of G. E. Moore, who greatly influenced the movement and is jointly with Wittgenstein its chief patron saint, though not himself strictly a linguistic philosopher (he practised it so well that he evaded this label), it was puzzlement by the paradoxical assertions of *other* philosophers. He explicitly states that he never found the world itself or science philosophically puzzling.*

Note that not only are the criteria of what starts the activity left fairly inexplicit, in as far as we are given clues they are semi-metaphorical, semi-psychological: puzzlement, perplexity. One does not know here, as so often with Linguistic Philosophy,

---

* "I do not think that the world or the sciences would ever have suggested to me any philosophical problems. What has suggested philosophical problems to me is things which other philosophers have said about the world or the sciences." "An Autobiography", p. 14, in *The Philosophy of G. E. Moore*, ed. P. A. Schilpp, 1942.

how literally to take this. (Would a perplexity induced by a drug count?) The least psychological of the terms employed is *paradox*. Professor John Wisdom even defined philosophy as the logic of paradox.

Alleged paradoxicality is indeed the starting point, and the characteristic beginning of a treatment of a problem by a linguistic philosopher is to bring out the allegedly paradoxical nature of (traditional) philosophic theories and problems: they characteristically asserted, it is alleged, what we know full well in our common-sense moments to be untrue (e.g. that time is unreal, that there is no such thing as causation, or beauty, etc.). Here, as elsewhere, the movement is greatly indebted to G. E. Moore, who systematically brought out the paradoxicality of philosophic theories and questions by treating them with a deliberate literal-mindedness.

This of course provides us with the clue to the unavowed substantive theory about the world: all paradoxes being due for "treatment" and being indices of linguistic pathology, non-paradoxical statements are exempt: the world is as non-paradoxical statements describe it, in other words as common sense sees it. The world is, substantially, as it appears. This doctrine, whilst not always avowed, is built into the criteria that initiate philosophic treatment, "dissolution" or "therapy".

What about the equally unspecified criterion of *termination* of the activity? We get, again, the quasi-psychological correlatives of the criteria for the start; the dissipation of the perplexity, of the mental cramp. "The fly is let out of the bottle." "One no longer wishes to ask the question", or "it no longer matters what answer is given". One gets the impression, just as the world is necessarily commonsensical, unparadoxical, unexciting, so the ideal set up for the successful philosopher is a kind of nonchalance or insouciance. All the flies having been let out of all the bottles, there is nothing left to be excited about—at any rate, nothing in or about the world (as opposed to language); or not philosophically. The vision of the world and of man implicit in the criteria for the *termination* of the linguo-philosophic therapy are the same, naturally, as those insinuated by the criteria for setting it off.

The social ideal of imperturbability has been turned into a principle of cosmology: the world must be such as to justify non-perturbation. . . .

One should add that no attempt has been made to cope with the fact that what seems paradoxical is not the same to all people at all times, nor even to the same person at different times. It is assumed to be obvious. Or rather: when an "ordinary" locution is hard to make sense of, this counts as a confirmation of Polymorphism, of the diversity and complexity of ordinary speech. If a "philosophical" assertion is odd, this confirms the thesis that philosophy is paradox. (One can of course play this game in the reverse direction, and some old-fashioned metaphysicians have done so. The complexity of ordinary language was an index of its *inadequacy*, and the difficulty of philosophic propositions, a sign of its *depth*.)

One can please oneself which procedure one prefers. This illustrates the fact that the paradoxicality of philosophy, like the other ideas of Linguistic Philosophy, is a definition rather than an idea, and is guaranteed and supported by the other elements and procedures of the system.*

The circularity of the game becomes particularly marked when, instead of "paradoxicality", linguistic philosophers claim "not to understand" a philosophical doctrine. "Unintelligibility" of this kind has the same role as paradoxicality, namely to trigger off the process which is only allowed to terminate by the abandonment of the allegedly paradoxical or unintelligible view.

Academic environments are generally characterised by the presence of people who claim to understand more than in fact they do. Linguistic Philosophy has produced a great revolution, generating people who claim *not* to understand when in fact they do. Some achieve great virtuosity at it. Any beginner in philosophy can manage not to understand, say, Hegel, but I have heard people who were so advanced that they knew how

---

* A striking example of both oblique communication and the philosophy = oddity equation was Professor John Wisdom's reaction to a challenge to specify his own views (rather than be ever diagnosing hypothetical models of what "sceptics", "metaphysicians", "logicians" say when misled.)

He replied, in a letter to the *New Statesman* in 1953, by constructing a wholly absurd, though not particularly philosophical, question, and challenging the original questioner to answer *it*. The question was so odd that the only possible response was "What makes you ask it?" What Professor Wisdom was trying to convey was that philosophical questions should properly elicit just this response.

not to understand writers of such limpid clarity as Bertrand Russell or A. J. Ayer.*

But there is a serious aspect of this: by deciding what one "understands" and "does not understand", one in fact tacitly prejudges the picture of the world one is prepared to accept. Linguistic philosophers have decided in advance that they only understand established ordinary usage.

Finally, let us look at the third suppressed or semi-avowed factor, the rules governing the *activity* whilst it is in progress, between the commencement and the termination. The statement that "we don't know what will let the fly out of the bottle" suggests that the various moves and practices have no roles, that *anything* can be tried; but this claim of total elasticity need not be taken seriously.

What characteristically happens tends to be:

Firstly, reminder of violation of non-paradoxical usage (generally the invocation of the APG and the Contrast Theory).

Then, detailed investigations of all the complexity of ordinary non-paradoxical usage. (Invocation of Polymorphism.)

Then, specification or insinuation of the alleged misleading models which may be in the mind of those tempted by paradox (misleading models in the sense of suggesting that an expression functioning in one way is functioning in another). If, for instance, a term which is not a name is treated as if it were, one then seeks, vainly, for a nominee, as a person who supposed that "Nothing" was a name might be puzzled—it is said—by how one can "see nothing". *What* do you see?

The treatment of the word "nothing" as though it were a name of *somebody*—when in fact the whole point of using that word is to convey that there is *no* "somebody"—is seen as a kind of model for philosophic error: (pre-linguistic) philosophers are said to have supposed, apparently, that a "cause", because it is between two things, is like a chain, or that a sensation is like a thing or a part of a thing, and so on.

Concerning these and similar activities that make up the linguo-philosophic investigation between its commencement and its termination, two things must be said:

(1) They are generally applications of the APG, the Contrast

* I have heard Professor J. L. Austin claim to achieve the latter feat, and Professor H. L. A. Hart, the former.

Theory and of Polymorphism, and they consequently suffer such weaknesses as have been found in those ideas.

For instance, the exposure of a "paradoxical" philosophical doctrine in virtue of its conflict with the APC, i.e. because it contradicts the customary use of the relevant words, may and generally does completely miss the point. The view, inspired by atomic physics, that "tables are not really solid" is *not* shown to be silly, or even misleading (who is misled?) by the consideration that the normal use of the term "solidity" is paradigmatically exemplified by the surface of hard tables. The claim that "tables are not really solid" rightly draws our attention to the fact that the properties of small parts of that table, or even of the table as a whole in certain circumstances, are not such as we used to expect, when following up the full implications of the connotations of "solid": which are, for instance, that the table or any part of it remains impenetrable however small the body that attempts penetration.

The view that "tables are not really solid" is only in conflict with the past denotation of "solid", but not with its connotation: or rather, it points out that the denotation is normally drawn mistakenly. It shows that a new connotation must be found for the whole range of application which, undeniably, is good enough in daily life. Linguistic Philosophy, through the use of the APC, systematically confuses the two and makes the limits of denotation as currently operating the chief or exclusive criterion of meaning, thereby making nonsense of all intellectual advance and indeed of the working of language.*

Or take an example drawn from the application of Polymorphism. It is true, though irrelevant, that the verb "to know" is used in a most varied set of ways according to circumstances. The claim to know Lloyd George conveys something quite different from the claim to know Venice, the multiplication table, or one's own mind. Certainly, the use of "to know" illustrates, and amply, the polymorphic thesis. It appears to undermine models of "knowledge" built up by previous philosophers, models such as contact between mind and thing, or as

---

* Professor J. O. Urmson, having noticed the inapplicability of the APC to problems of value, still supposes it to be applicable to problems like these.
   Cf. *Essays in Conceptual Analysis* (ed. Flew, 1956), p. 132.
   Cf. also "Use and Meaning", *The Cambridge Journal*, 1951.

strictly valid inference, or as flash of insight, or as the accumulation of sensations, and so on. It can be any or none of these, and no one of them exhausts the ways in which "know" can be used.

But how totally irrelevant this is to philosophic problems of knowledge! These arise as consequences and reflections of social and intellectual change, when people are unclear about what kind of authority, inside and outside of themselves, they should consult or prefer. The empiricist model of knowledge then tells them only to refer to experience or the experimental scientist, to remould all questions in such a way that he can handle them, and to disregard or forget questions which cannot be so remoulded. The Kantian model tells them to do this only up to a point, and to use other criteria for a limited set of special questions. And so forth. These models, though they are indeed very simplified accounts of how we use the word "know"—and they were not intended to be accounts of it at all—give reasons for choices that have to be made, and some of the reasons are better than others. It is the job of philosophy to assess the rival merits of these "models", if we must call them such, and not to abrogate them all in virtue of the fact that they are simplified and general. All interesting ideas (even those of Linguistic Philosophy itself) are, disclaimers notwithstanding, simplified and general. Their merits *qua* models are what matters. *That* they are models is irrelevant—and inescapable.

The linguo-philosophical answers to the problem of knowledge, to the effect that the word "know" is used in a great variety of ways, or that it is used to convey a guarantee of the truth of the assertion on the part of the speaker, are irrelevant to the issues involved (even if true in a way), and display, on the part of those who uphold such theories, a remarkable capacity for misunderstanding what a problem is about, and/or a preference for the most trivial possible interpretation of it.

(2) The descriptions of "how we use words" are anything but neutral.

Old-fashioned philosophers generally begin by indicating what concepts they are going to employ and giving reasons why those concepts are basic to their thought.

Linguistic philosophers, on the other hand, give themselves *carte blanche* to use all the concepts in current ordinary use, without justification and without limitation. Are not the usages that are to be described pieces of verbal behaviour, acts within publicly played language games? And in describing the world in which these acts take place, and those acts themselves, are not ordinary concepts, whose ordinary employment guarantees that they "have a use", just the kind of concepts that do not require justification? Is it not, on the contrary, all new or allegedly general concepts which need to be justified and explained in terms of them?

The circle is complete. The procedures, just as the criteria for initiating and terminating them, guarantee that the results will confirm the predisposition towards the world being what it seems, and in favour of concepts already in use.

3. FLASHBACK

The emergence of Linguistic Philosophy was foreshadowed by L. Wittgenstein in the *Tractatus* * (6.53):

"The right method of philosophy would be this. To say nothing except what can be said, i.e. the propositions of natural science, i.e. something that has nothing to do with philosophy: and then always, when someone else wished to say something metaphysical, to demonstrate to him that he had given no meaning to certain signs in his propositions. This method would be unsatisfying to the other—he would not have the feeling that we were teaching him philosophy— but it would be the only strictly correct method.

6.54. My propositions are elucidatory in this way: he who understands me finally recognizes them as senseless, when he has climbed through them, on them, over them. (He must so to speak throw away the ladder, after he has climbed up on it.)

He must surmount these propositions; then he sees the world rightly.

7. Whereof one cannot speak, thereof one must be silent."

What Wittgenstein says there about "the correct method in philosophy" is what he conspicuously failed to do in the *Tractatus*, where he did *not* restrict himself to saying things which had nothing to do with philosophy and merely exhibiting the lack of sense in philosophical statements. On the contrary, he uttered

* *Tractatus Logico-Philosophicus*, London, 1922.

many most characteristically and avowedly philosophical propositions, senseless ones on his own account, and then, having
conveyed something or other by them, disavowed them. That
was the famous "throwing away of the ladder" by which he had
ascended.

To this extent however the programmatic remarks at the end
of the *Tractatus* were accurately prophetic, in that the method
outlined is really the defining characteristic of Linguistic Philosophy. The ladder is no longer visible and no longer avowed;
sometimes it is explicitly disavowed. My contention is however
that a ladder is now insinuated and/or presupposed: it alone
gives both point and justification to the "activity" which alone is
now practised. The "ladder" is of course the set of mutually
supporting doctrines about the world, about language, and
about philosophy: the common-sense theory of the world, the
Functional or Game theory of language, the Pathology or
Euthanasia or Prophylaxis theories of philosophy.

Without the set of beliefs, background models or what not
which are the disavowed "ladder", the practice, the activity
recognisable as Linguistic Philosophy is devoid of any rules or
criteria; criteria for starting or terminating the therapeutic
activity, rules to govern what counts or does not count as a
move in the process.

The ladder is still there, only it happens to be heavily camouflaged.

In one sense Linguistic Philosophy is the fulfilment of the
programme of the *Tractatus*; it is the saying of things "which
have nothing to do with philosophy", so as to bring out ineffable
truths concerning the impossibility of philosophy and the relation of the world to language. In another sense Linguistic
Philosophy, as carried on by Wittgenstein in his later years and
by his followers and successors, is a *reversal* of the doctrine of the
Tractatus. *Philosophical Investigations* is both a completion and a
denial of the *Tractatus*. It is a completion of it in this sense: it
takes over the doctrine that nothing can be said outside a proper language game; nothing can, for instance, be said about its
general conditions or its relation to reality. One cannot speak
outside all speech; and hence, as this is just what philosophy
would *ex hypothesi* be saying, there is nothing that philosophy
can say—but it can *do* or *show* things. This idea, programmatic
in the *Tractatus*, is the actual procedure of much of the *Inves-*

tigations, which in this way carries out what the earlier work promised.

In another sense however the *Investigations* are a denial of what the *Tractatus* maintained. The early work maintained that the proper language game, outside of which meaningful discourse was impossible, was *unique*. The later view is that no language game has or can have such pre-eminence; that no language can have the characteristics attributed to the ultimate language in the *Tractatus*; that the multiplicity of possible forms, the compromises with concrete aims and circumstances, is an *essential* attribute of language, not a distortion of its true nature. Everything said about language is contingent—except perhaps certain denials, namely the denial of absoluteness, of private language (which would be a kind of primary, basic and hence absolute language if it were possible), or of pre-eminence.

The essence of Linguistic Philosophy proper is the denial of the possibility of standing outside language, the insistence on a contingent, naturalistic, pluralistic view of language.

A difference between the programme of the *Tractatus* and actual later practice is that the statements whose utterances Wittgenstein programmatically recommends in the *Tractatus* are "the propositions of natural science", whereas in fact propositions of "ordinary language" now assume this role. In the actual practice of Linguistic Philosophy, it is seldom if ever the propositions of natural science which are uttered in the process of bringing home to someone that he has "failed to give sense" to some expression. And the explanation is not (at least not wholly) that some linguistic philosophers are not familiar with many propositions of natural science.

The real explanation is more fundamental.

In the *Tractatus*, genuine propositions are conceived to be all of one simple kind. Atomic propositions are envisaged as mirroring atomic facts—a notion which is a picturesque hypostatisation of the fact that communication requires some concomitant variation between the two communicating centres, and knowledge has traditionally been viewed as communication between fact and mind (or, in Wittgenstein's case, fact and language). Then, *non*-atomic propositions are seen simply as reiterations, combinations and denials of atomic propositions, built up from them and owing their truth or falsity entirely to them. The propositions of natural science are conceived to be of this kind, appearances notwithstanding. Strong arguments exist * against seeing science in this way.

Wittgenstein was aware that ordinary language does not even look as if it fitted this model, but, at the time of the *Tractatus*, he thought this of little import. He comments on it briefly:

"Man possesses the capacity of constructing languages, in which every sense can be expressed, without having an idea how and what each word means—just as one speaks without knowing how the single sounds are produced.

"Colloquial language is a part of the human organism and is not less complicated than it.

"From it it is humanly impossible to gather immediately the logic of language.

"Language disguises the thought; so that from the external form of the clothes one cannot infer the form of the thought they clothe, because the external form of the clothes is constructed with quite another object than to let the form of the body be recognized.

"The silent adjustments to understand colloquial language are enormously complicated." (*Tractatus*, 4.002.)

In the *Tractatus*, Wittgenstein thought that ordinary ("colloquial") language was a camouflage thrown over the real logical form, the one unique and fundamental language game or system, played between language and reality or man and reality. No doubt the camouflage did little practical harm, but one had to realise it was there. The deviants from meaningfulness, philosophical pseudo-propositions, were, however, not deviants from ordinary language, but from the logical skeleton alleged to underlie it. (Wittgenstein does not appear to have wondered at the time of the *Tractatus* how in general one could distinguish the innocuous camouflage of colloquial speech from a philosophical proposition in which one had failed to give sense to some of the signs. Given the fact which he stresses, namely that the "adjustments . . . are enormously complicated", one should have thought that one could never be sure whether one was faced by a very complicated adjustment, or by an expression lacking in sense.)

In the terms of his later doctrine, the *Tractatus* commits an enormous fallacy, namely the supposition that only one unique

* Powerfully expounded by Professor K. R. Popper.

language game was played and playable. All the diversities found in the real life of language are, according to it, but "enormously complicated silent adjustments". Those "enormously complicated silent adjustments", tucked away as a subthought, three decimal places * away from the main argument of the *Tractatus*, were destined to become the cornerstone of a new and messianic philosophy.

The fallacy of the *Tractatus* which later Linguistic Philosophy spent its time in castigating and correcting is just this notion of a unique logical structure underlying all discourse. Ordinary discourse was not to be seen as complicated adjustments of the underlying skeleton, but to be seen for what it is, as used in life. That *something*, of which the silent adjustments were the adjustments and distorted appearances, is now seen, not as a substrate, but as a *mirage*, and the clue to the pathology of language, in other words to old philosophy.

In a way, the diagnosis is still the same—philosophic propositions are those to whose constituents no sense has been given. But the manner in which "sense is given" is now conceived differently: it is by use and the manifold variety of uses, not by attachment to the "atomic" constituents of the world, whatever they may be. Hence the sense-less propositions are not those that have strayed from the alleged substrate, but on the contrary those which, deluded by the mirage of a substrate, have been deflected from ordinary language.

4. LOGICAL ATOMISM

Some general features of the doctrine of the *Tractatus* have already been indicated—notably those relevant to the transformation of Wittgenstein's early views. The relevant features were mainly the idea that there is a pre-eminent "logical form", a fundamental manner of saying things which alone succeeds in referring to reality; so that other modes of expression, notably the variegated and untidy ways of natural languages, are but distorted and camouflaged versions of it.†

* All propositions in the *Tractatus* are numbered; decimal numbers indicate thoughts which are subsidiary to the main ones so that the more decimal places the number of a proposition has, the less central the proposition.

† For a fuller discussion, see Professor J. O. Urmson's *Philosophical Analysis*, Oxford 1956.

A slightly fuller sketch of Logical Atomism may perhaps be required. The crucial intuition underlying *Logical* Atomism is the same as that underlying ordinary, physical atomism: things are divisible into parts, yet the divisibility cannot carry on indefinitely—one must come to a stop somewhere (Cf. *Tractatus*, 2.021) otherwise nothing would exist.*

Logical Atomism applies this idea to knowledge and language. There must be ultimate items of which knowledge or meaningful discourse are built up.

A second notion which contributes to the basic model in terms of which this Logical Atomism is thought out—a notion particularly prominent in Wittgenstein's version—is what I shall call the idea of *concomitant variation*.† The idea is a simple and persuasive one—namely, that knowledge presupposes an interaction between knower and object known, or, in terms of language, between a sentence and the state of affairs described. This idea, in one form or another, underlies a great deal of theory of knowledge—and rightly so perhaps: knowledge is knowledge *of* something. The knower (or language) must somehow vary concomitantly with that which is known.

The simplest version of concomitant variation is, I suppose, *impact*. Indeed some theories of knowledge are worked out in terms of it. They see knowledge as the impact made by a passing object on mind or consciousness, plus the mark left behind by that impact.

This mark mirrors the object or situation in another medium, so to speak. Wittgenstein in the *Tractatus* worked this out a little more fully in terms of *language* and reality. He was not, at any rate directly, concerned with how one would *know*, with the impact itself, but rather with how one would meaningfully assert something; with the parallelism, the nature of the meaning-relation. Nevertheless, his view had obvious implications for the theory of knowledge, namely—that knowledge which did not mirror was always built up from atoms which *did*.

* Strictly speaking, this is not true of Wittgenstein's view in the *Tractatus*, where he says "Even if the world is infinitely complex, so that every fact consists of an infinite number of atomic facts . . . even then there must be . . . atomic facts" (4.2211). In other words, his atomism is based on the idea of divisibility alone and not on that of the inevitability of its termination.

† I prefer this to "picturing" or "mirroring", expressions that were used and which have unfortunate associations which further—and unnecessarily—weaken the case for the theory they are intended to convey.

"4.01 The Proposition is a picture of reality . . .

"4.014 The gramophone record, the musical thought, the score, the waves of sound, all stand to one another in that pictorial internal relation, which holds between language and the world." (*Tractatus.*)

As can be seen, Wittgenstein elaborated the idea into a kind of Mirror theory of meaning and language. In a sense, the idea is valid, and had indeed been one of the bases of communication theory: a code can only communicate information concerning the same number of possible objective alternatives as happens to be the number of its alternative possible messages . . . (and then it can be said to mirror them). Any greater richness in the world cannot be conveyed by it. On the other hand, any greater richness in the code (i.e. more signs than are necessary for the number of alternative messages liable to be conveyed by it) is redundant.

It is not difficult to think of a "language" in exemplifying this: a railway semaphor will serve as an example. Its position varies concomitantly with ("mirrors") whether there is a train on the line, etc. The difficulties which arise for Logical Atomism, arise from the fact that what is sought is not a limited language for a limited purpose, but an all-embracing, fundamental language describing the world—and presumably not leaving anything out—and incorporating all meaningful discourses. Furthermore, scientific *theory*, which after all only refers to concrete facts at a great remove, must somehow be seen as an abbreviated shorthand of the absolute, basic language, whose innumerable little atomic tentacles cling limpet-wise each to its corresponding little atomic fact in the world, which it "mirrors" . . .

It is interesting to sketch roughly why atomistic theories should have been revived at that time, and why they should have the "logical" guise they had. In part, it was a reaction against the holism of Bradley and the unrealistic picture of the world associated with it. Atomism seems more realistic, if less consoling, than the view that the world is a kind of all-pervasive *blancmange*, as the Absolute was once called by Russell. In part, it was a re-affirmation of empiricism. Atomism almost unavoidably suggests empiricism: the picture of "building up from constituent parts", when applied to cognition, naturally suggests the priority of the individual observation as against all-embracing theory.

Apart from being a re-affirmation of a realistic outlook and empiricism, Logical Atomism was stimulated by certain advances in logic. The holism of Bradley had as one of its props a quasi-logical doctrine of the "unreality of relations": it seemed possible to attack this doctrine, and hence holism, with the help of a new logical notation and associated logical doctrine which, for independent reasons, incorporated "relational statements" (as opposed to traditional logic which only catered for subject-predicate statements).

The new developments in logic stimulated the philosophy of Logical Atomism in other ways, too. The sheer existence of the powerful and suggestive new notation aided the programme of building up a general scheme of language. As Russell said in his introduction to the *Tractatus*, "This view [that it is impossible to say anything about the world as a whole] may have been originally suggested by notation . . . a good notation has a subtlety and suggestiveness which at times make it seem almost like a live teacher" (*Introduction*, p. 17).

The new logical notation and doctrine also made room for a new view of the status of logic and mathematics which no longer made them a stumbling block to an empiricist-atomic theory of knowledge. The notation also facilitated the building up of an empiricist theory of knowledge not open, as others had been, to the charge that it neglected judgments or propositions.

Another important factor was the so-called Theory of Types, a doctrine which overcame some difficulties in logic by excluding certain kinds of expression as *meaningless*. This suggested the possibility of drawing the boundaries of *meaning*, rather than the boundaries of the knowable as had been more usual in philosophy, and this anticipated an important feature of both Logical Atomism and of the subsequent forms of Linguistic Philosophy.

These factors, and perhaps others, stimulated the emergence of a philosophy whose basic image was knowledge—or rather, in this case, the linguistic *expression* of knowledge, inseparable from its content—split up into its ultimate constituent parts, leaving room for nothing other than what is built from those parts. Moreover, these parts were joined to each other, and internally organised, in ways conveniently expressible by the

currently developed notation of mathematical logic. This, incidentally, opened the way to a dualistic vision of the basis of
knowledge—a dualism long associated with empiricism—as being either wholly *given* or wholly man-made: factual truth was
a matter of (very) brute fact, whilst formal and necessary truth
was somehow supplied from inside, constructed and owing nothing to fact. The truth of the latter was fully intelligible—it
managed to be true, ultimately, by not saying anything, but
only providing the shell within which something was said. The
basis of factual truth on the other hand was also divested of
mystery by making its mystery so impenetrable as to be beyond
all questions: facts simply were what they were, they could not
be explained. That which is normally called explanation was
really but a convenient summary or abbreviation of many facts.
(This aspect of Logical Atomism, the dualistic manner of making knowledge intelligible, is one which survived into so-called
Logical Positivism proper.)

Two notions thus provide the clue to the nature of the world:
the notion of *mirroring*, and that of *part-and-whole*. Language
and the world both split up into parts: and their ultimate parts
mirror each other. *That is all.*

The logical atomist manner of looking at the world and language gives rise to many problems, some of them technical and
not all of them relevant to our argument. It is however important to specify some of the difficulties and features which
were either taken over into later Linguistic Philosophy, or provoked the developments leading to the elaboration of that attitude.

There may be something fundamentally wrong with the
adaptation of physical analogies (of dividing a thing into parts,
and of mirroring or concomitance) and applying them uncriti-
cally to something radically different, namely units of communication or meaning. There may also be something wrong
in envisaging statements outside all practical relevance and use.
And the claims constituting the theory of Logical Atomism were
not meant to be rivals to science, and yet what were they? How
were they to supplement or supplant the truths of science and
daily life?

Logical Atomism also has difficulties of a more specific kind.

One of the very marked difficulties for Logical Atomism was
the finding and identification of the atoms, be they the atoms in

language or atoms in reality, that were to be the bases of the alleged pyramid of cognition or assertion. Perhaps it should not worry an atomist that he does not find his atoms at once. Nevertheless in the long run, as G. E. Moore has reported,* the fact that an atomic sentence had never been found, that nobody managed to think up a plausible example of one, did bother the theorists of language who maintained that ultimately language was made up of them. Although at first sight Logical Atomism seemed a more realistic doctrine than Bradley's holism, with the passage of time a doctrine which maintained that both discourse and the world was made up of constituents which could then never be located seemed just as unrealistic. It was probably the failure to find the atoms, plus the failure to give plausible accounts of how scientific and ordinary discourse was built up of the atoms that were surmised, that jointly destroyed confidence in that logical atomist world picture and in the "reductionist" philosophic programme that was associated with it and similar philosophies.

A second difficulty facing Logical Atomism is related to the first. The alleged cognisable atoms of the world, postulated to correspond to the ultimate atoms of language, were not merely hard to locate and identify and describe plausibly, they also had a metaphysical air. It is difficult to resist the impression, at least with hindsight, that they are simply a kind of reduplication of a surmised linguistic atom, invented as its shadow.

The features of Atomism mentioned so far were those which have led to a *reaction*. Let us now look at some others, which, though possibly transformed, were *taken over* into later Linguistic Philosophy. One obvious corollary of the logical atomist picture of language was the drastic limitations of possible meaning. For instance: if all discourse was either atomic sentences or conjunctions or abbreviations of them, what room was there for the assertion for instance that all discourse is made up of atomic sentences? In other words Logical Atomism leaves no room for the doctrine of Logical Atomism, or any other philosophical doctrine for that matter. That *other* philosophies were excluded, could hardly be expected to worry its authors: in fact it seemed quite a merit of the doctrine. That the assertion of Logical Atomism *itself* was barred did however present a difficulty of kinds. Wittgenstein solved the difficulty by the famous device

* *Mind*, 1954.

of the ladder that he throws away at the end of the *Tractatus*. The ladder that was to be thrown away when its purpose had been served, in other words the *Tractatus* itself was declared meaningless in virtue of the criteria of meaningfulness contained in it.

A problem which also arises in the *Tractatus* is in connection with "formal concepts". The ideal of the *Tractatus* was the *mirror*, or, as I prefer to put it, language seen as concomitant variation between a symbolic system and a real system. But in order to describe the symbolic system Wittgenstein has to use certain terms or concepts which did not themselves mirror or reflect or vary with any one *thing* in the world, terms such as "thing", "fact", "relation", which in the *Tractatus* he called "formal concepts". They indicated places where real terms, which *did* reflect something, could stand in atomic sentences. But the need one had for formal concepts, and the interesting way in which they differed from what he then considered real concepts, were clues to an important truth, namely that to speak one requires concepts of radically different kinds. In the difference between formal and proper concepts in the *Tractatus*, and in the necessity for this difference, one can perhaps see the germ of the later doctrine of Polymorphism and of the differentiation and multiplicity of categories of linguistic functions.

Another difficulty which Logical Atomism faced was in connection with the existence of people and of minds. The difficulty arises as follows. The state of affairs describable by saying that Jones believes that the cat is on the mat, cannot easily be interpreted as a simple conjunction of two or more atomic sentences: for one of the requirements of the logical atomist picture was that all the atoms were wholly independent of each other (that any one true atomic sentence can be replaced by any other true one, or a false by a false one, and everything else remains the same, and notably the truth of the complex expression as a whole). When on the other hand sentences get involved with what are called propositional attitudes, i.e. when sentences are said to be believed or doubted or supposed by people, they lose their independence. For although it is true that Jones believes that the cat is on the mat, and it is true that the cat is on the mat, and it is true that the dog is in the kennel, we cannot substitute "The dog is in the kennel" for "The cat is on the mat" and rely on the result still being true: for quite possibly Jones does not believe that the dog is in the kennel (even though he is). This shows something very important—namely that, on occasions at least, sentences such as "The cat is on the mat" seem *not* to enter into larger complexes as independent atoms, replaceable by other true sentences without affecting the whole.

Wittgenstein dealt with this difficulty in the *Tractatus* in a very summary way by a kind of schematic indication of a behaviourist solution. Complex statements of the form that somebody thinks something were all to be interpreted as variants of the statement that somebody *says* something. (About this there is presumably no difficulty: the fact that somebody says something can be interpreted as a more or less complex description of his physical state.) The preoccupation with interpreting statements about states of mind and about propositional attitudes survived from the *Tractatus* into Linguistic Philosophy and fed one of its chief preoccupations, the philosophy of mind.

The interest in this subject was of course later reinforced by other factors. An activist philosophy of mind went hand in hand with an activist or functionalist theory of language, and the two reinforced each other. Both provided explanations of why the very presuppositions of Logical Atomism, the assumption that knowledge must always be a case of fact-sentence parallelism or mirroring, should not be presupposed at all (for speech acts were *acts*, not mirror-images). On to the need of showing propositional attitudes to be compatible with the Logical Atomist picture, there came to be superimposed the need to interpret them in such a way as to show Logical Atomism not to be necessary in the first place. The need then was to show that believing and knowing were not cases of being related to atomic propositions or complex propositions, but that it was possible on the contrary to interpret knowing and believing in a behaviourist way which can wholly dispense with having as "objects" those ultimate bricks, logical atoms, on which Logical Atomism insisted.

There was finally a rather more general, diffuse difficulty facing Logical Atomism. Where in its scheme does one find room for the human world of values, for ethics, aesthetics, religion and so forth? This form of Logical Atomism catered for atomic reports of experience, it catered for the formal knowledge of mathematics (though it gave them rather a derogatory status of tautologies). It catered for science in an indirect way, as a derivative of those first two classes. It catered for some of daily speech as complicated subtle adjustments, compromises with practical purposes. But where in this vast accumulation of little grains of disjointed facts is there room for some elusive features of the world which seem to make it a place of interest and of value? For much of what gives richness and fullness to life it seemed to leave no room at all. Was transcendence or mystery to be seen as so much nonsense, or as mysticism? Or, as Wittgenstein saw it, as *both* of these? The exile of an important part of human discourse from the field of meaning, or at any rate from the field of determinate discourse, was taken over from Logical Atomism by Logical Positivism, and it was this above all else which gave it its notoriety. The defect, if defect it is, was remedied by Linguistic Philosophy which reacted against both in this respect, and restored all the manifold human activities and uses of language to their places, though it did so, as I shall try to show, in an *extremely* left-handed manner.

5. LOGICAL POSITIVISM

Logical Positivism, as for instance expounded in A. J. Ayer's *Language, Truth and Logic,* is a system fairly similar to the Logical Atomism of the *Tractatus,* but it is more lucid, less dramatic and less aphoristic. It also differs from it on points of doctrine. It has no murky ineffability doctrine. Instead, it rather rudely castigates all that violates the bounds of meaning, as specified by it, as "nonsense" and makes no attempt at saying it. Its main differentiation from Logical Atomism is perhaps that it is more emphatically—or tries to be—a doctrine about language and not about the world.

In the *Tractatus,* we seem to be told a lot about the structure of facts as well as about sentences, and are left with a feeling that the world is somehow filled with an invisible camouflaged net or basic structure. Logical Positivism attempts to outlaw— and avoid—inferences from the structure of language to the structure of the world. (On the other hand, Logical Positivism embraces phenomenalism, the view, roughly, that sensations are the stuff from which we "construct" matter, in order to complete its theory of language—so as to account for the logic of expression about material objects. In consequence it at least *seems* to give us in addition a theory of the world—of a world ultimately composed of "sense-data".)

Of all the movements or styles of thought proceeding from, or associated with, Linguistic Philosophy, the ideas and the name of Logical Positivism have made by far the greatest impact on the unspecialised educated public, and rightly so perhaps: for whereas the other clusters of ideas tend to be ultimately philosopher's philosophies, combinations of themes contingent upon particular historical situations amongst thinkers, conjunctions of particular influences and so forth, Logical Positivism on the other hand is a forceful and elegant formulation of one of the most archetypal, so to speak, and most fundamental possible outlooks for man. Logical Positivism is radical empiricism formulated as a doctrine about language and meaning.

The impact which Logical Positivism has made on the general educated public has had as a consequence that the name Logical Positivism came to be applied by non-specialists to the whole group of philosophies, and not to the rather narrower Logical Positivism proper. This usage is now so well established in journalism and elsewhere that it is probably useless to try to change it. The resulting confusion, if confusion it be, is a good deal resented by linguistic philosophers, who consider the differentiation between their own doctrine and that of Logical Positivism which preceded it to be of the utmost importance. They are technically right in insisting that there is a difference, whilst the general public is in some ways right in ignoring the difference. For general human purposes the difference need not be very important. Furthermore, although linguistic philosophers deny it, logical positivist premisses are employed to buttress up in a very essential way the views of Linguistic Philosophy where necessary (notably when some metaphysical alternative has to be excluded). Admittedly, it is *equally* essential for Linguistic Philosophy to have techniques (as indeed it has) for avoiding and forgetting the doctrine of Logical Positivism when it suits it (notably, when it is necessary *not* to exclude some actually employed class of expressions which does not happen to fit the positivist model).

Logical Positivism had a certain *succès de scandale*. In essence it is an overwhelmingly simple doctrine. It consists of the claim that all knowledge, or, in the linguistic formulation, all meaningful discourse, consists of two kinds: first, reports of experiential fact, whose claim to truth resides exclusively in that the facts bear them out; and, secondly, logic, interpreted as conse-quences of calculations within systems whose rules are conven-tionally established. This dichotomy, and the mystery-dispel-ling diagnosis of both scientific and mathematical truth, is shared by Logical Positivism with Logical Atomism. A further idea that is shared is the denial, the exclusion of anything out-side these two categories from the realm of knowledge or mean-ing.

The most conspicuous thing about Logical Positivism was perhaps a certain *élan*. It was a philosophy which seemed to do justice to the conspicuous and immense successes of natural science and at the same time gave a brutal but necessary diag-nosis of the sterility of traditional philosophy, of religion, and so forth. What matters most about it is perhaps its negative as-pects, its denials of ethical, aesthetic, religious and other aspects of human discourse, its expulsion of that kind of talk from the realm of determinate meaning. This brutal legislation is what is primarily associated with Logical Positivism in the general mind, and rightly so. (One of the reasons for the current or recent acceptance and success of Linguistic Philosophy is that it claims to reverse this, to reinstate everything that the soul desires in its old place, and yet to do it in a way which seems as hard-headed—or rather, more so—as the preceding Logical Positivism.)

The doctrine of Logical Positivism is contained in the famous Verification Principle. It is probably fair to say that all its other tenets are corollaries of that principle. The precise formu-lation of it has come, with time and the attempt to cope with objections, to be a lengthy, involved and technical matter.* But those technicalities do not concern us, and the underlying idea is extremely simple (and none the worse for that).

This idea is: a statement can have meaning either in virtue of saying something verifiable about the world, or in virtue of fol-lowing from the meaning of the words occurring in it. There is no third possibility. A formula which can be checked neither by observation of the world, nor by deduction from our definitions, has no meaning.

Why did Logical Positivism seem true?

* Cf. Professor A. J. Ayer, *Language, Truth and Logic* 1936, and in par ticular the Introduction to the Second Edition, 1946.

At its roots lies a certain model. Given that model, the conclusions are inescapable. It is also difficult to see how the model itself could be escaped.

Think of either mind facing the world it knows, or alternatively, *language* facing the world it describes: in either case, mind or language will consist of parts, bits or items of putative knowledge, cognitions or propositions. These would fall into two classes: those which in some way or other vary with, depend on, something in the outside world, and those which do not. It is the dependence of those of them that do vary with something in the world which gives knowledge or description its objectivity, its reference.

It is best to think of these "bits" as forming a kind of structure —and indeed they do: the various statements that we make are related to each other by implying, contradicting, etc. each other. For a system of statements to be about the world, or about anything, it must vary with the world or that "anything": for instance, whether the system contains the sentence "It is raining" or, on the contrary, the sentence "It is not raining", must *vary with* whether or not it is raining. This is merely the requirement that the sentences of the system be "about" something. If they "varied with" nothing, they would not be about anything.

But over and above these "variable" or sensitive or world-reflecting parts, a system of language also needs to have parts that do *not* vary with the world, parts that are rigid, to provide a kind of framework for the sensitive, variable kinds. The system will after all employ a variety of terms, and in order to be used for recording or communicating, the use of these terms must be constant. (If "rain" meant one thing today and another tomorrow, sentences employing the term would convey nothing.) The interrelations of such stable terms are *definitions*. But from definitions, further statements can be inferred. The definitions plus the multiplicity of statements deducible from them form the "rigid" part of the system.

If, inspired by this model, we look at our language, we find some kinds of expressions, "experiential reports", which correspond to the sensitive part; some, pure logic and mathematics and definitions and their consequences, which correspond to the rigid part; and, finally, a multiplicity of statements which do not at first sight correspond to either. The Logical Positivist programme is to show the consonance of some statements with the model by means of breaking them up into constituents, each of which fits in by clearly falling into one of the two exhaustive pigeon-holes, and to exclude as meaningless those that *cannot* be fitted in.

It is noteworthy that versions of this model have often been available since reflection on knowledge began; but they have not in general been dominant. The reasons are various. For one thing, the relativising, subjectivising and certainty-destroying implications of it are ethically or politically unacceptable. Secondly, in societies where religious, legal, metaphysical or literary thought—all of them carried out in a way which does not seem to fit the model—are prestigious, the model lacks appeal. What has led to the success of the model at last has been, first, the prestige of experimental science and the corresponding decline in prestige of other forms of putatively cognitive activity, and, second, the emergence of an interpretation of logic and mathematics consonant with the model. (Previously, mathematics had been a stumbling block.)

Can Logical Positivism in its narrow and proper sense be refuted? Can the philosophy of David Hume be refuted? The question comes to much the same. There is no simple answer to this but certain observations are worth making about the way in which Linguistic Philosophy "overcomes" Logical Positivism.

Logical Positivism is itself not an empirical but a deduced doctrine. This is not a defect (though some have claimed it to be such), still less an inconsistency, but it is worth noting. It is deduced from a model. This model again is far from arbitrary or implausible. If the model is accepted it seems extremely doubtful whether Logical Positivism can be refuted.

But the model can be questioned in various ways.

The main way of denying the model is by denying its most conspicuous general feature, namely what might be called its First Person approach. The First Person approach is traditional in the theory of knowledge. It consists of envisaging a world from the viewpoint of an individual or impersonal knower, and asking oneself how the world can become known to him. But normally in daily life we do not look at knowers in this way, with the possible exception of ourselves. We look at most men and their cognitive processes or attitudes in the Third Person, as things and events in the world, not as ultimate centres which construct or receive the world into their cognitive bosoms.

This is the core of the overcoming of Logical Positivism by Linguistic Philosophy. Now the adoption of the Third Person viewpoint is not in itself anything new: many of what are called naturalistic philosophies have in the past adopted it. The Third Person approach as such is nothing new and it cuts little ice; indeed it has the reputation in philosophy of being shallow and avoiding the problem by missing the point. What differentiates Linguistic Philosophy in its use of the Third Person viewpoint is that it was camouflaged as a theory of language, just as the First Person viewpoints of Logical Atomism and Logical Positivism were also camouflaged as theories of language. Linguistic philosophers think they are substituting a realistic theory of language for an unrealistic one, but what they are really doing is substituting a Third Person viewpoint, rightly or wrongly, for a First Person one. The alleged "realism" and "unreality" of these viewpoints are really red herrings: what matters are the independent grounds for preferring the Third Person viewpoint as such to the so-called unrealism of the logical positivist model constructed on the assumption of the primacy of the First Person view.

Underlying the plausibility of the logical positivist model is an old argument in the theory of knowledge: before there can be a world, that world must be "built up" from the little parts that are given to the knower in the course of experience. . . . As in Logical Atomism, the part-and-whole picture is applied to knowledge. This makes the knower pivotal, gives him a priority over the world that he knows—for it is *he* who "constructs" or "assembles" it, i.e. sees it as a unity after being "given" the constituent parts (and, possibly, supplements their gaps).

Linguistic Philosophy "overcomes" this model by refusing to allow the knower, or the language he uses, to be pivotal, central, to be the creators of a world: on the contrary, it sees both him and the language he uses inescapably as processes or events *in* the world. In so doing it takes the world for granted, so to speak: it does not refute the argument by which Logical Positivism reached the conclusion of two-and-two-only kinds of knowledge, nor does it argue about the merits of the model which provided the premiss for the argument: it simply refuses to use the model, or to re-interpret the world in the light of it

(i.e. it refuses to see the world as "constructed" from constituents compatible with the model, that is, from bits of experience plus a logical scaffolding, or indeed to think of the world as requiring such construction. It refuses to do so by, as it were, insisting that the world was there first and language is a process within it, and hence language must be seen as in the world, rather than the world re-interpreted so as to fit a model of how language or cognition is possible. A part—"language"—cannot challenge or sit in judgment on the whole—the world—of which it is a part, it might be said.)

The second step is then to look at language-in-the-world and insist that, when investigated as it is rather than as it is supposed be in virtue of the preconceived model, we do not find the two species and their exclusiveness, but, on the contrary, a vast multiplicity of language uses. (So linguistic philosophers say. In fact, the species we find depend on the classification we choose to employ, and what is really at issue is not whether the logical positivist dichotomy fits at first sight—plainly, it does not—but whether it can be *made* to fit.)

But this new kind of "empiricism" with regard to language, leaving it as we find it, enables the linguistic philosopher to abstain from re-interpreting the *world*, in the manner in which the positivist inescapably, if unwittingly, did: as made up, constructed, out of contingent disconnected atomic parts (or sense-data, or the contents of basic observation reports, or what not), plus a man-made or language-made framework which alone was responsible for any seemingly non-contingent features of the world. On the contrary, the linguistic philosopher leaves the world alone. (That is his function.)

The situation is somewhat complicated, for, strictly speaking, Logical Positivism only had or presupposed a First Person view of *knowledge*—the world had to be built up of little pieces of experience which in the end was *somebody's* experience. About *language*, though it spoke in a simplified and schematised way, it spoke in a Third Person, public kind of way (although it spoke of a "sense-datum language" which referred to private experiences, from it a public language was supposed to be built up by rules that were not private).

Linguistic Philosophy in the first step destroys or prejudges the First Person vision of knowledge, and in the second step destroys or prejudges the simplicity of the already more-or-less

Third Person picture of language (which in Positivism was associated with the epistemological First Person approach) by insisting on taking note of the complexity of actual language.

The first step, which is the crucial one, is based mainly on simply refusing to look at things in any way other than the Third Person one, by insisting on the natural standpoint that takes the world for granted, and by claiming "not to understand" any other, and also by claiming that deviations from it are the pathology of language. It is however *also* reinforced by a specific argument, one claiming to show the impossibility of a private language. (The denial of a pre-eminent or logical language is directed at Logical Atomism, the denial of a private language is directed at the phenomenalism of Logical Positivism.) This attack is based on the contention that the terms that would occur in a private or sense-datum language, names for sensations and so on, are only intelligible, identifiable and so on (if intelligible at all) in the wider context of a public language in a public world, and hence that a basic First Person language out of which the public world is to be constructed is an impossibility. It presupposes the public world and language which it is to explain: hence, it is somewhat oddly argued, this public world cannot be a problem.*

The circularity of the whole position lies in this: if indeed the world is not a problem but a datum, then, naturally, it follows that it is not a problem, and hence that arguments making it appear that it *is* a problem must be mistaken and are to be dealt with in some other way—for instance, as cases of a disease of language. The argument remains circular even when reinforced by the case against private language, for that argument (assuming it valid on its own grounds) only shows that men speaking to each other in a public world, i.e. seen in the Third Person manner, cannot explain their notions of a private, First Person language to each other without using terms or notions of a public language first. But this does not refute the

---

* All that really follows if the argument is valid is that, if it is a problem, it cannot have an empiricist solution. But non-empiricist solutions are already excluded by Logical Positivism. The logical positivist one is then excluded by a rejection of the epistemological First Person viewpoint. *All* solutions now being excluded, the conclusion is meant to be that there cannot be a problem. Note that the elimination of all solutions uses mutually incompatible premises at various stages.

old arguments in the theory of knowledge for the *need* of starting with a private language, with some datum given to someone. The most it can show is that such a need cannot be satisfied.

However, whilst circular, the circle is of a curious kind: in order to break out of it, we must refuse to take the world for granted—and we can easily be made to look foolish doing that. We know that "we'd better" accept this world. Linguistic Philosophy tries to make us do so, tries to make us take the world for granted and to think only about the oddity of philosophy emerging in it, rather than to think philosophically *about* it. It tries to make us do so by sheer dogmatic insistence, by repetition, by just pretending that there is no other way to talk, by means of a theory which treats anything else as pathological, by means of a procedure which does not allow anything else, by means of an argument (the claim of the impossibility of private language) which is to deprive us of the language by means of which we could hope not to take the world for granted but speculate about its knowability. The key question about Linguistic Philosophy is the merit of this circle.

It ironically consists of a *down*-grading of the importance of language in that it insists on seeing language as a natural thing, one amongst many others, *in* the world, rather than as fundamental, as a key clue to how our awareness of the world is built up. What it calls the new realisation of the importance of language is only the awareness of its alleged importance in the ætiology of one minor disease within the world, namely the disease of asking philosophic questions. It is true that this truth about language, if indeed it is true, has been under-estimated in the past.

The merits of the new angle of vision are best discussed in the context of the rejection and alleged "overcoming" of the theory of knowledge in general, rather than of Logical Positivism in particular. The arguments, if valid, "overcome" all theories of knowledge, all theories which attempt to answer the question of how we "build up" the world from some epistemic bricks. It does not militate against Logical Positivism specifically. It just happens that Logical Positivism was one of the last theories of knowledge on the scene before the arrival of the Wittgensteinian Revelation, and, also, that its partial re-formulation of the problem of knowledge in terms of language (not: "how do we know the world" but "how does language refer to the world?") aided the shift to the Third Person approach.

Moreover, intimate if unavowed and disclaimed connections remain between Logical Positivism and Linguistic Philosophy. The positivist doctrine is re-invoked any time there is any need to exclude an inconvenient interpretation of or within that world that is now being taken for granted. The two-and-two only principle is resuscitated when required, which is not infrequently. Linguistic Philosophy absolutely requires and presupposes Positivism, for without it as 'a tacit premiss, there is nothing to exclude any metaphysical interpretation of the usages that are to be found, and allegedly "taken as they are", in the world. The trouble is that usages "as they are" are quite passive: to give an account of them "as they are *in* the world" requires principles of interpretation, and amongst these the exclusion of metaphysical ones, based on the positivist argument, is the most important. Linguistic Philosophy is only possible as the second stage of a process of which Logical Positivism was the first: if all transcendental theories are first eliminated by Logical Positivism, Linguistic Philosophy can then overcome Positivism. But it would not prevail if the transcendental theories were still in the running. Positivism is like the paper in the children's game that can wrap the stone but can be cut by the scissors. Linguistic Philosophy is the scissors, that could not affect the stone though it can cut the paper. It is parasitic on the Positivism which it also destroys.

Thus Logical Positivism is invoked as a tacit premiss when necessary. And, of course, it is *also* in all seeming sincerity disavowed when *that* is convenient, in virtue of being a theory of knowledge and hence *ex officio* "philosophical", i.e. paradoxical, over-general, etc., etc.

Thus the general educated public is not so far off the mark in its persistence in equating Logical Positivism with Linguistic Philosophy. Their relation may be characterised as follows: Linguistic Philosophy rejects all theory of knowledge, as such and in principle, but if there *were* a theory of knowledge, then Logical Positivism would be the correct one.

6. LOGICAL CONSTRUCTIONS

The philosophic programme implicit in the theories of Logical Atomism and Logical Positivism was fairly similar. This common programme can be divided into two parts: the programme of salvation and the programme of damnation.

Damnation

The programme of damnation consists of exorcising or otherwise disposing of those kinds of discourse which, according to the doctrine in question, were illegitimate, notably, of course, metaphysics.

Salvation

The programme of salvation consisted of somehow showing that those kinds of discourse which were supposed legitimate, notably science, and some common sense, but which did not *look* like the model prescribed by the appropriate philosophy, nevertheless could be shown to fit in by some kind of expansion or translation. A most characteristic kind of way of doing this was by the so-called method of "logical constructions". . . . This method tried to show that some kinds of discourse to be saved were translatable into the approved language, though not in any straightforward way. The expression "logical construction" was to convey that though a kind of translation was possible, it was not a straightforward translation with absolute replaceability of units from the one language by units of the other. It was hoped to show, for instance, that material objects were logical constructions out of sense data, or, that minds were logical constructions out of behaviour, propositions from sentences, and so forth. If this programme succeeded, then the manifoldness of actual discourse or of reality could be held to be, after all, reducible to the simple elements required by the theories. The actual complexity and reduplication of discourse could be seen as merely a kind of complicated shorthand.

The important thing about both Logical Atomism and Logical Positivism is that their programme or programmes generally failed. Both damnation and salvation failed to work. The translations which were to establish the Saved status of what was approved seldom if ever sounded right, and the damned also failed on the whole to disappear into the hell which was prescribed for them. They continued to haunt the earth. This, in conjunction with some difficulties already pointed out, such as the failure to find plausible instances of atomic propositions, was what led to the replacement of these philosophies by Linguistic Philosophy. Patience snapped at a certain point.* These philosophies were not *refuted*: they failed to deliver the goods, and this failure prepared the ground for the switch in viewpoint which is the essence of Linguistic Philosophy. Logical Positivism, which had tried to damn so much, ended by being itself damned by this shift of vision.

As already indicated in the preceding section, Linguistic Philosophy is parasitic on the theories which preceded it. It is parasitic both on their success and on their failure.

7. COMMON SENSE

The third doctrine that was essential in preparing the ground for Linguistic Philosophy was G. E. Moore's so-called Philosophy of Common Sense.

It is not clear whether Moore should be called a philosopher or a pedant of such outstanding ability as to push pedantry and literal-mindedness to a point where it became a philosophy.

He was, as he confessed in a famous passage quoted earlier, not puzzled by the world or science: he was only puzzled by the oddity of the statements of philosophers.

His thought *is* characterised by great pedantry, literal-mindedness, carefulness, painstakingness. Taking the statements of philosophers literally and examining them with great patience, care and perseverance, he found them (not surprisingly) wanting. He generally found that the dramatic slogans contained many claims and not one claim, some plainly false and some unsubstantiated.

He was deeply imbued with the conviction that Common Sense was right—that our most obvious convictions were true, did not call for justification, and were *not* called before the bar of philosophy. If anything, it was rather philosophy which had

---

* The point at which faith in the way of "logical constructions" is said to have failed, was Professor John Wisdom's series of articles of that title in *Mind*.

to be judged by whether it was compatible with common sense, and not *vice versa*.

He was in consequence inclined to feel that philosophy made no difference to life. He firmly refused to entertain general doubts. The things we normally feel commonsensically certain about, he maintained, really are *ipso facto* certain. Descartes once started a new philosophic tradition by trying to doubt everything. Moore started another by firmly refusing to doubt anything.

It has in the past been of the essence of philosophy that when philosophising we were ready to doubt what in daily life we could not seriously question—be it for practical or other reasons. I think it would be hard to exaggerate the usefulness of such deliberately far-fetched questioning and doubting. What *seems* commonsensical and unquestionable, and cannot for practical reasons be seriously doubted, may nevertheless be worth doubting. It may either be false, or require reformulation or detachment from false associated ideas; or, even if true, doubting it may bring out hitherto unconsidered possibilities and vistas. Moore's philosophy of "common sense" is essentially a flouting of the convention that, in philosophy, we suspend belief: Moore refused to leave common sense at the door with his umbrella when he came in to do philosophy. This was perhaps a brave gesture, and at any rate it required a great deal of social courage—and skill—to do it in a manner which led him to be admired and emulated, rather than otherwise.

Some philosophers have considered the deliberate suspension of belief, of the natural attitude, to be of the essence of philosophy. Husserl called it the *epoché*, a kind of putting-of-the-world-in-brackets and suspending judgment so that one could have a better look.

The essence of Moore is a kind of *inverted epoché*. He refused to put the world in any brackets.

Moore's inverted *epoché*, his conviction or principle that things in general were substantially as they seemed, reappears in Wittgenstein and in Linguistic Philosophy proper *with a rationale* —namely, that assertions to the effect that things are radically other than they seem are always misuses of language. In brief, Moore displayed many of the characteristics of Linguistic Philosophers, without being led to them by the ways and reasoning of Wittgensteinianism. He did by nature that for which Wittgenstein's Revelation found reasons.

He introduced a kind of argument (anticipated by Dr. Johnson in his "refutation" of Berkeley) of checking a philosophic idea against what seems obvious: on a famous occasion, he "refuted" all doubts about the reality of the external world by pointing out that he, Moore, had two hands, so that at least two material objects were known to exist. (Moore, unlike Dr. Johnson, was taken seriously and is thought to have contributed something to philosophy by doing this.)

His use of this kind of argument is extremely similar to the Argument from Paradigm Cases, as later used by Linguistic Philosophy proper.

The difference between the "common-sense" attitude of Moore, and Arguments from Paradigm Cases, is that the former is a piece of simple dogmatism, whereas the latter is a piece of dogmatism deduced from an interesting though mistaken theory of language (to the effect that the applicability of words to their Paradigm Cases of application cannot be doubted). The two kinds of argument have a great deal in common—they make it impossible for us to doubt important notions and put us at the mercy of the prejudices and superstitions of our predecessors in the use of language, provided they are sufficiently well diffused to count as common sense; and, when used to "validate" beliefs against allegedly queer doubt, their validation is of a left-handed, useless kind. To prove that matter exists, or free will, or rightness, etc., in virtue of the fact that this seems commonsensical or that the relevant terms have a use and paradigm uses, is to prove something quite different (and trivial) from that which the questioner doubted. Unfortunately users of the argument are not always clear about this and pass off the one proof as if it had the value of the genuine article.

Another important aspect of Moore's thought was that relevant to the difficulty or impossibility of "analyses" or "reductions". Whilst his apotheosis of common sense, by making it difficult for philosophy to claim insights of its own beyond or contrary to common sense, contributed to turning philosophy into "analysis" (explicating what is known, as opposed to procuring new knowledge), at the same time his work on ethics led to the view that analyses are very hard to come by and that the answer to the problem of analysing our concepts must very frequently be that they are "un-analysable", irreducible. This was his conclusion concerning the concept "good", and the very significant motto borrowed from Bishop Butler which adorns *Principia Ethica* tended to bring home and generalise the moral. (The motto is: "Everything is what it is and not another thing". In other words: it is impossible to give analyses of concepts in terms of others.) This moral was also brought home later by the famous "paradox of analysis", which consists, essentially, of the fork: an analysis, an account of the meaning of an expression, is either trivial or false. For if true, are we not simply presented with synonyms (and why should *that* throw any light on the concept?)—yet if we are presented with two expressions which are *more* than synonyms, then *ipso facto* the analysis cannot be valid—for that "something more" that is found on one side and not on the other must *ipso facto* upset the absolute equivalence which is the condition of a true analysis. This leads one to expect most concepts *not* to be "reducible" to others—which is *just* what the Polymorphist view of language also teaches.

The most famous case of finding a concept un-analysable was his doctrine concerning "good"; *its* un-analysable status led him to label all ethical doctrines which attempt to analyse it as guilty of the "naturalistic fallacy". The evidence for the inadequacy of given analyses was that it always made sense to ask, about the thing offered as the analysis of "good", whether *it* was good. In as far as the question made sense (irrespective of what the answer might be), the two terms occurring in the question could not be identical: for if they were, the question would be silly and its answer trivial.

It is interesting to note that the two main themes in Moore's thought are mutually inconsistent: the kind of proto-APC which he invented, the checking of doctrines against Paradigm Cases by calling their normal interpretation "common sense", is in fact a case of systematically committing the Naturalistic Fallacy, in a general form, of confusing the connotation of terms with their denotation by assuming that a term *cannot* be applied falsely to its characteristic application.

If seen alone, both these themes anticipated and prepared the ground for Linguistic Philosophy. The "unanalysability" of concepts reappears as the doctrine that each type of notion has its own role and cannot be reduced to others, that "reduction" is the chief philosophic sin. The habit of checking of philosophic theses against common sense reappears as the APC. Many other themes reappear: the notion that philosophy makes no difference; that it is a neutral account of concepts which does not interfere with them and does not and cannot evaluate them; the suspicion that old philosophic doctrines are all erroneous and that their error is best shown up by careful, protracted investigation of the terms occurring in them, and so on. An alienation from the modern world and real issues, a curious artificiality, pedantry, an ivory-towerism, procrastination, all these are characteristics and values shared by Moore and linguistic philosophers. It is important to note that his work and approach generally receive kind treatment and recognition from them, even in cases where he maintained views (as in ethics) which in fact are repugnant to common sense. Whereas Linguistic Philosophy sees itself as *reacting* against the doctrines of Logical Atomism and Logical Positivism, and indebted to them only in this negative way, as exemplars of how *not* to do things, their debt and attitude to Moore is more positive and cordial.

It is arguable whether Moore's views should be seen as an apotheosis of *common sense*, or on the contrary, of common *language*.* I am not myself concerned with Moore-an exegesis. It seems to me that in his positive views was a cult of *common sense*, but that in his demolition of the views of philosophers he made great use of their unacknowledged deviations from common *language*.

One might in consequence say about him that he *practised* much of what Linguistic Philosophy practises—the insistence on neutral and platitudinous conclusions, the destructive attitude towards creative, reformative philosophy—without however subscribing, even tacitly, as linguistic philosophers do, to a general *rationale* justifying those practices. But just this makes his practice flawless: for it is a part of the theory of linguo-philosophic practice—a part not lived up to—that there is no theory behind it. . . . One might say that Moore is the one and only known example of Wittgensteinian man: unpuzzled by the world or science, puzzled only by the oddity of the sayings of philosophers, and sensibly reacting to that alleged oddity by

* Cf. the issue of *Philosophy* on G. E. Moore's philosophy (July 1958), and especially "Moore's Appeal to Common Sense" by Mr. A. R. White.

very carefully, painstakingly and interminably examining their use of words. . . .

The "game" model of language and all the other theories of meaning and philosophy which underwrite the philosophic practice of linguistic philosophers, seem absent from among Moore's convictions. Also, his way of arriving at the practices appears to be his own: it shares with Linguistic Philosophy a sense of the alleged "oddness" of philosophy, but does not spring from a disappointed hope of constructing a perfect language. *Psychologically*, he really did seem innocent of any general theory. (Wittgenstein tried to behave as if he were, but he was not, and the truth always slipped out.) But *logically*, such claims of innocence, still made by some philosophers, are and must be *always* false. The tacit general theory is incapsulated in the practice, in its criteria and rules, in what it counts as clear, etc.

In as far as Moore simply *did* philosophy in a certain way, without secretly or semi-avowedly holding and insinuating a theory entailing why the practice must be successful and is the only possible one (and this differentiates him from linguistic philosophers proper), one may, according to taste, consider him superior or inferior them. My own inclination is to consider his approach *inferior*. A simple dogmatic cult of common sense, caution and literal-mindedness seems to me to have little to commend it, unless it be that sometimes (though hardly at the present time) it is salutary as some kind of corrective to excessive verbal extravagances. By contrast, the later theories of Wittgenstein, the immanentism, linguistic functionalism and so forth, which are used to justify such procedures, are, though mistaken, at least interesting, stimulating and can be discussed, provided of course one disregards their associated taboos.

In the development of Linguistic Philosophy since the death of Wittgenstein, however, there has been one strong trend that would reverse this valuation, and commend Moore for merely doing and for being genuinely free of underlying doctrines justifying the doing. The doctrine-less-activity theory of philosophy was a semi-conscious delusion with Wittgenstein and his followers, but it has since become fashionable to try and live up to it and emulate Moore in really having no ideas at all. The claim of doctrinelessness amongst contemporary linguistic philosophers, though still far from true, attains some semblance of plausibility when they abandon the claim that usage-observing is philosophically therapeutic, and come to see it as "pure research". Such research can perhaps be done without any presuppositions, though it then has little merit or interest; and the practitioners tend to see their patron saint in Moore.

One should add, finally, that in certain respects Moore's thought was very much unlike Wittgenstein's. His practice of carefulness as the key to philosophic truth was associated with an old-fashioned view of mind which Wittgenstein did much to eradicate—namely, that thought, or at any rate philosophic thought, was a matter of attentively observing concepts before the eye of introspection. The activity-theory of mind and the role-theory of meaning and language are directed largely at this kind of view, and on this point Linguistic Philosophy considers itself to have progressed significantly beyond Moore.*

It is interesting to note that Moore is himself a striking refutation of the view he has made fashionable, namely that carefulness is the key to philosophic truth. His own indisputable painstakingness did not save him from expounding a wholly incredible theory of morals in *Principia Ethica*. Ideas, and even the detection of errors, require more than care and caution. The universe does not surrender its secrets to a combination of pedantry and dogmatism under the name of Common Sense. This combination is not even a guarantee of avoiding error, let alone of attaining truth.

8. TRANSITION

In the course of describing Linguistic Philosophy as a theory of *philosophy* we have described the three philosophic trends which preceded it. The two which it replaced were Logical Atomism and Logical Positivism. Yet it would be incorrect and misleading to say that Linguistic Philosophy consists of a *refutation* of those two outlooks in any ordinary sense of refutation. It is not the case that those two trends had some specific difficulties and that Linguistic Philosophy is a new theory which solves those difficulties or copes with them better. Of course those movements did have plenty of difficulties which they did not quite succeed in coping with, but Linguistic Philo-

* Cf. Mr. G. A. Paul on "Wittgenstein" (Ed. Ryle), p. 88 in *The Revolution in Philosophy*, 1956, esp. p. 90 *et seq.*

sophy is not a new theory *of the same kind* which just happens to cope with some difficulties better or solve them. The innovation it introduces is far more radical than that. It is a new way of seeing the problem, not a new solution of an old kind.

Linguistic Philosophy appeals to the familiarity * of the phenomena which give rise to philosophical problems; to the fact that *we* use the relevant expressions; to the fact that we *use* them; to the fact that we use them for *communication,*† and that we are successful in this.

There is a much-quoted passage in St. Augustine in which he remarks that he knows what time is, until he thinks about it, and then he does not. He might have said that he knows how to *use* the concept but not how to say what it *is*. This situation, which seems common with regard to many philosophically crucial concepts, is in a way the starting point for Linguistic Philosophy : it treats it not as a problem, but as the solution. We know how to *use* the concept, but not how to account for it : but if concepts are the *use* we make of words, do we not become also capable of accounting for them, as soon as we realise that indeed a concept is what it *does*? Manners makyth concepts as well as Wykehamists. So it was not some knowledge or insight that we were lacking, in each individual case, when we were philosophically perplexed, be it by time, goodness, induction or anything else : what we lacked was, ironically, the *general* idea applicable to all these problems—namely that the *use* is all there is to know with regard to concepts, and hence the exploration of it is the only solution a philosophic problem can have. It is also true that one important aspect of that use is that each word or concept is used in a multiplicity of diverse ways, and moreover that different concepts have different kinds of uses. (At *this* level, generality is rejected, and diversity is the clue; but this does not exclude the fact that a very general insight is what is crucial for the understanding of Linguistic Philosophy.)

Linguistic Philosophy can be seen not merely as reading St. Augustine's famous remark backwards, but also as reading backwards the type of philosopher—Bradley, for instance— who declares some ordinary, customary way of speaking as im-

---

* Cf. Mr. G. A. Paul in *The Revolution in Philosophy* (Ed. Ryle), London 1956, esp. pp. 92 and 93.

† Cf. Mr. R. Rhees' preface to Wittgenstein's *The Blue and Brown Books*, Oxford 1958, p. xiii.

possible and contradictory, and argues that, in consequence, true reality is different. Once one looks at language as *use*, as something *done*, this type of thinking becomes difficult: how can something *done* be contradictory? (Something that is *thought* or *said* can be, even if it is thought by many many people, and for a long time. But if thinking *is* a kind of doing . . .?) If what is done contradicts some alleged standards of possibility, of logical propriety—well, then, perhaps it is the job of philosophy to unravel and neutralise those standards, to show that they have no authority, and to leave what is done, what is said, "as it is". The old kind of philosophy took language for granted and puzzled about the world. Linguistic Philosophy takes the world for granted and puzzles about language. Instead of asking whether the world can be what we think it is, it asks, given that the world *is* what we think it is, given that language is true, how language functions and why we should have supposed that it should function in another way, a way which would leave no room for our normal beliefs.

Note that the very insight—the view of language as a set of behavioural games—is not really a *theory*, but a truism: in a sense, this is indeed what languages *are*. One might suppose that *theory* enters in the form of the prediction that, following up the implications of this truism, we shall "dissolve" philosophy. But in fact this prediction is treated not as a testable *theory*, but as a necessary and self-evident truth, a corollary of that naturalistic outlook which was insinuated in the course of expounding the notion of a "language game" and the reasons why it is superior to a constructed "ideal language".

9. APPEARANCE AND REALITY, OR MONSIEUR JOURDAIN'S REVOLT

One can see the quarrel between Linguistic Philosophy and its predecessors in terms of the old issue about Appearance and Reality, the old issue now fought out in terms of language.

The predecessors considered actual language a kind of appearance, a veil which, if torn away, would reveal a Real Language, based on a logical notation, and connected to the world in a more intimate manner, without redundancy and spurious admixture.

Linguistic philosophers, and in particular Wittgenstein, have done what has so often been done before: the carrying out of a revolution which inverts everything and installs appearance as true reality, and condemns the "reality", as previously conceived and sought, as a chimaera, a snare and a disease. Once again—only, this time, with special reference to language—the Real is proclaimed to be the Rational. And, as usual, the ultimate justification of this apotheosis of the actual is the absence of anything outside it which could be its yardstick.

There are, of course, special reasons why this particular cult of the actual should take a *linguistic* form. In Wittgenstein's case, it was the aftermath of an intoxication with a notation. (This could also be called Monsieur Jourdain's revolt: something snapped, and he refused to go on believing that he was ever talking *Principia Mathematica* without knowing it.) His early philosophy was in effect an atomism based on the idea that the world could best be seen through the notation of *Principia Mathematica*.* When this intoxication abated, the hangover was, in Wittgenstein's case, so powerful and persistent that he built a philosophy, an idolatry of ordinary language, from it, like a man who in the morning is so revolted by the visions of the preceding night that he treats the morning view of the world as a great revelation, and swears to abide by it henceforth. Unfortunately, he switched from the Procrustean attitude of his youth into a Protean, undiscriminating acceptance.

There is perhaps nothing new in such a cult of ordinary speech: it reminds one of the vehemence, for instance, of the early German nationalists in combatting the seductions of the French language (and of many other nationalists, combatting an alien language, since then). The language of the untutored is said to be somehow closer to reality than a polished, self-conscious, rule-bound manner of speaking. What is new here is that the vehement reaction is not against the language of an alien culture, but against the invented notation of formal logic. As so often, the first generation of the movement is led by those who had felt the blandishments of the alien diction most strongly; the second generation consists of those who have not, but who are delighted to hear that their old practices, of which

---

* This idea gave rise to a tradition of philosophy by "typographical jargon", as Collingwood called it. Cf. *An Autobiography*, Pelican Ed., p. 29.

they had come to be ashamed, had an unsuspected merit and excellence.

One can see this revolution both as an anti-Copernican attempt at putting the focus of thought back at something human—*speech*; and yet also as a genuine Copernican revolution with regard to language, seeing *it* as something *in* the world, rather than central to it.

CHAPTER IV

OF THE WORLD

I. THE SECRET OF THE UNIVERSE

W E H A V E D E S C R I B E D the views of Linguistic Philosophy on language and on philosophy, and it is time to turn to its view of the *world*. Officially, it has none. (Officially it is sometimes claimed not to be a theory of *anything*.) It often considers the pursuit of world-views to be *the* cardinal sin of thought. Alternatively, it claims to be neutral with regard to all substantive questions about the world. In fact, however, it does have an interesting, indeed striking, view of the world, which can, as shown, be elicited from its presuppositions, its procedural rules, its criteria of what counts as a solution, and from certain key slogans, and from occasional confessions.

The kernel of that view of the world is something that may strike one as so true, so all-embracing, so accurate a proposition as to merit being called *the* secret of the universe. I shall now disclose this Secret of the Universe. Its first formulation is:

The world is what it is.

It will be objected that this is a trivial tautology; to dress it up as the secret of the universe, a feeble joke; to attribute it to a serious philosophic movement, a silly travesty.

On the contrary, suitably interpreted, it is a powerful idea. Far from being a mere joke, the joke is on those who do not see its full implications: for past, pre-linguistic philosophy implicitly denied this principle, trivial though it may seem when so simply formulated.

Pre-linguistic philosophy implicitly contradicted it by supposing that the world could somehow be a different place according to whether this or that concept was employed to describe it. The power of the seemingly trivial proposition emerges if it is read in the light of the theory of language expounded earlier. For philosophic questions generally do not concern individual cases: they do not enquire whether this or that individual falls under some concept; whether *this* action is right, *that* painting beautiful, *this* inference valid. They enquire, on the contrary, whether rightness, beauty, inference as such exist or are of some general nature: and it was supposed that the answer to such questions about the acceptability of a general concept would show whether the world was of one kind or another.

Hence the insight that the world is what it is (in other words that philosophic theories are such that their truth or falsity would not succeed in making any difference to it) is one way of conveying the doctrine of Linguistic Philosophy. It often has been conveyed in this way. For instance, in Wittgenstein's *Philosophical Investigations* (p. 156):

> "Philosophy only states what everyone admits."

Or (p. 49):

> "Philosophy may in no way interfere with the actual use of language; it can in the end only describe it. For it cannot give it any foundation either. *It leaves everything as it is.*" (Italics mine.)

Or (p. 50):

> "If one tried to advance *theses* in philosophy . . . everyone would agree to them."

Or, already in the *Tractatus* (5.5563):

> "All propositions of our colloquial language are actually, just as they are, logically completely in order."

Or consider Professor J. Wisdom's slogan,

> "Philosophy begins and ends in platitude",

or again, the importance given by G. E. Moore (and others following him) to the quotation from Bishop Butler, which he made the motto of his *Principia Ethica*:

> "Everything is what it is and not another thing."

This has always been interpreted in Linguistic Philosophy as meaning that everything is what it is said to be and should not be explained in terms of something else.

Consider also all those numerous recent philosophers who insist that philosophy must be a "second-order study", which is to say that its findings cannot be about "first-order" issues, or, in plainer words, about the world. The underlying notion is similar throughout: philosophical truths do not indicate or exclude possibilities about the world, they leave it as it is: there are no general alternatives about the world. (Their motto might have been: "Things are what they are and will be what they will be—why should we seek to be confused?")

That this must be so can be made to follow from various premisses: from the fact that philosophy is a conceptual and not a substantive enquiry; from respect for the basic truths of common sense; from the fact that we lack cognitive channels for truths other than factual or formal ones.

One may ask about this idea—is it a thesis about philosophy, or a definition of what Wittgenstein means by "philosophy"? If the former, it is false; if the latter, it is trivial. In fact, of course, it vacillates between the two.

As a thesis, it is false. If we mean by philosophy what men in the past have meant by it, it is plainly untrue. If we mean by it what we sensibly can and normally do mean by it—thought about fundamental issues—it is again untrue. It is untrue either that we can do without such thought, or that we can replace it by mere description of how we speak—which is what Wittgenstein recommends. (*Philosophical Investigations*, p. 47.)

As a definition, it perhaps describes a possible activity, but not an important or sufficient one.

To Wittgenstein, it did seem sufficient. But this was only because the horizon of his intellectual life included so little other than his own wrestlings with the views of the *Tractatus*.

At the heart of his thought lies the tautology: things are as they are. The language games in which we describe them are so to speak formal and make no difference to those things (this idea—formal concepts say nothing—is already present in the *Tractatus*). Moreover, the games are themselves activities, things in the world, and not privileged. (*Philosophical Investigations*, p. 44. *This* idea is opposed to the *Tractatus*.) Moreover, these things are infinitely various, and nothing can be said about them, they can only be described. (*Philosophical Investigations*, p. 11. The idea that nothing can be said "outside" is found in the *Tractatus*, and the idea of diversity is added to it.)

Wittgenstein thought he had the secret of the universe—by

seeing that there could be *no* ultimate secrets, because language was a thing like any other.

There is an alternative possible formulation of the secret oı the universe, which we may call the second version:

The world is what it seems.

With this formulation of the Secret of the Universe, one's difficulty is exactly the opposite from the one encountered with the first formulation: there one was struck by the apparent triviality, whereas here one is impressed by the apparently questionable nature of the statement. Past philosophy, and indeed any reflective man, has always been willing to contemplate the possibility that the world might be radically other than it seems. There is little reason to suppose that our current prejudices are ultimate truth, and there are ample reasons for suspecting that we may be mistaken.

But again, suitably interpreted, this principle conveys something implied in the relevant theory of language. Of course, linguistic philosophers do not wish to deny that the concrete world is full of little surprises. What is denied is the possibility of surprise with regard to general, abstract concepts: to suppose Rightness, Beauty, Inference, etc., to be absent, or to be different from what the use of the relevant words suggest, is not to imagine a different world, it is—unwittingly—to change one's way of looking at the same world. Denials of these entities or categories, or the postulation of counter-usage theories about them, is not the presentation of new theories, but possibly unwitting conceptual revision. (Kant once tried to show that we could not be wrong about our categories because *we* supplied them. Wittgenstein tried to show that we could not be wrong about them because *language* supplied them.)

The plausibility of this argument, as indeed of the one connected with the idea that "the world is what it is", only extends to "categorial" or "formal" concepts, to language games as opposed to moves within them. Hence much depends on the possibility of distinguishing the two. It also depends on the view that there is no point in denying or changing a whole category, *or* that to do this is extra-philosophical. We have discussed this earlier, and we shall return to these themes when assessing the philosophy.

Wittgenstein liked to point out that the steps in philosophic arguments which we think of as most innocent are in fact the most dangerous ones. The boot is on the other foot. *His* step, seemingly innocent, of recommending *description* for philosophy, and declaring *explanation* as impossible, in fact insinuates the preposterous theory that the world is always as it seems: for the description must itself be in the ordinary terms which incorporate the ordinary assumptions.

And, in the end, it insinuates this theory not in some subtle, ethereal interpretation of it (for instance, as merely the denial of the doctrine of the *Tractatus* that there is a logical substrate of the world) but in the disastrous literal sense, as an underwriting of all the prejudice and simple-mindedness of our unreflective selves and our ordinary ways of speaking. In his youth, Wittgenstein discovered that there were no surprises *in logic*: in his age, that there were no surprises.

2. NATURALISM

So far we have made sense of the ideas of Linguistic Philosophy about the world mainly by stressing that they can be understood best in the light of its theory of language. This might be taken to show that it does not really have a theory of the world, that concerning the world it is neutral, as is claimed. This would be a mistake. In fact, it both insinuates, and is dependent on, a theory of the world which I shall call Naturalism: roughly, that the world is unmysterious, that, in the preceding formulations, it is what it is or what it seems, and "no other thing".

There is a kind of reciprocated suggestiveness: the naturalistic view of the world implies a naturalistic view of language, and that in turn implies a naturalistic view of the world. This circle is further confirmed by seeing any non-naturalistic idea in terms of an elaborated pathology of language, and in making the elimination of non-naturalistic ideas the criteria of successful therapy, of successful "dissolution" of a philosophic problem. . . . There is no breaking out of this circle: by going round it, the naturalistic picture of the world confirms itself. . . .

In substance, Linguistic Philosophy conveys, insinuates, insists on a naturalistic view of the world. It does so by means of the terms in which language and its use are described; by means of the criteria employed for when this description is to count as completed and successful; by means of its tacit criterion of what is pathological or paradoxical, and what is a cure; and it does so by combatting the type of philosophy which argues from a kind of use to the existence of a kind of entity or a special realm: instead of allowing the invocation of entities or realms, Linguistic Philosophy insists on interpreting any kind of assertion as one further kind of *use* of language, within the natural world. Either a plausible, naturalistic account is found —and this confirms their view—or, if not, linguistic philosophers are not abashed: the fact merely illustrates one of their favourite themes, namely the complexity and manifoldness of the uses of language.

The argument can be put thus:

Here is man. He thinks and speaks. Thought and expression cannot occur without some kind of medium, of which the most familiar is words. But the units employed, the tokens, in this case words, cannot be employed without there being some kind of rules for their use: these rules are the meaning of those tokens, and systems of such rules are, in a broad sense, a language. That there must be such rules is obvious: a token used without rules, at random, cannot convey anything.

But, this being so, what questions can there be? There may be questions internal to the language-systems, decidable in accordance with the decision procedures appropriate to the system in question and forming part of its rules.

These questions are not philosophical. Secondly, there can be questions *about* such systems. They are philosophical, and the answers to them *are* philosophy. But these systems are observable: they either already exist in the actual habits of the men employing them, or, alternatively, they are systems specially invented. In the former case, we observe those customs and elicit the rules; in the latter, we work out the implications of the specifications of the designer of such an invented game.

Having done either of these two things, how *could* there be any questions left? To carry out this programme may be a little difficult, particularly the observing of actual languages and eliciting their rules, for the observation may be hampered by great complexity of actual living languages, whilst the eliciting of the rules may be a matter of tricky interpretation. But, though possibly difficult, there can be no doubt but that it is possible, and that, when completed, no philosophic questions can remain. The "dissolution" of philosophic problems *must* be possible, it seems.

But whilst the naturalist, common-sense "things are as they seem" outlook acts as the central premiss of the various procedures and doctrines of the Linguistic Philosophy, it can also be deduced *from* them: the circle is complete.

For instance, it can be deduced from the assertion (axiomatic within Linguistic Philosophy) that old-fashioned philosophic theses are odd, paradoxical, as follows:

Old philosophical theses are paradoxical, odd, countercommonsensical. True philosophy removes the temptation to make them.

Conclusion: The true vision (remaining when the pathological paradox has been cured), is the commonsensical one.

Or, for instance, it can be deduced from the Game model of language: The games are carried on by ordinary people, including children or stupid people, in ordinary circumstances, and must be described in the terms in which we describe ordinary activities in ordinary contexts. Being explicable in those terms, it follows that those ordinary concepts are adequate accounts of the world, for it is in terms of *them* that we have explained the use and place in the world of those various concepts *in* the language game that we were initially concerned with.

Or again, it can in a very similar manner be deduced from the Activity ("know-how") theory of mind: Mind being an activity or set of dispositions *in* the public world, the ordinary notions we employ to describe doings of people (including children, simpletons, etc.) are adequate to describe the world conceived by "mind".

Thus, there are many ways of showing that the ordinary view is right. Voltaire once defined philosophy as what everyone knows and what no one will ever know. It now seems to be only what everyone knows, but proved in a way no one would ever have suspected.

The philosophical job is to persuade us of the adequacy of ordinary conceptualisations. It is the story of Plato over again —only this time it is the philosopher's job to lead us back *into* the cave.

3. A SPECIAL KIND OF NATURALISM

How does the naturalism of Linguistic Philosophy differ from the many familiar versions of it which abound in the history of thought? Linguistic Philosophy is a Naturalism, a naturalistic or common-sense metaphysic, which maintains that things are much as they seem. It is, however, a Naturalism with a set of very peculiar features, which distinguish it from ordinary, old-fashioned kinds of naturalism, and make it much more novel and successful. These peculiarities are:

It is not asserted—it is insinuated. It is insinuated by the practice of examining usages in their actual context—i.e. naturalistically—but without postulating Naturalism.

It is not so much proved, or argued for, as it is presupposed, yet in a manner which makes it appear innocuous. It is presupposed by approaching the problem as a problem about the use of words (in the world)—but at the time the naturalistic answer is presupposed. It is built into a circle of practices, values and tacit presuppositions: words are not used at random, and the rule of their non-randomness *is* the solution. (And: nothing other than a set of observations about use counts as a solution. Until it is found, the chase continues, undiscouraged by the fact that some problems do not look as if they were soluble or dissoluble this way.)

It is a naturalism containing an appealing account of how non-naturalistic, counter-common-sense doctrines and problems arise. It contains, so to speak, a pathology. This pathology is or claims to be a "logical" doctrine, which distinguishes it from the merely sociological or psychological explainings-away of earlier naturalisms.

It is a naturalism which is prepared to make very great concessions to non-naturalistic views if this is required: it is wholly pliable without loosing its essence.

Or rather one should say it is a naturalism without tears, a naturalism which enables one to have one's cake and eat it; to give in fully to the compulsive insight that after all the world is but a natural thing unhaunted by elusive mysteries—the mid-morning view of the world—and yet not to have to suffer any of the sacrifices which naturalism in the past has brought with it, sacrifices which used to be necessitated by the fact that many of our doings, convictions and traditions seem to pre-suppose non-naturalistic elements. Linguistic Philosophy is like a magical looking-glass which enables everyone to see in it just what he wishes to see. The view that every kind of proposition is perfectly in order as it is, and the movement's linguistic functionalism, its polymorphism, and the resistance to any kind of reduction or elimination, enable everyone to preserve just those kinds of uses to which he is attached, *and yet* to see them as *"uses"* and hence naturalistically. He may, if he wishes, support this retention by finding an account of how that use works, but even if he fails or is too lazy, the outlook guarantees that some use, some function is there to be found. If it cannot be found easily, this merely shows that it is a complex one—and this, after all, is a part of the general doctrine. This also is just what one is led to expect! This provides an omnibus and watertight defence of any kind of discourse against hostile critics of that kind of discourse. These are reductionists—it is said—who are misled by a simple model which they use as a criticism, etc., etc. And in as far as all criticism has to be based on a model or a norm, and the very possibility of applying these to kinds of discourse is just what is denied, this defence against criticism is totally invincible within the general context of Linguistic Philosophy. Thus seeing language as a *game in the real world* makes Linguistic Philosophy hard-headed. The permissibility of all kinds of games, on the other hand, makes it pliable and conveniently non-radical, a way of re-incorporating whatever one wishes.

There is of course another strand hidden in Linguistic Philosophy which can be used if one wishes to get *rid* of some kind of discourse, namely, the logical positivist doctrine of the exhaustiveness of the dichotomy of "either factual or logical". This brand is less advertised, and in connection with Logical Positivism it is ever being attacked. Nevertheless, it can be invoked when necessary—it is invoked in Wittgenstein's *Philosophical Investigations*, in the form of the exhaustive opposition of "empirical" (or "scientific") and "grammatical" (pp. 43 and 47).

It can then be used to destroy what one does not like, notably genuine critical philosophy. With the help of the two techniques, the omni-tolerant linguistic functionalism and the old restrictive two-and-two-only-kinds-of-discourse doctrine, one can adjust the contents of the mirror so that it contains exactly what one wishes.

Past naturalisms have tended to be defeated, at any rate in philosophy, by one great obstacle—the theory of knowledge. The theory of knowledge has perhaps been the main intellectual bar in the way of a victory of naturalism, for everything else favoured it: the success of natural science, the bankruptcy of transcendentalism, the general secularisation of modern life.

But epistemology, the theory of knowledge, has always succeeded in presenting powerful objections to a naturalistic world view. Roughly and briefly, it has always been able to point out that nature, in terms of which everything was to be explained, had after all to be *known* before things could be explained in terms of it, and hence knowledge was prior. Moreover it was extremely difficult to account for certain features of knowledge in naturalistic terms, for instance the necessity and the objectivity accorded to natural laws. Naturalism was a kind of Third Person outlook on the world reinforced by the range and precision of science. Epistemology was always able to point out that before there could be a Third Person view of the world, there had to be a First Person view of the world. By making the Third Person view derivative, and the First Person view primary, it made nature derivative of knowledge and placed knowledge outside it.

Linguistic Philosophy has overcome this obstacle, or so it seems to those who subscribe to it.* It has done so by claiming to undermine and destroy the whole science of epistemology, as shown, by claiming that it rests on what are considered confusions, a kind of pseudo-psychology.

Thus this form of naturalism seems to overcome the philosophic difficulties of the previous kind of naturalism, without, however, sharing its political or ethical disadvantages. It appears to commit no one to any disagreeable naturalistic view such as subjectivity of value, and so forth. Other aspects of Linguistic Philosophy—Polymorphism, acceptance of actual usages—come into play and obviate "paradoxes", un-commonsensical or "substantive" conclusions. Once the Third Person view is accepted, linguistic functionalism and tolerance is invoked, and any required kind of discourse, such as ethical discourse, religious, aesthetic, and so on, is then defended on the

* "The analysis of skills, competences, learnings, knowing-how . . . reintroduced into philosophy as one of the rightful heirs of the condemned pseudo-science of epistemology." Mr. S. Hampshire, *Mind*, 1950, p. 238.

ground that it, like any other kind of discourse, is all right as it is, need not be defended, and cannot be criticised.

The linguistic basis provides for this kind of naturalism not merely a premiss, but also a camouflage and a certain *freshness*. This last is not unimportant in accounting for the success of Linguistic Philosophy. Non-linguistic naturalisms are stale. Camouflage, for that matter, is also very important. The general convenience of this kind of have-it-as-you-wish naturalism has already been pointed out. The camouflage adds to it. Its protagonists do not see this doctrine as a naturalism, they see it as something quite neutral, although they borrow all the appeal of naturalism.

It is worth while elaborating further the difference between linguistic naturalism and the old-fashioned traditional kind. In both cases there is an overcoming, or attempted overcoming, of epistemological problems by a switch from the First Person to the Third Person view. The old-fashioned variety in effect said: but surely knowledge is a biological, psychological, social, etc., process in the world, so there cannot be problems about knowledge which are not soluble by any investigation of those natural and social processes—an investigation carried on like any other. Linguistic Philosophy in effect says: knowledge is after all something that occurs within the context of a language game. So—there cannot be problems about it other than such as would be soluble simply by the investigation of the structure and rules of the language game in question.*

Though similar in their Third Person twist, the practical and programmatic implications of the two kinds of naturalisms are vastly different. The old kind commends scientific investigation and commits the philosopher either to becoming a scientist or at least to making a serious study of the result of the work of

---

* It is sometimes supposed, mistakenly, that Linguistic Philosophy could be refuted by showing that there is non-verbal thought or that concepts manifest themselves in ways other than linguistic ones. Indeed they do, and indeed there is thought outside language, if we mean by "language" a natural or constructed system of sounds or marks. But if we investigate those non-lingual manifestations of thought or concepts, we will find that they also involve a system of alternatives and so forth describable as a "language game": in an extended sense of language, indeed, but a legitimately extended one, which bears out the points made by linguistic philosophers. Though this philosophy has many weaknesses, this one is not amongst them.

scientists. It was and is a spur to the emergence and development of psychology and sociology. In thus orienting those interested in the solution of fundamental problems towards the sciences, it pays the price of naturalism. The answers so obtained then have to share the original sin of all scientific results, corrigibility and a kind of essential incompleteness. A naturalistic philosophy of the old kind is doomed to share the eternal progress of natural scientific enquiry.

The practical and programmatic implications of *linguistic* naturalism, however, do not entail a pursuit of, or regard for the sciences. On the contrary, they are a rationale of a rigid separation of philosophy from science and a disregard for it. The programmatic implications tend to be stated somewhat as follows: philosophy is a second order study, the study of concepts and not of things. (The fact that concepts are now linguistic *things* of a certain kind—moves within language games—does not appear to affect this point.) Therefore the results of natural science do not concern us. We are free and independent of them. (Linguistic philosophers concede that there may be philosophic problems concerning the concepts employed by natural scientists, problems within the philosophy of this or that science; but they do not suppose that science is relevant to the general philosophic problems which—they say—arise in the general language and not in its scientific subparts.)

So, the ideal of old-fashioned metaphysics, a closed kind of thought, is curiously maintained within linguistic naturalism. The old naturalism was an invitation to intellectual adventure, and the assessment of the fruits of such adventure. The new version is, on the contrary, the enclosure of a nice neat circumscribed little world, complete, safe, without danger of innovation: as stable as the old invented worlds of the metaphysicians, without even the disadvantage of making transcendental claims, or *any* claims for that matter. This discovery or invention of a safe little world for philosophers to tend, a world safe from science—being "second order"—*and* safe from transcendentalism—language being naturalistically interpreted—is probably the main appeal of Linguistic Philosophy in the circles in which it has succeeded. Professor K. Popper's interpretation of Plato has shown how Platonism can be seen as a means of attempting to arrest intellectual change. The historic achievement of linguistic philosophy has been to show how the same aim can be pursued through an extreme nominalism.

If we are to abandon epistemology and the First Person approach—and there may be something to be said in favour of this, given the relative sterility of philosophy and the successes of science with its Third Person approach—then let us do so in favour of *science*. Nature, man and society can then be investigated by means of the natural and social sciences.

What seems crazy is to ignore science on the basis of a crypto-epistomological argument ("common sense came first") *and* then reject epistemology too on a different basis: and all this for the sake of a cult of alleged common sense.

4. THE BAIT AND THE TRAP

The Linguistic Philosopher presents himself as having no specific doctrine of his own, but, on the contrary, as being either altogether beyond all philosophy, or philosophically neutral. He wishes to sell you nothing, he says: neither naturalism nor any other doctrine. All he asks in his strikingly modest way is that for a while you should accompany him in his examination of the concepts you employ, the concepts which have led you to feel that there is a problem. If you will only consent, he will, or he may (this depends on the degree of his confidence), show you in the course of a careful and minute examination of those concepts that the problem does not really arise.

Linguistic Philosophy was first sold to the academic public with this kind of promise. Those, however, who agreed to indulge in this protracted examination of terms and concepts were seldom, if ever, in fact rewarded by the therapy, by a real dissolution of the philosophic problem which initially led them to it. What does happen, however, is that the custom of examining concepts endlessly somehow becomes habit-forming and obsessional. After a time, it goes on without further expectation of or confidence in a "cure". It is then called "pure research", without therapeutic or philosophical basis. Once one has entered the trap, the bait is removed. The psychology of this is interesting and suggests some comparison with psychoanalysis. It seems that the habit of confessing our concepts can be as habit-forming and obsessional and as transference-producing as confessing our emotions and memories. Our concepts in their confusion are perhaps as shameful and guilt-inspiring as our emotions, if not more so. We bind ourselves to him who listens, especially one who does not confess any doctrine of his own but merely silently insinuates that he sees through and beyond the confusion from which we are trying to get. In both cases, an institutionalised rule excuses him from illuminating us. The psychoanalyst is *ex officio* silent, or merely "suggests interpretations": the linguistic philosopher, also *ex officio*, abstains from expressing any general view, though somehow or other it is tacitly understood that he has, or is nearer to, an ineffable insight which makes him see why nothing other than this kind of conceptual confession can do one any good. One then comes to live in a strange new world created by this endless free-associative confession and loses interest in the real issues of the world. According to one defence of this kind of practice, one is supposed to be led back to it in the end, but this is not frequently observed to happen.

One might ask whether that which is insinuated by Linguistic Philosophy should properly be called *naturalism*. I do not insist on that term. There is no illuminating non-circular way of defining what is and what is not "natural". In any case I only use the term as a kind of first approximation. It might be more correct to say that what is insinuated is a kind of conceptual conservatism. Linguistic Philosophy being in essence the insinuation of the concepts customarily employed in describing the world, it will confirm everyone, unwittingly or otherwise, in the employment of previously used concepts. It makes him redefine any problem that is puzzling him in those terms, and go on doing so until he either loses the interest in doing anything else, or, instead (if it ever really happens), "dissolves" the original problem. Thus Linguistic Philosophy confirms everyone in his preferred or older speech habits and their associated world view. In our period, the conventional world view tends in fact to be a kind of mitigated naturalism (using that term in a narrower sense), but, I suppose, it need not be so. In a society in whose language and way of life the concept of witchcraft is deeply embedded, on the other hand, the techniques of Linguistic Philosophy would confirm *it* (rather than what *we* now consider naturalism). By " dissolving", so to speak, any problems about the existence of witches by means of an examination of (the terms occurring in) witch-language, it would confirm their existence. In the end one comes back to the customary language. "Philosophy ends in platitude." *Whose* platitude?

We are here faced with a veritable mystique of ordinary language. This has often been said, but one must stress that it must be taken literally. What has happened is that people under the influence of Linguistic Philosophy talk themselves into absurd beliefs such as that there is no genuine problem of free will or mind–body interaction. They talk themselves into a state of mind when they genuinely think this, just as earlier philosophers, whom they frequently ridicule, have talked themselves into a state of mind where they thought they knew what they meant by the Absolute, and so forth. The models to which linguistic philosophers tacitly subscribe do not allow for such problems; so there *could not* be such problems. The fact that patently there are such does not bother them very much. The mystique took care of that.

This mystique of ordinary language or common sense is a set of high-powered, high-brow, doubly-sophisticated devices for inculcating an alleged common-sense or ordinary view. It has many parallels, such as pretending that the shepherd's life is best; or middle-class revolutionaries pretending that the worker's life is somehow fundamentally superior to their own.* The doubly sophisticated linguistic philosopher who talks himself into what he calls a naïve realist outlook is doing something in the same tradition, although perhaps less arduous and less interesting.

5. THE TURN OF THE SCREW

So far, we have looked at Linguistic Philosophy as a camouflaged naturalism—a naturalism which looks at man as a speaker, a language user, and sees philosophic issues as soluble by attention to some idiosyncrasy, nuance or complications in those speech habits. Where old philosophy has seen a complicated problematic world, Linguistic Philosophy sees only a complicated set of speech habits, occurring within an unproblematic world.

But although this is central and esssential to Linguistic

---

* Bertrand Russell has pointed out the similarity between Wittgenstein's prostration before "common sense" and Tolstoy's before the peasants. Fortunately, Tolstoy's muzhiks were not able to take up and propagate his doctrine. Wittgenstein's did. Cf. *Encounter*, Feb. 1959.

Philosophy, it does not exhaust it. There is a further turn of the screw.

It is true that some linguistic philosophers, some studies within this tradition, do work on this principle. But others are subtler than this. This above version can be called the Ordinary, or Primitive Linguistic Philosophy. Linguistic Philosophy can be classified as follows:

Straightforward (or Ordinary or Primitive): (1) Insinuates naturalism by simply describing usages *in* the world, until you see (if ever you do) how the non-naturalistic illusion was a by-product of misunderstandings of it, or until you can be persuaded that you *will* see this in the future.

Triple Star: (2) Alternates or supplements this insinuation with the contrary one: "Of course the non-naturalistic 'paradoxical' way of speaking *also* has certain attractions— we have no objection to their also being brought out."

De Luxe: (3) To people familiar with (1) and (2), it is possible to proceed to the stage of insinuating nothing. Some of the linguo-philosophic aphorisms are *so* obscure, some of the usage-collections *so* pointless; this stage is like the last, blank card in a T.A.T. Those with a well-trained eye of faith continue to see. They have come to like this game anyway.

6. TRIPLE STAR

The procedural practices and underlying ideas of straightforward Linguistic Philosophy are easy to describe, and have already been indicated.

The second level of sophistication is what I call the *Triple Star* form of Linguistic Philosophy. The Triple Star method consists of insinuating *both* a naturalistic *and* some alternative picture, by describing the "ordinary use", but at the same time heavily hinting at something inaccessible and beyond it. Not only *use*, but *misuse* too is claimed to be illuminating. The general picture conveyed by this method is not so much that past problems and theories merely arose through the interpretation of one use of words as though it were another, as that past philosophers did try to get at *something*, though unfortunately that something cannot be said, or cannot be said straightforwardly. It is then said that those theories were dramatic and misleading ways of bringing out something that might be illuminating or important.

Within the Triple Star method one could distinguish what may be called the Dialectical method, which has an interesting resemblance to certain views associated with Hegel. The idea is that successive assertion of seemingly incompatible general statements is essential and valuable, not merely because each of the rival assertions and denials conveys something or other, but because the very process, this kind of alternation, conveys something or other that could not be conveyed in any other way. The characteristic form assumed by the linguistic dialectical process is that of fluctuation between platitude and paradox. We have here an interpretation of philosophy as a game whose chief and crucial moves are a succession of blatantly platitudinous or blatantly paradoxical assertions.

To exemplify: In order to solve or "dissolve" the problems of, say, the nature of material objects and our knowledge of them, it is necessary not merely to describe in full our use of material-object expressions (as in crude Linguistic Philosophy), but also to present, in succession, the various opposed old, non-linguistic theories. (For instance, to present in succession the theory that material objects are something other than sensations, and, on the other hand, that they are nothing but assemblages of sensations.) This kind of alternating current will result in illumination: by seeing the temptation to each of the opposed theories—the features of our use of material-object expression which suggest each of them in turn—we shall come to see the truth about that class of expression, and not feel compelled to subscribe to either. They will thus contribute towards their own "dissolution". The best exponent of this kind of method is Professor John Wisdom.*

The criticism to which the Dialectical method is specifically open is that in its omni-tolerance it misses all points. If any philosophy "brings out" some kind of insight, and nothing is really false, we have not got very far: moreover, once one sees the mechanics of the oscillations which are said to be of such importance, one will hardly be tempted to indulge in them.

This kind of rather flabby omni-tolerance is indeed implicit in the whole Wittgensteinian approach. It is best conveyed by

* The theory of this is expounded by Professor J. Wisdom in *Philosophy and Psycho-Analysis*, Oxford 1953.

the slogan which Professor Wisdom once popularised "Say it if
you wish, *but be careful*". The point that was to be conveyed by
this was that you may, if you wish, and in order to communicate
some insight or other, put forward *any* philosophical theory (and
even, or especially, mutually incompatible ones). They are
alright in some sense or other; there is only the danger that
you may take them too seriously, or in some sense other than
the one—whatever it is—in which they are true or insightful.

This kind of relativism is implicit in the Wittgensteinian approach for the following reason: the notion of a language game
can after all *also* be applied to philosophers' games: there is
some context—or one can be found—in which even the utterances of philosophers are a move. The only danger is that you
might think that you are playing some more serious game when
you are merely playing a philosophical one.

If one sees one's philosophic pronouncements in such a light,
one will not waste one's breath on them.

Improving slightly on David Hume, one might summarise
this position by saying: "If we take into our hand any volume;
of divinity and school metaphysics, for instance; let us ask,
Does it contain any abstract reasoning concerning quantity or number?
No. *Does it contain any experimental reasoning concerning matter of
fact and existence?* No. Well, *don't* commit it to the flames, all
the same; but *be careful*, for it contains some illumination
cloaked in paradox and platitude."

There are, really, two possible attitudes implicit in Wittgensteinianism—a total relativism, as just indicated, or a rigid
conservatism. (Professor John Wisdom seems to have chosen
the former, most of the post-Wittgensteinians the latter.)

Santayana remarked somewhere that our nationality is like
our relation to women—too involved in our moral natures to be
changed honourably, and too accidental to be worth changing.
The Wittgensteinian view of our conceptual schemes and languages is similar: we are too involved in them to be able to
change them without confusion, and they are too accidental and
contingent to be worth changing. From this one can conclude
either that we can choose any we like—the liberal, relativistic
conclusion of John Wisdom—or again, as after all there is and
can be no philosophical reason for preferring one to another,
that we should stick to the old ones.

There is also a non-dialectical, simple version of the Triple

Star method. It consists of insinuating that over and above the complex facts of usage there is something—albeit not directly communicable—which can be the object of insight, and that old-fashioned philosophy was right in striving to attain this insight, and only wrong in attempting to articulate it.

This kind of Linguistic Philosophy is of some interest. It does not fit the charge to which crude Linguistic Philosophy is open, namely that it reduces philosophy to a set of contingent truths about how we happen to use words (thereby insinuating naturalism and inescapably committing the Naturalistic Fallacy). The truths insinuated by *this* kind of technique do not appear to be contingent. This is both an insight and a let-out. It can conveniently be invoked against those who make the obvious and important charge against Linguistic Philosophy, namely that it reduces all issues to questions about verbal ritual.

But if this let-out is invoked, one has to ask how literally these insinuated non-contingent truths are to be taken. If they are to be taken literally, then something *can* be said about language over and above what can be described in the course of specifying individual language games. If so, let it be said and discussed, rather than obliquely insinuated.

This is not the place to discuss the merits of individual instances of such non-contingent truths "about language". What is relevant is that they do not profit from being associated with the more normal techniques of Linguistic Philosophy, or interpreted as being instances of the application of its method. On the contrary, they are obscured by it.

For instance, Professor Hare, after lucidly expounding the case for ethical subjectivism, disclaims holding it and convinces himself that he "does not understand" ethical subjectivism. He is, of course, as capable as anyone of understanding the thesis that values are not confirmable, being unlike, say, mathematical theorems: indeed he not only understands this view, but subscribes to it. The reason why he claims "not to understand" ethical subjectivism is presumably that, if true, it is a necessary doctrine which has no contrast, and hence in virtue of the linguo-philosophic model of meaning, it does not constitute a thesis and hence there is nothing to understand. Moreover, by claiming that he does not understand it and that it does not exist, he obscures the fact that he does hold it and the fact that it is not "neutral", that it does *not* "leave everything as it is".

It may be true that (assuming it to be valid) ethical subjectivism has only confused or contradictory antitheses. But those confused or contradictory antitheses of it, which assimilate values to facts, happen to be parts of the ideology of most societies: only sophisticated ones have discovered the independence of fact and value. . . .

The unfortunate thing about Linguistic Philosophy is that it prevents the formulation of such ideas, and is committed to believing that they are as it were *un*-ideas. Hence even these rejected views, like the naturalistic basis of crude Linguistic Philosophy, have to be insinuated or disavowed. This is no aid to clarity or critical discussion.

It is important to add that the Triple Star style is not typical of Linguistic Philosophy. This is true for two reasons: first, appeals to how language happens to be are more frequent than insinuations of how it *must* be. And if there is a *must*, this is not something about how a given and optional language game happens to be. The second and more important reason is that this style is parasitic on the crude version. It is the crude version which gives Linguistic Philosophy its appeal; there is no mystery, it is all a matter of our speech habits, of seeing their complexity and not being befuddled by simple models, of seeing that allegedly key words have uses as humble as any others. It is only by being mixed up with, and identified with, that kind of playing down of mystery that the Triple Star exercises come to be classed as linguistic at all, as having any particularly intimate connection with language. One should also note that when a non-crude linguistic thesis is upheld by a linguistic philosopher, it is inevitably interpreted as a support for "linguistic naturalism"—whereas in itself it would merely be a case against, say, some specific "reduction". On their own, Triple Star exercises would never suggest or call for the thesis that language as such matters for philosophy, or that illumination follows on understanding something about language or attending to it. They can, it is true, be formulated para-linguistically, just as in the past they could be and were once formulated para-psychologically or in terms of alleged realms of being.

7. DE LUXE

Finally there is what I call the *De Luxe* method. It is as rarefied and refined as those dishes or wines which are so sophisticated that their taste is barely perceptible. The nature of this method has already been indicated as the last stage that one reaches after prolonged habituation to the crude method. Whereas the crude method insinuates a naturalistic picture, and Triple Star method insinuates that and its opposite in succession, the *De Luxe* method may insinuate nothing whatever. It is a kind of final blissful state when the mystical exercises of Linguistic Philosophy have done their work, when there is no puzzlement left to exorcise, and the delights of usage observation can be indulged for their own sakes. This stage is not for beginners. Linguistic Philosophy would never have succeeded in selling itself to anyone had it *begun* with this. The blandishments and promises of the crude and Triple Star methods were required to persuade people to devote themselves to the new pastime. However, this pastime once established, its practitioners numerous, the league tables of skill and reputation set up, its practice made customary and prestigious, the stage was now set for the wholly unsweetened *De Luxe* method, unadorned by any promises, the taste of the connoisseur.

This style is of course parasitic on the preceding two, and in particular on the crude version. It feeds the tastes acquired in practising it, without serving its ends, or any ends.

CHAPTER V

OF KNOWLEDGE

I. THE CIRCLE OF KNOWLEDGE

LINGUISTIC PHILOSOPHY HAS no theory of knowledge, but only, as indicated, a theory of why the theory of knowledge is redundant and impossible. It really amounts to saying that we know what we normally think we know, and that no radical criticism or re-evaluation of the nature and limits of human cognition * is possible. Just as in ethics, Linguistic Philosophy tends in effect to underwrite the norms that happen to be built into current usage, so in epistemology it underwrites the criteria of intellectual adequacy that underlie current practices. (Linguistic Philosophy is an impossible position in as far as current practices are not mutually consistent in either of these fields, but, in practice, individual linguistic philosophers simply select for their exegesis just those current practices which suit them.)

Thus Linguistic Philosophy can be seen as a claim to have overcome, in a radical manner, the problems of knowledge which were at the core of past philosophies.

It is worth indicating how the new way of looking at these problems is related to the old. "Informal logic" replaces "epistemology": the quest for the rules and conditions of invoking a kind of sentence—the specification of the situations which must be the case if the sentence expressing a claim to knowledge is to be permissible—replaces the search for some para-psychological processes which were once supposed to precede cognition.

The quasi-logical way of seeing the matter was not introduced by Linguistic Philosophy, but was already well established when Linguistic Philosophy emerged and came to work out some of its possible corollaries. Analytic philosophy in general, under the impact both of the emergence of symbolic logic and

* Such as has in fact occurred, for instance, in consequence of the secularisation of the Western world—but in the a-historical atmosphere of Linguistic Philosophy, little note is taken of that.

of Moore's method of analysis, tended to formulate its questions in linguistic or near-linguistic terms as concerning statements or propositions rather than psychological or quasi-psychological entities. Linguistic Philosophy pushed the matter further by two additional steps: Behaviourism and Diversificationism (Polymorphism).

By Behaviourism (or it might also be called the Third Person approach) we may mean in this context the insistence that it is not some disembodied spirit, some world-cognising ego which is not in the world, a mystic camera which can never be in the picture itself, that learns to use language and uses it: it is, on the contrary, a concrete person in concrete situations. Doctrines such as Logical Positivism proper, though they spoke of language in a Third Person way and formulated the problem of knowledge linguistically, nevertheless remained in thrall to the vision of this language ultimately used by a kind of Humeian bundle of sensations, a consciousness aware of things but not one of them.

The reason why doctrines such as Logical Positivism still half-explicitly subscribed to the assumption of a cognising-self, a transcendental ego that is not in the world, was not just naïvety. (In any case they did not call it by such names: but the notion is implicit in the procedure which, in order to account for how we know, assumes away the natural world, including the natural self, and then speculates how that world of the natural self can be assembled out of purely "given" constituents, "sense-data" or what not.) These epistemologists did not literally believe in such a cognising ghost: but they did suppose it a legitimate fiction for purposes of investigating the foundations of knowledge, and good reasons—not naïvety— impelled them towards it.

Those reasons for supposing it were, in essence: We may not assume the facts we normally claim to know about the world, when we wish to explain our knowledge of the world as a whole —for to do so is circular. We may not, for instance, explain knowledge in terms of a causal story about light waves, nerves, etc., for to do so is to assume that we *already* know about waves, nerves, etc., and that we know this knowledge to be reliable. On the contrary, to theorise about knowledge is to *suspend* our normal convictions and re-examine them. A naturalistic account only examines knowledge in presupposing it and prejudging the issue (presupposing the natural facts invoked in giving a causal account of knowledge).

For *this* reason—and not from some prior assumption of a pure self or sense data or what not—theoreticians of knowledge, including those who, like Logical Positivists, were determined to be hard-headed, assumed away the natural self and its natural doings, and postulated in its place variants on the ghostly-knower theme, such as "sense data". The important point about "sense data" for the theory of knowledge is that they are not just events in the world—like the ones we normally speak of as events—but events logically prior to the natural world from which that world is built up. Of course, the notion of "sense-datum" is produced as a cross between the pure world-brick and something tangible, it is an attempt to give the logical atom, from which all knowledge was to be built up, an interpretation in terms of something we also recognise and experience, and this was done by making it a kind of *sensation*. A "sense-datum" is a hybrid notion—and not therefore necessarily a bad one—produced by crossing the ultimate atom of knowledge (in the *Tractatus* no attempt was made to identify this atom concretely) with something experienceable, namely sensation.*

Whatever the demerits or implausibilities of postulating ghostly knowers, sense data, etc., the reasons for so doing seem overwhelmingly strong: the only alternative is to look at knowledge realistically, as concrete doings by concrete people, and to do this is to prejudge the whole problem of knowing. (Linguistic Philosophy consists of attempts to show that this *is* legitimate.) When we investigate knowledge as such, it seems illegi-

* It is perhaps worth adding that this identification was never wholly successful, for sensations do not behave in a way fitting the ultimate constituents of knowledge: they are not always, or ever, fully determinate; we often are not quite sure just what the sensation is that we are having. An example often given is that when we have the visual sensation of an area with a number of spots, we are not always certain concerning the number of spots. But if the sensation is to be one of the atomic bases of our knowledge, it cannot, *ex hypothesi*, be checked by anything else, for all checking will in the end be by reference to such sensations, which are hence themselves beyond all checks. So, in the case of the ambiguous sensation, we are compelled either to seek some *more* ultimate appeal (contradicting the initial hypothesis), or to say that reality is inherently ambiguous. Neither is satisfactory.

timate to assume that we already know about people's habits, or doings, or nerves, etc. This argument, more than any other, kept the epistemological tradition in philosophy going, and prevented a philosophical victory of the old kind of naturalism, despite the triumphs of that experimental science which seemed to embody and exemplify the naturalistic outlook, the habit of investigating things (including people) "in the Third Person", as objects.

Wittgensteinian Linguistic Philosophy overcame this argument, or so it claims. It claims to have superseded the epistemological approach in philosophy. Wittgenstein did succeed in convincing philosophers, by means of a few impressionistic observations of language, of something about which science, with its great triumphs, failed to persuade them. How did he score this triumph? How did his version of naturalism escape circularity?

It did not, but it was made to appear to do so. For one thing, philosophers are familiar with the circularity of ordinary naturalism, but they did not recognise it clearly when the circle re-appeared in linguistic guise.

Secondly, the circularity had already been *half*-committed by the manner of speaking of those philosophers influenced by the new notation in logic, and by Moore's style of philosophising, and by the "rejection of psychologism" (i.e. by the insistence on treating propositions as independent of their subjective concomitants). These manners of speaking already spoke at least of *statements* in the Third Person, or impersonally, in abstraction from the knower and hence also from the ghostly knower, and *vis-à-vis* these philosophies, Linguistic Philosophy appears as an advance, a more consistent approach which looks at both the linguistic unit, and the piece of the world to which it is alleged to refer, and the speaker himself, in the Third Person, unghostly manner.

Thirdly, the new naturalism was far more acceptable to philosophers, in that it did not entail their departure from their armchairs in order to go to the laboratory, but only a reform in their habits *in* the armchair: instead of speculating about ghostly knowers or ultimate elements of cognition, they only had to think, in the Third Person, about how one uses language. This re-orientation is not quite so painful. This may not be a powerful argument logically, but it may be, historically, one of the decisive reasons for the academic success of linguistic naturalism.

Fourthly, this naturalism has an uncheckable rationale: the type of notion required for the suspension of the natural standpoint—notions such as the disembodied knower, the ultimate atom of cognition, or the sense-datum—are declared meaningless and unintelligible; their employment, or that of any notion, is to be allowed only if first explained in terms of its "use" (in the world) or of "ordinary language", i.e. from just that natural standpoint which they meant to put in doubt, and this is of course impossible. Thus the questioning of the natural standpoint is not allowed to proceed, such questioning being treated as pathological and the concepts it employs as unintelligible. (Of course, as indicated, the naturalism is tacitly contained in the criteria of health and of intelligibility.)

Finally, Diversificationism seemed to confirm it: if "knowledge" is a great variety of things, it is less tempting to suppose it out of this world.

The upholder of traditional epistemology may rightly sneer at the Wittgensteinian linguistic philosopher for the circularity of his procedure, but the latter tries to avoid the appearance of circularity by insisting that we must start from the world as we normally suppose we know it—and he then claims he "fails to understand" the concepts necessary for placing that world "in brackets", so to speak, so as to see how we know it if we start from scratch. (Epistemologists from Descartes onwards have always tried to start from scratch so as not to prejudge anything —though they have disagreed as to the identification of the scratch.) The linguistic philosopher then derides the epistemologist for not indulging in the circular argument, for *not* "taking the world for granted": and of course we can be made to feel foolish about that, for we know that, like the lady philosopher who said she "accepted the universe", *we'd better*. Thus the circularity is not merely camouflaged, and protected from challenge by outlawing the terms required for challenging it, but is also reinforced by skilfully bringing out the terrifying intellectual and social hubris involved in *not* committing it. . . .

2. MULTIPLICATION BEYOND NECESSITY

In the preceding section the logical and, to some extent, temporal progression to the linguo-philosophic position was sketched as a behaviourism superimposed on a linguistic formulation of the problem of knowledge, with Polymorphism tagged on as a convenient addition which reinforces it. But, in fact, Polymorphism could also be seen as central (with behaviourism as an attached theme), and the emergence of Linguistic Philosophy outlined in terms of *it*.

The antecedents of Linguistic Philosophy, if seen in this light, are the discoveries by Russell to the effect that (*a*) language is richer in "logical forms" than had previously been supposed, and (*b*) "logical form" does not always correspond to grammatical form. The former discovery centred round the fact that, whereas it had previously been supposed that all propositions have a subject-predicate form, that they consist of an attribution of some characteristic to some subject, it was now found to be essential to see "relational" propositions—those asserting that two or more subjects are related in some way—as an independent class of their own. The second discovery focused attention on facts such as that a proposition which seems to be, say, a subject-predicate one, was in reality more complex. (A famous example is the statement "The present King of France is bald", which cannot be construed as attributing baldness to a subject, for there is no such subject—and yet the statement has meaning. The explanation given was that logically it is, despite being grammatically *one* sentence, a conjunction of a number of statements.)

Russell, who made these discoveries, did not multiply logical forms beyond necessity, and though he distinguished logical form from grammatical form, he supposed that there *was* a logical form under the grammatical form to be discovered. Linguistic Philosophy can be seen as emerging when these views are pushed further. What is the criterion of "logical form" if it is something to be discovered *under* the verbal form? Ultimately, the criterion can only be what is *done* with the verbal utterance, its general context in the world of things and of other utterances. But if so, there is no need to stop at any limited number of logical forms, for the contexts of speech are legion. Conversely, if the multiplication of logical forms goes far enough, it calls for a behaviourist interpretation: Platonic logical realms are plausible or attractive if they effect a kind of economy, but if not—if logical forms are as numerous as manners and contexts of speaking—no advantage is obtained in going beyond the actual speech acts. . . . So, the behaviourist (or naturalist) view of language, and a diversificationist or invertebrate view of language, both reinforce each other in a kind of circle, and both can be seen as springing from the sophistication concerning "logical form" which took place earlier in the century. (Linguistic Philosophy is a kind of inverted Occamism: entities, logical forms, must not be eliminated but multiplied. Wittgenstein's view that in philosophy one must describe and one cannot explain is correlative with his view that there are countless species of discourse: if one only describes, one cannot unify and reduce the number. Conversely, if there is an endless variety, one cannot unify and explain, but only describe. Those who drive manifold oxen must themselves be manifold, it appears.)

Equally, one can see it as the culmination of a progression, which starts from no longer accepting verbal form as a reliable index to logical form but still thinks of logical form in the image of grammatical form, and proceeds from this, via the appeal to behavioural and contextual criteria as a means to discerning true logical form, to a doctrine which equates logical form with behaviour and context, and sees no need for a notion of logic other than the rules and context of the verbal behaviour in question, the *use*. One can also see how both behaviourism and diversificationism undermine the idea, basic to Logical Atomism and the doctrines of the *Tractatus*, that there is an underlying pattern of the world (to be discovered through a correct appreciation of logical form, discernible by a kind of logical X-ray). This aids the overcoming of epistemology by underwriting the "natural viewpoint". If logical form is nothing but the behavioural context and use of utterances, and if these are endlessly various, then no underlying pattern of the world can be inferred from logical form. Or rather, what is inferred is that the world is as it seems, is that it consists of things like those acts and contexts of speech which give speech meaning.

3. SOME CONTRASTS

As indicated, the emergence of Linguistic Philosophy can be seen as the replacement of the epistemological viewpoint, of the critical evaluation of what we know, by an anti-epistemological outlook, which denies such a possibility, and sees the cognising ego as a thing amongst others in the world, manipulating language which is also just one activity amongst others *in* the world. Thus, mystery is excluded from the start—and so is the possibility of *general* criticism. (This is held to be a merit.) Alternatively, one can see it as the replacement of the doctrine of hidden and homogeneous "logical form" underlying discourse, by the insistence that discourse is behaviour, and very manifold behaviour at that, and hence that there is no homogeneous *or* hidden underlying structure. The two ways of looking at things support each other in a variety of ways, diversificationism providing behaviourism with a diagnosis of why anyone is tempted to adopt anything but the behavioural viewpoint ("because they are misled by the supposition of a simple homogeneous picture of language"), whilst behaviourism provides a guarantee that the role and meaning of expressions must be found in the activities and contexts envisaged in the natural way. There is no breaking out of the circle.

Both these progressions or transformations can be illustrated in terms of changes undergone by Wittgenstein's views between the *Tractatus* and the *Philosophical Investigations*.

Concerning the cognising self, the *Tractatus* says

"There is therefore really a sense in which in philosophy we can talk of a non-psychological I.

The I occurs in philosophy through the fact that the 'world is my world'.

The philosophical I is not the man, not the human body or the human soul of which psychology treats, but the metaphysical subject, the limit—not a part of the world." (5.641.)

Concerning simplicity, it says

"Men have always thought that there must be a sphere of questions whose answers—*a priori*—are symmetrical and united into a closed regular structure.

A sphere in which the proposition, *simplex sigillum veri*, is valid." (5.4541.)

Both these assumptions are indeed central to the *Tractatus*, and indeed to most of the varied theories of knowledge which make up the main Western philosophical tradition for at least three centuries. They are reversed in Linguistic Philosophy. They are replaced by the insistence on the concrete knower and language user, and on a view that *simplex sigillum falsi*.

One can also see Wittgenstein's later views as a *development* of the idea of the *Tractatus* that "formal concepts" do not designate anything *—with the difference that formal concepts are now seen to be numerous, and inherent in natural language and "humble" † (not special and set apart) rather than few and somehow absolute and above ordinary ones. But unfortunately, whilst multiplying and so to speak naturalising "formal concepts", linguistic philosophers persist in treating them as neutral *vis-à-vis* substantive issues. This grave mistake is in part a survival from an earlier stage in which it was at least plausible.

In the *Tractatus*, Wittgenstein indicated a few very general concepts which provided the framework for saying things about the world, but did not themselves mirror any thing (and which could plausibly be held to be neutral). Faulty philosophy was said to arise from treating them as names of *things*.

The view that formal concepts provide the framework of saying, but do not themselves say anything, and that the philosopher's job is concerned with them and not with saying things, and that about *them* it is difficult to say anything, but that one can show or exhibit them, remained with him. But in his later view, there were *different* formal concepts connected with each one of very many possible language games—and some of these games could be of very restricted and local application and relevance—rather than that these formal concepts be connected with one unique, ultimate and all-embracing language game (the one sketched in the *Tractatus*). The neutralism and formalism survived into Linguistic Philosophy, without justification and with disastrous results.

* "My fundamental thought is that the 'logical constants' do not represent." (4.0312.)
† *Philosophical Investigations*, p. 97.

4. REALISM AND IDEALISM

There are also respects in which the earlier and later views of Wittgenstein do *not* stand in opposition to each other but exhibit the same—and mistaken—assumptions.

These mistakes are the supposition that there is such a thing as "seeing the world rightly", an absolute insight without intermediary, so to speak; and associated with this fallacy, as a consequence of the awareness of the difficulty of expressing such insights, there is the idea of ineffability. On the surface the claim to "seeing the world rightly" is abandoned; in fact, it is still operative in his later thought, and the persistence of ineffable insights is a clear index of the persistence of that idea. He sees, early and late, that absolute knowledge is incompatible with the general conditions of *saying*. But, having in his mind some absolute claims, he has to assign them to the ineffable, or to the insinuated.

Consider Linguistic Philosophy as a new vision which replaces the old philosophical habit of looking at the mind-world relation, by concentrating instead the language-world relation. (This characterises *both* the doctrine of the *Tractatus* and that of Linguistic Philosophy proper.) Far from it being the case that this re-orientation obviates the old problems of the theory of knowledge, these questions—how can mind (now: language) get at, reflect, incorporate, the objects which it knows (now: speaks of)—all reappear, albeit in new form.

The greatest amongst these problems is perhaps the question of the *Ding an sich*, the thing-in-itself. The very notion of knowledge requires that there be something independently existing, outside knowledge, for knowledge to be the knowledge *of*, and similarly the notion of a language requires that there be something extra-linguistic for expressions to refer *to*.

So far so good: but reflection soon brings forth the problem. If all knowledge is knowledge by, through the medium of, some mind (or, all statements being in some language, of some rule-bound set of concepts), then how can we ever know (say) what that unknown (unmentioned) X is like prior to, independently of, being known (being described in speech)? How can we even know (say) that it exists at all, let alone what it is like?

A Realist is one who, impelled by the reflection that knowledge must be *of* something, insists that, despite all such difficulties, there must be something there. His opponent may, as cogently, point out to him * that to speak of what something is like prior to being known is to speak of what, *ex hypothesi*, you do *not* know (or that you are trying to say what things are like when *not* spoken of).

An exact replica of this problem reappears in the linguistic formulation of the situation. But, as the situation is described in terms of language and meaning and its limits, not in terms of knowledge and *its* limits, so the X-prior-to-language becomes not something unknowable, but something *unsayable, ineffable*. Ineffability doctrines are the linguistic form of the Idealism which declares the *Ding an sich* to be out of cognitive bounds. And just this is of course what happened in the *Tractatus*. The *Tractatus* was a description of what the world and language were supposed to be really like, under all superficial appearances, and what enabled the one to describe the other. But to describe this it had to say what each of them was like *without* the other. But to do this it had to say what things were like prior to anything being said about them—what they were like so that one could say something about them. Wittgenstein said it and, notoriously, then declared his own statements to be meaningless, in virtue of their violation of the plausible argument that one cannot say what things are like without saying something.

So, in terms of the old opposition, the *Tractatus* was both a Realist and a Subjectivist work. It was Realist in that it did in fact say what (and how) things were prior to their reflection in language. But it also takes full cognisance of the subjectivist argument that to do this is impossible. If one stresses the doctrines at the beginning of the *Tractatus*, which give it content, then the work is a linguo-Realist one. If one stresses their disavowal as meaningless at the end of the book, then it is a linguo-Subjectivist work. Yet the convenient doctrine of ineffability and "the ladder", also enables it to choose both horns of the dilemma at the same time.

5. WHAT ONE LOOKS LIKE WHEN NOT LOOKING

But the dilemma is also not overcome in his later work, in Linguistic Philosophy proper, though it is better camouflaged.

* Cf. R. G. Collingwood, *An Autobiography*, 1939, Pelican Edition, 1944, p. 34.

Throughout his life, Wittgenstein was like a man obsessed with the question of what he looks like when he is *not* looking in a mirror. *Ex hypothesi*, he can never know. In the *Tractatus*, he tells us in detail, and *also* tells us, summarily and at the end, that he *cannot tell*. (Please yourself which half of the story you believe.)

In his later work, the balance between peeping into the mirror to see what one looks like when one is *not* looking, and the expansion of the reason why such peeping is impossible, is altered. There is more of the latter, less of the former. His later work is a far more detailed examination of language, in order to show that it is impossible to say what things are absolutely, what they would be like without the intermediary of language. (Strictly speaking, the theme of his later work is the impossibility of a perfect, pre-eminent or private language, but this amounts to the same: for these languages would, if they were possible, each in its own way show what things are really like, irrespectively of being spoken or thought about in the terms of some particular language. A perfect language would mirror the world without redundancy or omission, and a private language would mirror the very stuff of experience.)

But he could not eliminate the peeping, the reporting of that which could not be reported, altogether. For one thing, something outside any and all languages had to be said, or at least conveyed, in order to explain the point and purpose of the exploration of the limits of individual, actual language. The truth that we cannot say how things are outside of all saying, cannot be a truth inside some particular language, but is outside and about all of them. So, at least one language-transcending truth remained (albeit a sadly negative one), and Wittgenstein was conveying it, *and* yet also saying that it was unsayable in virtue of being outside any given language game.

So, the ineffability doctrine remains in various forms, such as that philosophy communicated insights which would only be misrepresented if articulated, or, most misleadingly, that it was "therapeutic". This idea is most misleading because the message that is being conveyed but not articulated is simply incapsulated in the concept of "health": the cured man is he who sees that message, or perhaps one who does or sees nothing which violates the doctrine of that message.

The doctrine that philosophic problems are "dissolved" is of course closely associated with this: it amounts to saying that philosophic problems have no statable solution, but that they simply disappear when one examines language sufficiently—i.e. the examination of actual language if protracted long enough, and carried out under the supervision of someone already familiar with the ineffable insights, will sooner or later induce the same insight in the observer.

Wittgenstein could not avoid still occasionally saying that which cannot be said (though the balance was now in the direction of only saying what can be said—descriptions of language), but he preached such abstinence from explicitness. He never altogether succeeded in practising it, though I believe some of his followers have, particularly those who have turned his practices into "pure research". (Once this is done, the need for transgressing the limits of what can be said, the need to explain the *point* of it all, naturally diminishes, for there no longer is any point.) He himself never succeeded in following the rule of not saying the ineffable, but he tried hard, and the result of the unstable compromise between silence and utterance was his most characteristic manner of exposition, the "stammer", the withdrawals, the apparent caution, the castigation of *all* formulations * of his position as misrepresentations. (In the nature of the case, they were *all* bound to say too little or too much: to say the ineffable, or *not* to say it.)

In consequence, his teaching and that of some of his followers is ever pervaded by *double-think*: the ideas which justify the therapeutic function must not be articulated, and must themselves be cured if articulated.

There were of course differences between the communicable but unsayable ineffable truth of his early and of his late views.

The difference can be conveyed as follows: the *Tractatus* said "The world is the *totality of facts*, not of things". (My italics.) His later philosophy in effect asserted that the world was the *totality of things*, not of facts. Saying that the world is a totality of *facts* (and language mirrors these facts, and then assembles

---

* Professor J. Wisdom attempted to cover himself against such a castigation by expounding Wittgensteinian views and adding, in a footnote, that he did not wish to suggest *either* that "Wittgenstein would approve of *this* sort of talk nor that he would disapprove of it". (Cf. *Philosophy and Psychoanalysis*, Oxford 1953, p. 37.) The inherent ambiguity of Wittgenstein calls for such all-direction acknowledgements.

the multiplicity of individual little mirrors) shows that, for all the linguistic formulation, he still took a First-Person, traditional-epistemological view of the problem, and not a Third-Person, naturalist view which is essential to his later position: for "facts" are what the world is when it is divided into units of *experience*, not units of *things*. To say that the world is a totality of *things* is to imply that amongst the things there happens to be a set of activities known as language, which does not *mirror*, but is a *part* of the world. In brief, when young he believed that language reflected the world, and when old, that it did *not*.

The early ineffable truth was that the pre-lingual world was such as would be reflected in the perfect language—a mass of individual little atomic facts (each mirrored in an atomic sentence), wholly independent of each other and, as a totality, making up the world. The sentences mirroring them (plus, perhaps, some condensed versions, abbreviations and congeries of such sentences) were all that could be said, and hence truths such as that this *was* all that could be said, could not themselves be said.

The *later* ineffable truths were not such as transcended *one* perfect language, but such as transcended *all* of an endless multiplicity of language games and natural languages: they try to say something valid independently of the rules of all or any specific languages. (For instance, that all truth is tied to specific languages and so to speak internal to them.)

So the content of the ineffable, as well as the method of conveying it, had changed.

6. "SEEING THE WORLD RIGHTLY"

But the need to say, *and* the need *not* to say, the ineffable doctrine had remained, and was rooted in the same basic fallacy in both cases: a cluster of notions, such as that there is such a thing as "seeing the world rightly",* and the unavowed assumption that knowledge, or at any rate *real* knowledge, was a kind of incorporation or *contact* unmediated by anything.

This preposterous idea underlies the whole of Wittgenstein's work, early and late, and he never liberated himself from it.

That it pervaded the work which found expression in the

* Cf. *Tractatus*: "He who understands me . . . then . . . sees the world rightly." (6.54.)

Tractatus is obvious: the truth of sentences resides in their mirroring, reproducing, being like the facts which they report. When this model of what knowing or representing is like was seen by him to be inapplicable to the doctrine itself, to *its* relation to *its* object, he claimed that this doctrine could at least be "shown". Showing was plainly a matter of exhibiting a kind of *Ding an sich*—the language-world relation itself—which could not in turn be made into an object of speech without infinite regress. *Both* the image of how individual sentences reflect the world, and of how that doctrine as a whole was itself to be communicated, were based on the image of knowledge-as-contact-with-the-thing-known. In the one case, the thing left an imprint, a mirror-image in the sentence; in the other case, such an imprint could not be allowed—its presence in the realm of mirror-sentences would have upset the theory—so there was *contact-without-an-imprint*: just this is what the "showing" in the *Tractatus* amounts to. Something is seen to be the case, yet there is nothing one can *say*. One sees the *thing itself* (it is "shown"), yet it is unmediated by any concepts, as it would be if it were articulated. "Mirroring" was the next best thing to *being*: "showing" was not the next best to that, but, really, the best thing itself!

In his later work, Wittgenstein emphatically rejected the Contact or Mirror theory of knowing with regard to all ordinary, non-philosophical knowledge. All the insistence on language games is meant to bring out that utterances or words do not function by mirroring facts, but by having a role within a system of behaviour. To this extent, he overcame the Contact theory of knowledge at one level (at *one* of the two levels at which he held it in the *Tractatus*). But: at the level of the ineffable truth communicated by philosophy, he had *not* overcome it. Language games, the functioning of concepts, were still *shown*, "described",* without, it appears, any intermediary theories. (It is this illusion which enables linguistic philosophers to suppose that their accounts of concepts are neutral, uncoloured by any theories of their own.)

The practice of not theorising, not saying anything which would utilise concepts, but just "showing", describing language systems, invented or existing ones, is based on the notion that a thing can somehow be known by coming into contact with it.

* *Philosophical Investigations*, p. 109.

But even *if* he and other linguistic philosophers really restricted themselves to *exhibiting* usages and language games, it would still be the case that the exhibiting of samples always insinuates or illustrates some idea. The notion of knowledge-by-contact, restricted by the later Wittgenstein to knowledge *of* languages and not applied to knowledge *inside* specific languages, is further reinforced at this stage by diversificationism: everything being very much unlike everything else, any description of it would necessarily be a travesty; so truth is only to be had by just looking at the thing in action, seeing *it*, doing it. And diversificationism is both a logical and an empirical doctrine; it follows, logically, from the alleged need in philosophy to *show*, describe, and not to explain or generalise—for one can only show the individual, not the general. It is also, however, meant to report on empirically discoverable diversity.

Various absurd claims of Linguistic Philosophy are the corollaries of this fallacy; notably, the claim that Linguistic Philosophy is neutral, employs no question-begging concepts of its own, but merely shows language systems for what they are in the hope of freeing us from cramps and misunderstandings, etc. It says, as it were, "I am a camera". Once it is realised that no such unmediated knowledge is possible, at either and *any* level— not with regard to systems of thought as such, any more than with regard to things specified *within* systems of thought—these claims to doctrinelessness and neutrality are seen in their full absurdity.

This diagnosis of Wittgenstein's fundamental error helps to explain the paradox that Linguistic Philosophy, proceeding from a sophistication about language, and almost obsessionally aware of the truth that most meaning-relations are *not* like naming, *not* like a contact or reflection occurring between symbol and thing, nevertheless systematically perpetrates this very error and is based on it. It castigates the error with regard to individual concepts, *inside* language games, but it systematically commits it with regard to language games or uses or types of discourse as *wholes*. This mistake at the heart of linguo-philosophic thought reappears in many forms: the Argument from Paradigm Cases, the committing of fallacious inferences from actual to valid usage, etc., are all special cases of it. Whilst acutely aware that moves within language games are in no simple way related to things, and are seldom if ever names, linguistic philosophers treat language games as wholes as simply related to their contexts, and not themselves committed to some wider interpretations. (If this *were* legitimate, the APC would be valid.) But, in fact, language games or systems as wholes, just as much as individual moves within them, have no such simple relation to their contexts. If this be admitted, one need have no objection to Linguistic Philosophy—and thanks to its inherent vagueness and elusiveness, it may be admitted or hinted at: but if indeed it *is* admitted, none of the much-advertised features— neutrality, therapy, passivity, etc., follow any more. For then, language games as wholes may be challenged, and such challenges must be discussed, not prejudged nor cured.

7. THE SAGES OF LAGADO

This fundamental error of Linguistic Philosophy is well described by Jonathan Swift:

> "An expedient was . . . offered [in Lagado] that since words are only names for things, it would be more convenient for all men to carry about them such things as were necessary to express the particular business they are to discourse on . . . many of the most learned and wise adhere to the new scheme of expressing themselves . . . which hath only this inconvenience attending it, that if a man's business be very great, he must . . . carry a greater bundle of things upon his back. . . . I have often beheld two of those sages almost sinking under the weight of their packs . . .; who, when they met . . . would lay down their loads, and hold conversation for an hour together. . ." (*Gulliver's Travels*, Lagado episode. Everyman Edition, p. 170.)

Wittgenstein was, throughout his life, one of the sages of Lagado. In his youth, arguing that words were but names of things, and conceding that we could not carry the things about, he thought that linguistic expressions were at least mirrors, simulacra of things, like those toys the sages of Lagado carried about in lieu of things like houses, too heavy to carry. (He also noticed that some words, expressing "formal" concepts, were not mirrors of things or of anything.) The inconvenience of having to carry too many simulacra about was avoided by the fact that apparently endless numbers of them could be incapsulated in a very small space, in ordinary language, thanks no doubt to its "immensely complicated silent adjustments".

In his age, he changed his mind. Ordinary expressions were not mirrors of things, they were moves in games. But those games, with which he was now preoccupied, *could* be carried about in a sack, so to speak; they were carried about, in our speech habits. When encountering another sage, the thing to do was to unpack the sack and exhibit the one, or set of them, that was relevant to one's business. . . . The inconvenience attendant on this procedure is exactly what Jonathan Swift prophetically foresaw: ". . . if a man's business be very great, and of various kinds . . ." his bundles must be great and numerous, and it takes a long long time to exhibit them and get on with the business. Anyone who has observed the sages of Lagado conversing, or lecturing—they have now migrated to Oxenford—will know that it does indeed take a very very long time.

The aspiration of the sages of Lagado is something more than impracticable, something totally alien to the real nature of language. Neither talk about things, *nor talk about language*, can be carried on by exhibiting samples.

The achievement of Wittgenstein was to see this with regard to most uses of language, and his failure consists of conspicuously failing to see it with regard to philosophy itself, that is to say with regard to thought about general issues, about the viability or desirability of whole species of discourse; with regard to thought about thought. The consequence of this failure was the institution of philosophy by insinuation and by attrition, by means of the Lagadian prolixity, the alleged exhibiting of samples of language games without saying anything; the myths of saying nothing, of having no doctrine, and of being "neutral".

Wittgenstein's *early* thought applied the Lagado model to all knowledge: concrete, specific knowledge was the next best thing to exemplification, namely "mirroring", repetition in another medium. Knowledge about knowledge itself could not be this and hence was the best thing itself—it was the act of exhibiting, showing, almost *being*. In his later thought, he rightly rejected the model in its "next-best" form, with regard to specific knowledge inside systems, but kept it in its best-thing-itself form for knowledge about conceptual or language systems! They were still exhibited, "shown". (They were also conceived as being concrete systems of behaviour, and as infinitely various, and this made it both easier and more necessary to "exhibit" them.)

This main fallacy of Wittgenstein's which remained with him throughout his life can indeed be expressed more dramatically as the notion that there is such a thing as "seeing the world rightly".

What it was that was seen in this beatific state changed, in his opinion, between his youth and his age—but not the notion that there was such a thing, nor certain formal features of it. In his earlier period, "seeing the world rightly" meant penetrating through the superficial complexity of language and appearance to a hidden underlying simplicity: in his latter period, it was a matter of seeing the manifest complexity of things and language *to be what it is, to require no emendation or correction or penetration.*

. The earlier "seeing the world rightly" was a difficult penetration of the veil; the later, was a matter of seeing that the veil *is* reality, and the only delusion—the supposition that it is but a veil. One might call this a matter of "seeing the world rightly" on the cheap—for it only requires one to equate appearance with reality, to accept everything for what it is. The world is what it seems. With regard to Wittgenstein this would be unfair, because for *him* it was not cheap—the overcoming of the belief that there was a fundamental reality underlying the appearance of language was unquestionably a painful and sincere inner struggle.

Wittgenstein now interpreted veil-penetrating visions of the world as conceptual *worries* or *cramps*, and predicted, wrongly, that they would be cured by his method. What did happen was that people who were profoundly *un*worried anyway invoked his theory and method as their rationale. The idea that some of the members of the smooth, bland variety of second generation of linguistic philosophers undergo "perplexity", let alone intellectual *cramp*, has an element of high comedy.

For his followers, there can be no doubt that he has provided an absolute ontology very very cheaply: everything is just as it appears, just as ordinary usage implies it is—and this all-embracing theory of the universe is conveniently underwritten by an ultra-sophisticated theory of language, which entails that

anyone supposing otherwise is muddled, semantically diseased
. . . (with the application of a few simple-minded devices such
as the Argument from Paradigm Cases, the inner secrets of the
world, of free will, of everything, are laid bare . . .).

Descartes had initiated the modern epistemological tradition,
the First Person vision, the starting from the subjective minimum and seeing how far one could get. By noting the presupposition of starting from the minimum—the fact that doubt
presupposed thought, and thought a self—he managed to get a
certain distance, painfully, and implausibly.

The new Wittgensteinian vision was to start not from the self,
the subject, but from language: doubt presupposes not so much
a doubting, thinking self—it presupposes a language in terms
of which the doubt could make sense.

And starting from *this* minimum, he could conjure up far
more, less painfully and implausibly, than Descartes did! A
language presupposes behaviour and a public world in which
the behaviour takes place: its formal concepts can all be accepted because they merely provide the frame and prejudge
nothing substantive, and also because to challenge them one
would need a set of absolute concepts and that is impossible. . . .
So, the whole natural world tumbles out, especially when it is
with the full richness and variety of natural languages that one
operates. . . .

If one treats the *Tractatus* as a Cartesian exercise in seeing
how much we can conjure out of inescapable presuppositions
without actually having to find out anything, we only get a
meagre harvest of logic and a few very formal, very general concepts as frames for "things". But *Philosophical Investigations* give,
or leave, us *everything*. What an improvement on Descartes!
Instead of "I think, therefore I am", we get "We speak, therefore the whole world is, and moreover it is as it has always
seemed". A rich harvest.

8. NOT TO ASK THE REASON WHY

Wittgenstein's situation in his later stage was this: he saw
humanity as employing a diversity of language games, which
were concrete activities in concrete contexts, governed by various contingent rules. So far so good: but furthermore, sometimes the operations of these rule-governed systems of speech-
acts went wrong. Very strange moves were made in the games:

untestable, pointless utterances were made, which played no part in the daily work of the system. Strange questions were asked for the answering of which there was no decision-procedure within the system, and so on. *This* was, for him, the essence of (old-fashioned) philosophy (including his own earlier efforts). Philosophy was the malfunctioning of linguistic systems. In effect, he equated philosophy with self-defeating thought.

What could be done about this? Each such disease could, *individually*, be put right. A word that was used in a manner contrary to its place in the system could be righted (use of the APC); a concept which had lost its "antithesis" could have its antithesis replaced (use of the Contrast Theory). A concept which was questioned on the assumption that there was some criterion of its valid use outside and above the system of which it formed a part, could be reinstated by reminding the questioner that there could be no criterion of the use of a concept outside the system of which it was a part (use of the view that actual use is the criterion of valid use). A concept which came to be used outside its own language game, or to be used as if it were a part of some other language game, as if it worked like a different kind of concept, could be righted by a reminder of its place and of the fact that concepts and games are so diverse that the rules of one cannot be applied to another (use of Polymorphism).

All this had to be done, shown, *in the individual cases* of the diseased concept, without, however, invoking the general theory of correct functioning that lies behind it. To do *that* is unnecessary: when we set right a machine, we do not read out the theory of its correct functioning to it, we only *apply* it by readjusting the malfunctioning part. And even when, in psychotherapy, we set right a mind and not a machine, it is still said to be incorrect and unnecessary to explain the theory in the course of the therapy. The cure consists of a kind of individual insight into the malfunctioning, and *not* of acquaintance with the theory of it.

And not merely is it unnecessary to state and explain the theory, it is positively harmful: we are coping with malfunctioning language-systems, and these are unfortunately capable of incorporating any verbal expressions that are presented to it or fed into it. The general theory of correct language-functioning (the Four Pillars, or any others), if fed into the diseased system, only *increase* its confusion. For remember that one of the possible diagnoses (the *Fourth* Pillar, Polymorphism) is that the diseased language-use consists of attempting to impose some general pattern of individual, necessarily diverse functions. But the general theory of correct functioning is indeed itself also a general theory, and its presentation to the individual, be-havioural language-machine or user must result in further mal-functioning, for if the general theory is accepted, incorporated, *it* will *eo ipso* lead to some additional undesirable unification. . . . So, the individual language user, who is, or is involved in, a behaviour-language-machine, has no business with general theories of language, of the world or anything: * his job is to *do* (not, anyway, to die)—and *not* to ask the reason why—certainly not in a general way and in isolation from the game he is play-ing. (He may ask "why?" *inside* his game. He may make the *why*-move in games in which it has an accredited place, and in which there is a pre-arranged procedure for recognising a *therefore*-move.)

The emphasis that the diseased language-user must *do*, but not ask the reason why; or rather that he must not be told (which would aggravate his illness)—on the contrary he must be *cured* of the temptation to ask this—is one of the most arro-gant aspects of Wittgenstein's philosophy.†

* This argument could be applied against any general theory of anything —such as those general theories of the world we call science. In fact, I have no doubt that had Wittgenstein's ideas been worked out in a pre-scientific age, they would have been used to prove the impossibility of science. (Perhaps we should interpret Heraclitean doctrines in this way, and see Wittgenstein as a revival of them, as the Heraclitus of thought and language.)

As he lived in an age when science is an established and indisputable fact, he contented himself with seeing it simply as mere content and insisting on the apartheid of form and content. His doctrines—both early and late— were about the "form" of knowledge. His early views were that there was a general form, his later one was that forms were legion and that one could not say anything general about them, or indeed anything: one could exhibit them, know them by contact or incorporation, so to speak, but not in any concept-mediated way. The fact of their diversity, and the fact that all concepts distort by generality, prevented this.

† There are two main forms of philosophic arrogance: one is to claim to incapsulate all past thinkers in one's thought; the other is to claim to be initiating an entirely new departure. One would have thought that these

Other men are thus seen as language-using automata, whose inner lives, if not non-existent, are at any rate irrelevant to their language-using functions,* and these automata, if they are to be set right in those unfortunate cases when they go wrong by violating their own rules, must not be further confused by being supplied with general theories about themselves, about language or the world (or any general theories, really), in other words, with statements for which there is no, and can be no pre-existing place in the language games. . . .

Once Wittgenstein adopted the view of language as systems of public acts, as language games, this kind of view of other people, and the need for the therapeutic, *in*explicit method in philosophy followed. Wittgenstein was compelled to be a practicing solipsist by his own theory—and, curiously, he reached solipsism from a premiss diametrically opposed to the one which normally leads to that position: he reached it from the view that language is necessarily public. Being a system of public acts, private experience was irrelevant to it. Moreover, a general theory of the language games, not being itself a move within the game, could not be helpful or relevant to the correcting of the game that was being played, and so should not and could not be stated.

To his credit be it said that he tried to be consistent and deny his own awareness of the situation as well as that of others: he strove not merely to restrict himself to curing others—and telling them nothing—but also attempted to abstain from telling

---

two claims could not be combined. But yes, Wittgenstein did succeed in doing just that. His pathology of philosophy was to sum up the past of philosophy; the unsayable "seeing the world rightly" to be a wholly new start.

A similar point is made by Mr. R. G. Mure, in his *Retreat from Truth*, 1958.

* After all, a private meaning is an impossibility, we are told.

One might say: In his age Wittgenstein saw the world as a language-using machine would see it, or rather fail to see it. On the other hand, the *Tractatus* of his youth was, in part, an interesting reconstruction of what the world may look like to an infant. Consider the following propositions of the *Tractatus*:

I am my world. The world and life are one. Death is not an event of life. The thinking, presenting subject; there is no such thing. Our life is endless, the way our visual field is without limit. The world of the happy is quite other than that of the unhappy. Ethics and aesthetics are one.

himself anything either. Fortunately he was not consistent and did not succeed.*

9. THE PROSELYTISING SOLIPSIST

Ordinary solipsism is a respectable and logical position. Bertrand Russell tells the story of a lady who wrote to him saying she was a solipsist and expressing surprise that more people did not adopt the same view. The difficulty which a solipsist encounters is not from logic but, as Russell's story illustrates, from other people's unwillingness to adopt *his* solipsism, to be converted to the view—against which *they* have some evidence —that they are behavioural automata, that *their* consciousness is only a figment of *his* imagination.

The irony of Wittgenstein's solipsism, deduced from his view of language, was that his experience was the opposite of that which is the lot of more ordinary, less inspired solipsists. He had some difficulties in permanently convincing *him*self—ever relapsing into having a general idea, over and above making moves in games and correcting defective games—but he had comparatively little trouble in convincing others that *they* were automata and unfit recipients for general ideas. An enthusiastic collection of followers proclaimed themselves automata, declared their own inner lives non-existent, or irrelevant to their use of language, and set about correcting each other's—and other people's—defective language uses, and yet keeping fairly mum about the underlying idea . . .!

The history of the Wittgensteinian fashion presents many entertaining features, not least the way in which it improves on the story of the Emperor's clothes. In it, the impostor succeeded in convincing the populace that one naked man was clothed: here, a whole clothed populace were convinced that they were all naked. With this are associated certain innovations in the style of persuasion, such as confusing listeners or

* There is a Central European fairy tale in which the hero is requested by his benefactress, an old woman, never to look in a certain room of her house. He disobeys and does so, and thereby liberates her from a spell and turns her into her proper shape, that of a young and beautiful woman. She was grateful for the disregard of her own request, which liberated her. Wittgenstein was never, apparently, grateful for the attempts to look into the forbidden room. Formulations of his general position were, apparently, *always* wrong and aroused his wrath.

readers by means of brief common words, rather than the quite dated technique of doing it with long and abstruse ones.* D'Holbach, and Goethe after him, remarked that where ideas are lacking, men make do by inventing a word. Linguistic philosophers attempt to meet the same need by *not* inventing words. (The programmatic implication of being an automaton is that one must *apply* the ideas which one must not in any circumstances name or avow.)

10. THE ELUSIVE BUT COMFORTING DOCTRINE

There are visual diagrams so constructed that they can be seen in alternative ways, and each of the alternative ways tends, after one looks at it for a time, to "jump" and be replaced by another. (The simplest example is a cube drawn in such a way that it successively appears either to recede back from the page or project forward from it.) Neither of the successive visions can be said to be the right one. Anyone who insists on treating it as such can always be corrected by drawing his attention to the other possibility.

Wittgenstein's thought is a system of ideas that have exactly this property. It has an inherent ambiguity which makes it "jump" from any one of a number of possible interpretations to the others, and this ambiguity is not accidental and due to inadequate precision, but essential and inherent to his thought.

Wittgensteinianism proper has a naturalistic way of looking at both subject and object, both languages and things.

It is a "realist" doctrine: it insists that things are what they are, in the sense that language, the conceptual system, the language game in which they are expressed, makes no difference. Formal concepts do not describe, and they can prejudge nothing. (This is exactly parallel to the old realism which insisted that knowing made no difference to the known.) No-

---

* Mr. G. A. Paul, a not un-typical linguistic philosopher, remarks in a rather starry-eyed manner (*The Revolution in Philosophy*, ed. G. Ryle, London 1956, p. 66) "Statements formulated in . . . 'technical' terms are protected from criticism by this very unfamiliarity. From it they can gain also an air of remote authority which discourages inquiry." The reader is advised to look at Mr. Paul's own essay on Wittgenstein in the same volume. Does Mr. Paul think that *its* style, or the elusive Wittgensteinian mysteries, or Austin's lectures, or Moore's manner as described by Keynes, *do* encourage enquiry, do *not* encourage an air of incontrovertible authority?

thing in the world is altered by whether we choose to use this or that language game—"things are as they are".

But note: there is still *also* the idealist strain in the position. Although things remain as they are irrespective of how we speak, we cannot speak of them without speaking; we cannot say how they are independently of any way of speaking about them. And as we *cannot*, it makes no sense to correct the way in which things appear within given language-systems, for we have no standard—and we cannot have—with which to compare them.

Thus, the insights of both realism and idealism are enlisted, and each by working out the implications of a tautology—of the view that *things are what they are*, and of the view that *we cannot speak without speaking*. (There is a sense in which Wittgensteinian Linguistic Philosophy is quite incontrovertible—quite apart from the endless qualifications, caution, smoke-screens and elusiveness—and *this* is it, I think. This accounts for the feeling that his views *must* be right, shared by him and his followers.)

But these insights are then fused with looking at both subject and object naturalistically and in the Third Person. This way of looking is after all already guaranteed by what I called the idealist insight: we cannot speak of things other than by speaking of them and hence they are as we speak of them, and that goes for the objects of knowledge and the processes of speech themselves. It is further guaranteed by the insistence that it is human babies, and not "cognising pure egos", who learn to use language, and it is concrete people, not transcendental subjects, who use language. (This view is further reinforced by an alleged proof that a language such as would be first learnt by a pure subject—a private language untarnished by concrete uses—is impossible.)

The fusion of both insights—the "realist" and the "idealist" one—with a naturalistic way of looking at things is the characteristic linguo-philosophic vision: the "things" that are unaffected by whether and how we speak are the ordinary, daily things: and the "subject" is neither a ghostly knower nor a ghostly language of the *Tractatus*, but the actually observable language games, and their users of daily life.

Thus Linguistic Philosophy gives us concreteness at both ends: we know ordinary things, as they are and as they always seemed, and we know them through the use of terms which we can see and observe just as we observe any other human habit or activity. All is clear, all is concrete. We cannot jump out of our linguistic skin—and yet we *can* observe it, for it is a thing in nature.

Thus our language is a prison which we cannot transcend *—and yet at the same time it is a contingent and observable thing in the world, not a ghostly mystery like the old "subject", a ghostly eye ever out of the picture. At the same time, things are what they are and unaffected by being known or spoken about—and yet these self-subsistent things (whilst guaranteed to be the correct vision by the idealist side of the argument—by the absence of a possible outside check) are also not hidden transcendent *Dinge an sich*, but the dear familiar things of our daily life.

This skilful superimposition of both idealist and realist visions, *and* of both the epistemological and the naturalist angles, gives one, as one begins to understand Wittgensteinian Linguistic Philosophy, that *frisson*, that compulsive feeling of necessary and yet endlessly elusive truth, which is so plainly a characteristic of the experience of its inventor and its devotees.

The insight can also be conveyed by saying that there can be no world without language, *and* no language without a world: we cannot say what the world is like without having concepts—language games—in which to say it; and, equally, we cannot say anything—operate language games—without there being

* The impossibility of speaking of the world-as-a-whole, or of the world-as-it-is-independent-of-all-speech—in other words, of metaphysics—can be made to follow not merely from the language-game model of speech, but even more strikingly from its Four Pillars: To say something of the world-as-it-*must*-be is to violate the Contrast Theory, for either what one says has a contrast and the meaning of that contrast provides an alternative, and then the claim cannot be necessary: or what one says has no contrast, and one is saying nothing. Similarly, the APC and the inference from actual to valid use can be invoked: an absolute assertion about the world presupposes a transcending of the contingent conventions that are inherent in any one language game, yet to say something one must needs use one of these games. Similarly, any attempt to say anything absolute about the world must fail through the fact that it will have some *form*, some manner or style of referring to the world, whilst there are (Polymorphism) innumerable ways of speaking of the world, no one of them pre-eminent, and all but one must be excluded from any unique assertion: and thus no one assertion or theory can be all-embracing.

a world, and a recognisable, familiar one at that, in which they exist and are operated. So, reflection on the nature of language enables us to conclude that the world is as we normally think it is (for it is in the world as normally conceived that we use words); and, similarly, reflecting on the world enables us to conclude that language is the public use of words within public games, and not a code acquired or elaborated by an extra-worldly spirit in the interest of characterising the world as such or as a whole. So, the circle is complete, everything is both what it is and what it customarily seems to be.

II. THE DELPHIC INSIGHT

Which of all these visions is the crucial or main one—the naturalistic reduction of concepts to rules of verbal behaviour? Or the denial of reductions in virtue of Polymorphism, the view that everything is what it is and not another thing, and that the number of kinds of thing is legion? * Or the super-imposition of the realist and idealist insights? Or did he intend to convey the insight gained by seeing the possibility of *all* and each of these?

I am inclined to the last hypothesis—but who can tell?

Note that whichever interpretation one chooses, if one proceeds to verbalise it explicitly, it promptly becomes susceptible to all the objections against the possibility of some absolute truth outside and about all language games, and verse and chapter can no doubt be found in the Master's work to show that it was not intended.

One's head begins to reel, and one would gladly obey the Master and retire into silence. There is *no* determinate answer in Wittgenstein's exegesis. Interpreting him is exactly like

---

* This kind of situation arises concerning whether we should interpret Wittgensteinianism as a denial of all *necessity*—for all language games and their rules are contingent—or as its re-affirmation, in view of the fact that the game, or set of moves, known as "necessary propositions", is also a game, or part of one, and hence also legitimate, and also to be left "as it is".

All language games are contingent (and, hence, there is no necessity). But, equally, "necessary propositions" are a legitimate game, like any other. (So, there *is* necessity. . . .)

Either interpretation is in a sense correct. . . . This just happens to be the wonderful plasticity of Wittgenstein's thought.

(Only an unregenerate philosopher would ask for a straight answer.)

trying to reach the absolute, metaphysical truth about the world —the ultimate, cosmic *mot juste*—all one can do is show why it cannot be had, why any claim to have captured it must be mistaken. . . . There can be *no* correct exegesis of Wittgenstein, any more than there is an absolute metaphysics of the world, and for much the same reasons.

Wittgenstein took great care to incorporate into the form of his thought those features of language which made an absolute picture of the world, a wholly faithful mirror of it, impossible. The need for contrast, for many forms, etc., is turned upon the doctrine itself. Any interpretation of his views also requires its contrast to complement it, just as the meaningfulness of any characteristic of things also requires the meaningfulness of its opposite. Any simple interpretation of Wittgenstein falls foul of the need for many approaches contained in his thought, just as any simple picture of the world falls foul of the need for many ways of speaking, and so on. In his elusiveness, Wittgenstein succeeded in truly mirroring the universe. . . .

Somehow he manages to say everything and nothing at the same time: he has managed somehow to bring out the difficulties of saying things; or rather, to insinuate them. He has managed to "show" us something without saying anything, and if we see what he has shown, it confirms his vision: if we do not— well, he did not say anything, and our failure to see it does not disconfirm anything.

The examination of how we use words is in his case only a kind of spiritual exercise which induces a state of mind receptive for the insight, rather than establishing it. It calls forth the mystical vision of the world as wholly unmysterious: a mystique of naturalism. (Some of his successors attempt to turn these exercises into a discipline on its own, without vision.)

The infallibility of Wittgensteinianism is due not merely to its rich equipment of face-saving devices, withdrawals, caution, ambiguity, etc.; it is also, at a deeper level, due to the compulsiveness of these insights, if such they are.

If a man says—"I have the idea X, which applies to things, except in as far as it does not"—we pay scant attention to him: *all* ideas have the property of applying, except in as far as they do not. To postulate one of them with such a proviso is not much of an achievement.

Wittgenstein succeeded in staking claims of just this form and getting away with it. He succeeded in incapsulating such an idea in a claim, which at the same time contained a procedure for camouflaging it. The claims were the various ideas about language and philosophy. The restriction of those claims to just the cases in which they happen to apply, did not call for an additional restrictive clause—which would give the show away: for the restriction, the withdrawal of the claim, was done by the initially claimed ideas themselves. Their reapplication to the question of their own range of application did the trick; and the whole, totally infallible Delphic procedure is further effectively camouflaged by ineffability, caution, *ad-hoc*-ness, etc.

Thus Wittgensteinian theses are all magnificent self-correcting formulae. They each of them contain an infallible self-righting mechanism and—oh marvel of design!—the mechanism is undetectable by the naked eye and does not spoil the symmetry of the missile itself: and for a simple reason—the self-correcting device is at the same time the missile itself.

Let us consider this with regard to the main theses. Take Polymorphism, the much-stressed insistence on diversity of types of proposition, and hence the need to avoid general formulae. Has it turned out to be wrong in some cases? Are underlying *similarities* what matters? This in no way undermines the idea: for *it is itself a general formula*, and thus it also (rightly, as it turns out) warned you against itself!

The much-vaunted theory of the need for contrast—the fact that expressions used "without antithesis" become metaphysical: does *it* turn out to be wrong?—are there cases where a contrast-less thesis is useful or true?—but did not the doctrine of Contrast itself also require, in virtue of what it itself says, a contrast? So it also warned you against itself! And hence, does not its own falsification, properly understood, really *confirm* it? But of course!

Or consider the Argument from Paradigm Cases, and the related fallacy of inferring from actual to valid usage: do not expressions such as "myth", "legend", "an error pervasively built into a given way of speaking", *also* have paradigm uses? And thus—cannot the APC be invoked to show that it itself does not have those absurd consequences—the validation of magic, witchcraft and everything—which its unkind critics have wished upon it? And similarly, is not the critical use of language, also "a use", one of the "games", so that criticism of a given language is but obedience to the actual rules of another kind of discourse? But of course! Wittgenstein's ideas *cannot* be wrong. And, indeed, they cannot. Their structure precludes it. (They provide their own feedback.) No wonder their adherents find them compulsive.

The fact that Wittgenstein abstained from indicating the limits in which his ideas were to apply—which view would make them less universally pliable—has even been claimed to his credit.

Moreover, these self-correcting homing missiles have the additional beautiful property that each man can make them home on what he wishes, for by suitable adjustment of the relative use of their straightforward, and of their self-correcting mechanisms, they can be directed anywhere one chooses. This, of course, shows not a neutrality but a total arbitrariness.

The basic, and invaluable, ambiguity of Linguistic Philosophy is this: the notion of "language games" faces two ways. *Qua* "games", that is, rule-bound activities in the natural world, the idea allows the philosophy which is based on it to be hard-headed, empirical, and down to earth. But at the same time, in as far each game is allowed to be in order and to be judged only by its own standards, it retains and justifies—in virtue of their having a place in some language game—all those notions occurring within them which might otherwise suffer from hard-headed, empirical criticism . . .*

So, by looking at language *games*, we hunt with the empirical-naturalistic hounds; but by accepting their *contents*, we run with the transcendental hares, or any others we care to run with. . . .

And moreover: by suitably determining the limits of "games" (language itself does not do it), and by choosing the terms with which to describe them, we can have our universe *just* as we wish, unchallengeable and beyond doubt.

12. THE ARGUMENT FROM IMPOTENCE

There is an aspect of Linguistic Philosophy which is extremely important and connected with the preceding themes, namely

---

* For instance: Is there objective moral value? Yes, or no. There are only rules of language. But, expressions expressing obligations "have a use". So. . . . And so on. . . .

what may be called its Formalism. Wittgenstein in the *Tractatus* was concerned with the "form" of things and of language, not the content: with the "how", not the "what". With the question as to *what* things were found and where, the *Tractatus* naturally did not attempt to deal: this was a concern for observation, for science. In this sense even the *Tractatus* was empiricist —and this is the old sense of empiricism. The *Tractatus* was a-priorist only with regard to the forms: later Linguistic Philosophy was *also* empiricist in the sense of seeing these "forms" as the sets of alternatives provided for in given language games, to be seen and understood as empirically observable sets of acts, connected by implicit rules.* It remained Formalist, however: it does not claim to *make* the moves in each of the individual games, or prescribe which should be made when. On the contrary, it protests—too much, perhaps—that this can only be done by the participants in the games in accordance with the situation and with the rules of the game in question. Linguistic philosophers are very anxious to stress that they do not, in their official capacity, take part in the individual games such as science, ethics, history, etc., etc., not to mention the large multiplicity of minor ones whose existence, importance and diversity were uncovered by Wittgenstein. In their private or other capacity, they may or must, and do, take part in these games, but as philosophers they are *ex officio* neutral. *Qua* philosophers, their job is, they think, to clarify which game is being played and what its rules are, *but not to take part*. The Formalism remains: it is only, so to speak, dispersed in this later view over a multiplicity of the forms of the many, many language games (whereas, in the view of the *Tractatus*, one kind of form was sufficient for all discourse, leaving out only nonsense and the mystical). A multiplicity of forms interpreted as activities *in* the world, has replaced a small number of forms inspired by logic.

One should add that Formalism is not something inherited by Linguistic Philosophy exclusively from the Logical Atomism of the *Tractatus*. All the philosophies which are its intellectual ancestors, and many others which are not but which contribute to the general spirit of the times, share this feature. The idea that philosophy, if it can be concerned with anything, must be concerned with the *how* and not the *what* is widespread and

---

* Cf. later remarks about the two dimensions of empiricism.

independently plausible. Some people's adherence to the views or methods of Linguistic Philosophy probably starts from Formalism as a premiss. They do not *reach* it as one of its corollaries.

The strongest single factor inducing people, rightly or wrongly, to Formalism is Empiricism. Modern philosophers do not observe or experiment: they "think". But how can unaided thought have anything to say about the world? The formalist answer is a plausible and attractive one: thought makes explicit the conceptual or linguistic forms into which the crude, empirically given matter is fitted.

Formalism receives a further impetus from the linguistic formulation of philosophic issues which is shared by Linguistic Philosophy with its predecessors.* The interest in language and logic led to the emergence and widespread adoption of the distinction between "first-order" and "second-order" language (sometimes also referred to as meta-language), the former being talk about things, the latter about concepts or linguistic entities. This made Formalism additionally attractive by making it appear more concrete, and less metaphorical: no elusive "forms", but tangible linguistic habits or rules were there for the attention of the philosopher who, by his professional commitment to the armchair rather than the laboratory, was not qualified to pronounce on *content*. Another reason for Formalism was that, for Wittgenstein, philosophy was always the *residue*—that which is left over when everything substantive has been said. (This is as true of his later views as of the *Tractatus*.)

The view that philosophy must be formal, second-order, that it cannot provide substantive guidance in any topic, receives a kind of unofficial support from the social position of the modern academic philosopher—a man commissioned by society to teach a recognised subject and at the same time without any source to tap the truths he should teach: he is credited with no special faculties or insights, provided with no revealed truth, no experimental technique and no region of the world to observe. He

---

* G. E. Moore's "philosophy of common sense" was also a most important preparation for the Formalism: it insisted that it was not and could not be the task of philosophy to challenge or assess the views of common sense, or indeed of individual applications of it, but that its task was merely to clarify what was meant by those beliefs.

may well feel predisposed by what one may call the Argument from Impotence to accept the view that philosophy *must* be formal, that it makes no difference, that it leaves everything as it is. Many professional philosophers—particularly amongst those who have embraced Wittgensteinian Linguistic Philosophy— are alienated from natural and social science (and hence from the exciting areas of intellectual advance), and are not deeply or originally involved in substantive moral, political and social issues.* If philosophy were substantive, they would have to concede that they are not fit to be good practitioners of it: if, on the contrary, philosophy is shown to be essentially formal, second-order, un-substantive, this could hardly be more convenient.

Linguistic Philosophy can be seen to provide a realm and an activity for philosophers, tailor-made for the requirements of some of the people who find themselves inheriting the task of teaching philosophy in the universities: a *neutral* realm, from which no guidance and no commitment on substantive issues is required; a *verbal* realm, which can be studied from the arm-chair without at the same time making any implausible claims to transcendental insights or faculties; a *conservative* realm, in which no surprising objects or conclusions can be found; and a *polymorphic* realm, in which no daring generalisations are allowed either and in which there is ample scope for continued, *minute* research.

By one of the coincidences of history, the spurious idio-graphic realm invented by Wittgenstein—the realm of purely second-order, formal, neutral, variegated, individually knowable ("showable" or "describable"), objects (language uses), never requiring either change ("philosophy leaves everything as it is") or a general idea ("we can only describe, we cannot explain"), was *just* what suited the convenience of people who were seeking such a realm, fearing the silliness of transcendental pursuits, or the ardours, aridities,

---

* Mr. Warnock appositely explains why a philosopher may feel reluctant to be anything but formal: "A . . . capacity for abstract thought is compatible with an 'attitude to life' entirely ordinary, or even dull. A philosopher's views in this area . . . might . . . be absolutely uninteresting". (*English Philosophy since 1900*, London 1958, p. 169.) Such a dull thinker might indeed welcome a definition of philosophy which excuses him from having anything of interest to say.

épatements and inconveniences of Logical Positivism and similar trends.

The Argument from Impotence is so deeply ingrained in some philosophers—it seems to stir so deep a cord, and correspond so closely to what they feel about the value of their own thinking—that for many of them it is the premiss from which the other linguo-philosophic positions are deduced, the initial and compulsive insight which calls forth the assent to positions which are shown to be connected with it.

For these philosophers, the Argument from Impotence is so self-evident that it can hardly be doubted, that any argument which requires suspension of belief concerning it is inevitably misunderstood and rejected in virtue of the Axiom of Impotence, as it should perhaps be called.

Yet, despite a specious, superficial plausibility, the Argument from Impotence is invalid. (It *is* intimately connected with the other linguo-philosophic positions, but this merely shows that they are invalid too.)

The formalism, or sense of substantive impotence, of Linguistic Philosophy falls foul of a number of things: for one, philosophic accounts are not so much accounts of how language games are played, as, on the contrary, of how they should be played or of how they can conceivably be played. (Hence actual games played are not conclusive; and, in any case, what game is really played is not a matter that can be seen in the "use of words", but only interpreted from it with the help of considerations of what game *could* be played!) This being so, the accounts then provided do favour some moves and condemn others. Theories of ethics are not neutral with regard to values, and theories of science are not neutral with regard to diverse scientific hypotheses.

The supposition that philosophy could be formal and neutral is based on a variety of absurdities. For one thing, it springs from the totally a-historical atmosphere of Linguistic Philosophy, which either disregards past thought altogether or treats it as though it were a contribution to the last issue of *Mind*. A modicum of historical awareness would show that philosophical re-assessments have not been neutral but have profoundly modified the substantive outlook of mankind. (Linguistic Philosophy could itself be quoted as an example: the new account *it* gave of philosophic propositions themselves has *not* been neutral with regard to the specific kinds of philosophic solutions that have been found acceptable.)

The absurdity which underlies the assumption of neutrality is the idea that formal and substantive questions are separated and separable. They are not. The kind of concept we use to describe things, the kind of general model we employ, automatically carries its values, preferences and suggested directions with it. Even if they were separable, they are not in fact separated. Most of the substantive issues, in science, ethics and elsewhere, are so tied up with the various philosophic, "formal" considerations that to discuss one is to discuss the other. Linguistic Philosophy, with its separation of form and content and its equation of philosophy with the clarification of the formal element and the cure of confusions arising from it, would only be a possible philosophy at the beginning or the end of time—when no philosophic issues have yet been raised and people only play language games, without having theories about them, or when all substantive issues have been settled and nothing but the reflection on language forms remains. But such a beginning or end of time never was or will be, or could be.

Apart from being absurd on general grounds, the Formalism can be shown to be silly from one of Linguistic Philosophy's own most cherished premises—Polymorphism. Formalism has some plausibility if the forms of speech are conceived of as something very, very general—the general form of *all* factual assertion, *all* evaluation, and so on. There is then some plausibility in saying that the form, the possibility of there being facts or values at all, etc., must not be confused with claims that specific facts obtain, that specific values are valid. But through its insistence on Polymorphism, Linguistic Philosophy insists that the forms, the language games, are endlessly various, that they are often tied to very specific situations, and that the idiosyncrasies of each minute game are essential, and that consequently the minute, *sui generis* games cannot be subsumed under some very general form.

If so—and to some extent this is correct—it is absurd to treat each of the many individual, minute, context-bound and idiosyncratic games, forms of speaking, as neutral and given. They may be relatively neutral with regard to the moves, *within* each of them, but they are themselves non-neutral moves within wider sets of alternatives. It is not conceivable that this vast population of games does not contain many alternatives—in the sense of containing various games serving similar purposes or contexts in different ways—and thus there are choices to be made about, as well as within, language games. This is in fact the case.

The fact that a "verbal-behaviour" account of religion, for instance, is in conflict with the transcendental claims found *within* religions, which is obvious, only illustrates the point which is ignored by linguistic philosophers, namely, that formal and substantive doctrines are so mixed up in human life through long history of inter-mixture that it is quite impossible to treat one without the other. Religions consist not of some "pure substantive" religious claims, but of these interfused with "second-order" theories concerning what religious assertions amount to. This probably holds for all fields of human discourse.

This is true not merely of doctrines which have transcendental constituents, such as religious ones, but equally of anti-transcendental ones. For instance, Utilitarianism may be seen as a substantive ethical theory—commending exclusive attention to human happiness in assessing institutions, codes, policies, etc.— but it is one which is bound up in an essential way with a second-order doctrine, empiricism, to the effect that only within human experience can there be non-arbitrary grounds for evaluation (or anything else). Any language is a way of categorising, classifying some field, some manifold. As such, it cannot but favour some practices, some aims, within that field, to the detriment of others. It cannot be neutral.

The same goes for the languages in which we describe other language games. To describe a use of an expression, or a language game, is to describe it in a world and to have a picture of that world. Moreover, uses and games, like other human activities, have their opportunity cost and must be assessed. Hence philosophic *accounts* cannot be neutral either. "Neutrality" is a notion which has application within a system of concepts or rules, and not when such systems themselves are under consideration. And note that language games, like any other thing in the world, can only be described by further sets of concepts, which in turn are not absolute and neutral. There is no knowledge-by-direct-acquaintance in this field any more than in any other. There is only insinuation masquerading as neutrality.

Language systems are like social systems (and indeed, he who sees language games as systems of behaviour cannot long resist this conclusion, and Wittgenstein did say that a language was a form of life). But social systems and customs, like conceptual ones, are generally affected by self-consciousness. Many deserve to be abrogated or improved, and some become positively unworkable as soon as they are understood. The transformation of life by reflection and self-consciousness is the history of thought. Thought does *not* "leave everything as it is".

13. CONCLUSION

What can be said for Linguistic Philosophy as a would-be overcoming of the theory of knowledge, and as (in fact) a crypto-epistemology?

It is tied up with a Formalism which is indefensible in itself and in any case in conflict with other linguo-philosophic insights, notably Polymorphism, and the denial of a perfect language.

The linguo-philosophic insights—that the forms of languages are neutral, and that they require contrast, that no absolute language stands outside them, etc., etc., are, perhaps, in a *very* left-handed sense, true. *Given* that something is a self-contained language game, system of concepts with alternative moves/assertions within it, it follows that the game as a whole is neutral in relation to moves within it, that there must be contrast, etc.

But: *we are never given this*. Not merely because, empirically, there is no non-arbitrary way of isolating such self-contained games within the flux of our thought and language (though this is also true): but because, logically, it is impossible. For to carry out such an isolation is already to prejudge all the issues. It is to say implicitly which values are to be served, which rules are to be the norms, and so on. There are no inherently isolated language games in the world, any more than there is an absolute, all-embracing one. To isolate one is to make one's choice. Linguistic Philosophy simply prejudges all issues under the cloak of a spurious neutrality.

The linguo-philosophic illusion of neutrality really springs from the fact that linguistic philosophers treat their own meta-language (the concepts in terms of which they describe others), namely ordinary language, as somehow sacrosanct and outside the fray, and neutral in virtue of some kind of fundamental and absolute status. But this is absurd.

CHAPTER VI

STRUCTURE AND STRATEGY

Explanation of the Diagram and Instructions for Use

The Diagram represents Linguistic Philosophy as a system made up of interlocking, mutually supporting parts.

Each box encloses a doctrine, idea, practice, rule, value or other constituent which plays a significant part in the maintenance of the intellectual atmosphere of Linguistic Philosophy.

Straight lines connecting boxes indicate support, a possible line of argument or transition, between the ideas, etc., contained in the connected boxes.

Jagged lines between boxes indicate incompatibility or strain between the ideas, etc., contained in the boxes so connected.

The most important starting points within this self-contained system have boxes with black margins.

Of these, three are due to Wittgenstein (denial of pre-eminent language, the game model of language, and Polymorphism), one to G. E. Moore (common sense is right), one to Logical Positivism (Factual—grammatical exclusive dichotomy), and one (argument from impotence) originates from no individual thinker but from some general background.

Suggested Parlour Games

The reader who wishes to teach himself to *expound* Linguistic Philosophy should pick any square at random and then proceed along straight lines to other squares of his choice, until exhausted. The arguments connecting the contents of the boxes are generally obvious.

The reader may also wish to learn to *defend* Linguistic Philosophy. He should, again, pick some box at random and assume it to have been refuted. He must then concentrate on showing that the remaining boxes, or some favoured set of them, are quite self-sufficient without the abandoned box, and indeed that

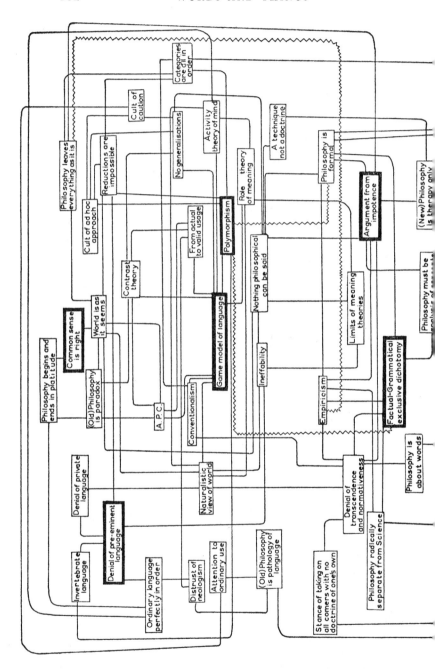

Philosophy leaves everything as it is

Categories are all in order

Cult of caution

No generalisations

Activity theory of mind

A technique not a doctrine

Philosophy is formal

Reductions are impossible

Cult of ad hoc approach

Role theory of meaning

Argument from impotence

(New) Philosophy is therapy only

From actual to valid usage

Polymorphism

Contrast theory

Nothing philosophical can be said

Philosophy must be analysis of separate

Common sense is right

World is as it seems

Game model of language

Limits of meaning theories

Philosophy begins and ends in platitude

(Old) Philosophy is paradox

Ineffability

Factual-Grammatical exclusive dichotomy

A.P.C.

Conventionalism

Empiricism

Philosophy is about words

Denial of private language

Naturalistic view of world

Denial of transcendence and normativeness

Invertebrate language

Denial of pre-eminent language

Ordinary language perfectly in order

Distrust of neologism

Attention to ordinary use

(Old) Philosophy is pathology of language

Stance of taking on all comers with no doctrine of one's own

Philosophy radically separate from Science

they imply something which is incompatible with it or with something it implies.

Note: certain items—notably "Cult of Caution" and "Limits-of-meaning theories"—can when desired be brought into conflict with almost any other item on the diagram, including each other. These particular potential conflicts, invaluable for defensive strategies (for showing that some abandoned output is not merely redundant but actually incompatible with the positions retained), are not indicated in the diagram, as they would make it too complex.

I. THE STRUCTURE OF LINGUISTIC PHILOSOPHY

THE IDEAS OUTLINED and their various supports form a highly integrated (even if not a fully consistent) whole, a structure which is so built up that it gives far greater strength and resilience to each of its parts than they would have alone. (The claim sometimes made, that there is no such integrated outlook and that we have here merely an assembly of independent ideas and devices, is absurd.)

Some of this integrated structure has been sketched, implicitly, by specifying the arguments in favour of the various doctrines. The structure is, however, quite complicated: those unfamiliar with its elements are unlikely to see the general pattern clearly. Indeed, some of those familiar with them also do not see it.

Having in the earlier sections discussed some of the trees as an aid towards seeing a wood, I now schematically portray the system of connected ideas by means of a diagram. The diagram can be used to illustrate a number of things: the interdependence of the various ideas of Linguistic Philosophy; the manner in which partial positions held by individuals contribute to the whole; the self-maintenance of the system—the mutual support the various ideas provide for each other, the limitation of the horizon, the completeness of the circle; the archeology of the movement, so to speak—the dependence on or influence of positions no longer held; the incompatibilities, apparent and real, that exist inside, and the strategies available and employed against criticisms and counter-example.

(To change the metaphor: I am interested in Linguistic Philosophy the *instrument*—its limits and defects. It is not denied that alternative melodies can be played on it, and within its limits.)

Note that it is quite unnecessary for any one individual to hold and explicitly defend the total set of the ideas I have listed. Indeed this may seldom be the case. What generally happens is that individuals hold or practise some of the constituents wholeheartedly, some lukewarmly, whilst they may be neutral with regard to others, or may hold them to be irrelevant, or even repudiate them.

What is important is this: any individual holding some of these ideas finds himself in a situation where a large part of his intellectual environment (or rather the *whole* of the intellectual environment that he takes seriously) consists of people who, collectively, add up to something like the interlocking scheme depicted. So, the logic of the ideas is in a sense also the sociology of the movement.

This system of logically connected ideas, each held by some even if not all of the people constituting the milieu, determines the kind of interpretations that will be put on what he says and does by others *and* by himself. It predetermines the kind of objections and the kind of agreement that he may expect. It implicitly contains the criteria of adequacy in terms of which he must build up and formulate what he wishes to say. The system, in this case, constitutes a complete circle, and its various compensating mechanisms prevent any breaking out. It can usefully be considered an ideology.

Note that not all elements of the ideology are literally *ideas*. Some are procedural rules, some are values and so forth. It is the mutual support provided by such items of diverse kinds that makes ideologies strong and resistant to criticism. For instance, a high valuation of clarity and caution, when combined with a theory of meaning and criteria of "clarity" which give an *a priori* clearance to all locutions sanctified by the Oxford English Dictionary but treat all philosophical neologisms as guilty until proven innocent (by virtually unsatisfiable tests), entails and constitutes a world-picture, *without having to articulate it*. To take the ideas alone, without the supporting pre-dispositions, would be to miss their force and point.

Some of the ideas constituting this system of thought are, however, in opposition to each other: for instance, the valuation of caution ("Say nothing general or what might conceivably be falsified") is not in harmony with the interesting and most questionable doctrine or prediction that philosophical problems can all be dissolved by careful examination of the use of the words related to them. Or again, the doctrine or necessary premiss that all truths must be either factual or grammatical, conflicts with the doctrine that there is a large or infinite number of kinds of truth. (Some of these oppositions are indicated by jagged lines on the diagram).

Again, this kind of conflict is a common feature of ideologies. Few, if any, manage to be wholly consistent. The conflict does not however lead to a breakdown if the conflicting elements can be isolated and the inconsistency camouflaged. Each of the conflicting constituents may be necessary to the system, but they can be invoked at different times and for different purposes. Moreover, there exist sophisticated devices for camouflaging the conflict: for instance, the view that every issue must be treated *ad hoc*—that there are no general principles—can be invoked against any simultaneous confrontation of contradictory ideas. Or again, the view that some important insights "cannot be said" can be used: ineffable truths presumably have no logical properties and, in particular, they lack the inconvenient one of contradicting one's other beliefs.

It is sometimes claimed—quite wrongly—that Linguistic Philosophy is not a homogeneous system of ideas, that differences of opinion exist within it. There are indeed divergencies within it, of two kinds: (1) Permitted ones which do not affect fundamentals: Linguistic philosophers may, for instance, disagree about just how a given term is used. (The linguo-philosophic discussion one Saturday morning, between Professor Tweedledum and Mr. Tweedledee, concerning the exact difference between the expressions "namely" and "i.e.", is still remembered in Oxford with bated breath.) This kind of "disagreement" is within the wider agreement about method, aims, and so on. The existence of this kind of disagreement in no way affects the claim that the system is homogeneous and closed. Most, or all, ideologies allow some free play inside. It is indeed a useful diversion of energies and attention. (2) Fundamental ones the implications of which are camouflaged.

Many linguistic philosophers have willingly given up, at least temporarily, individual positions of the system: indeed, some of the individual positions have been shown to be mistaken by linguistic philosophers themselves. But the system as a whole does not suffer, for the total structure can survive, at any rate for a time, without any one or small set of its parts. Moreover, the interconnectedness of the parts is such that, once the attack ceases, the abandoned part is, and has to be, reoccupied almost automatically and imperceptibly.

The game of evasion-and-retreat is made easy by a number of more specific features of this defensive system. A large number of the positions are reduplicated: there is an outer, exposed position, and an inner redoubt. The inner redoubt is impregnable: it consists of a position so reduced that one cannot really attack. For instance: the idea that *some* philosophical theories *may* be based on verbal confusions—one neither wishes to disagree with this, nor could one conceivably disprove it. But of course the linguistic philosopher only retreats into such an inner redoubt when under attack: at all other times (and especially when some other position is attacked and has to be aided), it is the outer, more exposed position that is occupied and that has a function within the whole system.

Furthermore, there are certain positions so placed as to facilitate retreat from an abandoned area whilst preventing the opponent from following up. For instance, as indicated, the idea that "each issue must be treated on its own merits" can be invoked to disconnect an abandoned position from those that are still occupied. Anyone insisting on seeing the various inter-related *and interdependent* positions jointly is guilty of "conflating" allegedly distinct doctrines.

Certain positions within the general structure are so to speak of archeological interest: they are survivals from the previous inhabitants of the area, and are evidence of the history of the movement. Of these positions, probably the most important one is the Logical Positivist doctrine of the exhaustive dichotomy of factual and grammatical truth. This position is not merely as a rule left unoccupied, it is even attacked. It is nevertheless an extremely crucial part of the defensive system, for it is *re*occupied when certain other parts of the system are attacked, and is invaluable in preventing those attacks from being effective. Roughly: a large number of other positions, such as the passivity of philosophy (both with regard to valuation and with regard to substantive knowledge), presuppose the impossibility of non-factual and non-deductive knowledge. When such a position is attacked, it can only be safeguarded by the re-invocation of the logical positivist premiss, by the re-occupation of the position: and this is precisely what happens.

It is interesting to note that certain connections which are *too* obvious may be left unexploited, for they would expose the general position and lay-out too plainly. For instance, the argument from the naturalistic view of the world to conclusions such as the denial of normativeness may be left unstressed. It may be preferable to camouflage it and give it an appearance of strength and subtlety by arguing via the theory of language.

Most criticisms of Linguistic Philosophy fail to make an impact on its devotees for one of two reasons:

They may concentrate on some doctrine or practice or promise of the system—and then this whole strategy of evasion, of inner deplacement and temporary evacuation, is brought into play, and the criticism makes no lasting impact on the movement. As the attackers arrive at what they suppose to be a crucial position, they are waved in by the retreating linguistic philosophers with friendly assurances that they never really wished to defend the position, and with offers of help in its demolition. One much-respected leader of the movement makes a habit not merely of conceding such positions, but of expressing utmost surprise at being told that it has ever been occupied—though it may have formed a part of an argument he has himself previously employed. But to point this out would, no doubt, be merely a sign of failing to realise the need for the *ad hoc* approach in philosophy.

Alternatively, criticisms have been directed at certain conspicuous features of the system as a whole, without bothering about its specific props. Thus, outsiders complain of the triviality, boredom, amoralism, obscurity, irrelevance of much of the work of the movement. These criticisms are again easily warded off: for, after all, they fail to show that what seems trivial is not, as linguistic philosophers like to give us to understand that it *is*, a subtle and nuanced way of saying something most important, of all that *can* be said; they fail to show that what seems obscure is not a higher form of clarity, and so on.

The aim of this book is, in part, to undertake the task of providing adequate guidance for the outside observer. Paraphrasing the immortal words of Groucho Marx—it seems trivial, but don't be deceived! It *is* trivial.

2. THE SPECTRUM

There is a kind of spectrum of positions * describable as Linguistic Philosophy:

(1) There are no philosophical problems. We use language in certain ways, that is all. (Language is a set of events in the world.) How could there be problems? (The insight that there cannot be philosophical problems, deduced from seeing language naturalistically in the world, is reinforced by the same insight springing from the two-and-two-only-kinds-of-knowledge theory. Neither insight would be as strong alone as the two jointly.) This outlook has its plausibilities. One can easily empathise it.

(2) There are no philosophical problems properly speaking, but there are important difficulties generated by language which can be clarified by understanding language.

(3) There are philosophical problems, but neither they nor their answers can be articulated, for they concern the very possibility of language and its relation to things, and that cannot be spoken of *in* language.

(4) There are problems, but their answers must not conflict with the actual use of words, for it is the actual use of words which gives them meaning, and a question or answer formulated in defiance of that use lacks sense.

(5) You may disregard ordinary language at the end, but only if you have taken care to give meaning to your neologisms. At the start, you must reflect on the actual use.

(6) Some problems *are* by-products of linguistic confusions.

(7) Some apparent problems *may be* by-products of linguistic confusions.

(8) *I like* knowing how I use words. (And make no claims

* Some of the positions analysed were characterised by Dr. J. O. Wisdom (not to be confused with Professor John Wisdom) as follows: "According to this phase of logical analysis its followers hold that philosophy arises from a state of perplexity, that all philosophical perplexity is NonSense, that there are no genuine philosophic problems, that there are no genuine philosophic answers, but that there are philosophical perplexities and problems that contain half-truths, and philosophic answers (equally NonSensical) that also contain half-truths: NonSense statement containing a half-truth and NonSense counter-statement containing a half-truth have a therapeutic effect upon each other." J. O. Wisdom, *The Metamorphosis of Philosophy*, Cairo 1947, p. 149.

whatever for its relevance. Kindly leave me in peace to get on with it.)

There are, in fact, people at each end of the points along this slippery pole. What is worse, some people are at a number of points at the same time, some slide up and down on it according to convenience, occasion and audience, and some are quite unclear about which position they are at.

Note some of the general features of the spectrum:

The higher up along it, the more interesting the position; the lower down, the more trivial and trivially irrefutable. The positions high up on the pole are interesting, by a variety of criteria of interestingness: they are challenging, novel, rich in implications for one's views of life; they have an appeal and a plausibility, fit in with certain other insights and experiences (the sterility and disagreements of past philosophy, for instance), and have all the stigmata of being an insight.

The positions lower down along the scale are hardly controversial. Nor, moreover, are they positions that merit the appellations *Revolution in Philosophy*, "an influential school", or claims of superiority over past ways of thinking, etc., etc. They merit nothing. (6) is a proposition on which I should stake my life without a great deal of nervousness: that some philosophers may have been confused is not something I wish to challenge. (7) is trivially necessary. (8) is not even a trivially necessary proposition, it is not a proposition at all. One distinguished, and rightly distinguished, member of the movement wrote to me after the earlier publication of some of these criticisms, saying that he agreed with much of the argument, but that, nevertheless, he just wished to continue finding out "how he uses words".

People who do not quite know at which point on the scale they are may be excused, to some extent, for the external appearance of the positions is strikingly—and one should add deliberately—similar. At the top, the philosophical position is unsayable, for deep reasons which are themselves unsayable.

At the bottom of the scale, the philosophical position is unsayable for the much more straightforward, less elusive reason that there is no philosophical position. This does not strain anyone's understanding or philosophic intuition.

When someone says nothing philosophical and practises the technique (of observing usages, or inventing language games) instead, it is hard for the outsider to tell whether his philosophical position is too deep for words or whether it is non-existent. It may be equally difficult for the man himself. (There is, perhaps, no privileged access to the ineffable.) He may not know whether he is at (1) or at (8). I rather suspect that when the *activity* way of doing philosophy becomes habitual and no longer a titivating novelty, he may simply *forget* at which point along this pole he is, and he may quietly slide down it.

Not merely are the movements along the pole camouflaged by the fact that the positions are not very distinct externally, but the pole is positively a greased one, the sliding is assisted. Having fully understood the position (1) one is encouraged to go down to (8)—"throw away the ladder", in Wittgenstein's metaphor. So one slides *down*. But also, the more "flies have been released from bottles" (i.e. the more problems shown to be amenable to the method) by activities lower down along the scale, the more does position (1) become acceptable and natural. So one also slides *up*. There is in fact a symbiotic relationship between positions at either end. Activities at the bottom may not in fact release many, or any, of the flies, but those watching them as students sooner or later catch on to the ideas of those at the top. Having seen the point, they see why sooner or later all flies *must* be releasable (on the assumptions that have been insinuated) and so come to take their eventual release on trust. But this confirms their implicit faith in the upper-end ideas again; that in turn confirms them in the practices, and once these become habitual, the ideas may even be forgotten, and certainly disavowed if challenged. Thus Linguistic Philosophy, the doctrine that philosophy is an activity, is a spiritual exercise that confirms the faith which calls for the exercise to begin with.

It is in this respect, as in others, curiously reminiscent of psychoanalysis. There, too, we have a doctrine and a technique in close symbiotic relationship. If we are interested in the technique and enquire about the statistics of its successes, we are hastily told that these in any case prove little: if we merely want a cure, why not go to Lourdes? The technique gives *insight*, which is more important than therapeutic success alone. But the insight, one imagines, must have some connection with the doctrines and ideas. If one investigates the ideas which constitute the insight, and becomes worried by their vagueness, lack of confirmability and confirmation, etc., one is assured—ah, but the doctrine can only be understood in the light of the technique, the *practice*. So one shuttle-cocks between the two. In both cases, there is only *weak* evidence that the technique is effectively therapeutic, but *overwhelming* evidence that it is powerfully habit-forming.

Linguistic philosophers go rather further than protagonists of psychoanalysis in that they also actually deny the existence (and not merely the sufficiency) of a general theory. The method has a curious analogy to Socratic ignorance or psychoanalytic passivity, enabling him who claims it to ask questions but to repudiate the obligation to answer any himself. Unkindly, one cannot but suppose that this is part of its role. We might say, paraphrasing Wittgenstein: "Don't look at what they say about the theory or lack of it, look at the *use* which they make of that alleged lack of theory."

This kind of behaviour has been well described in Miss Iris Murdoch's novel *Under the Net*, where one character is always very surprised if his interlocutor extracts a generalisation from his own way of discussion, and denies holding it as if such a generalisation were a lapse of taste. The author appears to take such behaviour at its face value, treating it as a kind of striking *concreteness*. But we are responsible for the presuppositions or premisses of what we say and do: it may indeed be difficult to get them right, but they are always present and it is inexcusable in a philosopher to pretend that they do not exist.

3. THE PRAYER-WHEEL

There is a story of a backward Asian principality: it contains many prayer-wheels, on which the various names of God are rotated. Under one of the technological aid programmes, the local prince ordered an electronic prayer-wheel that would go through all the possible divine names at much greater speed than the old mechanical models. The new "prayer-wheel" was duly delivered and installed. It was set in motion. The engineer who installed it thought that it would take the wheel about a day to go through all the possible names, and decided to wait and see it work well.

At the end of the day, the machine approached the end of its task. But lo!—as it ended, the moon faded, the stars disappeared, and the world folded up: for it had no further *raison d'être*.

This happily apocryphal story is however an excellent parable for philosophy as conceived by the post-Wittgensteinians. What conceptual problems *could* there be other than about how we use words? (Non-conceptual problems cannot concern the philosopher.) So, when all usages are listed—and without some electronic device it will take very, very long, admittedly—what reason could be left for thought?

4. THE NEEDLE IN THE HAYSTACK

Linguistic Philosophy, in the sense of observing the nuances of the actual employment of words rather than thinking about things, began as the view that the solution of problems, the liberation from "cramps", the "dissolution" of perplexities, *must* be found somewhere in the immense haystack of our actual speech habits. It was worth looking for the needle despite the tedium and difficulty of the search, for the needle *must* be there.

There were, *au fond*, two good reasons for the firm conviction that the needle *must* be there. (1) Where else? There are no transcendental realms, no subsistent norms, etc., etc., in which the solution to philosophic problems could be sought. This is the argument to Linguistic Philosophy from the conclusions of Logical Positivism. (2) The Game model of language.

Each of these arguments for the view that the needle *must* be in the haystack is extremely powerful, and each was in fact operative in making philosophers seek it.

The needle has not turned up. But the burrowing in this haystack has become habitual and established, and a cessation of it would leave many men in a bewildered state. Some have no other skills. So, some alternative positions have emerged and are to be found: there *may* be needles in the haystack. Haystacks are interesting. We like hay.

5. PHILOSOPHY BY FILIBUSTER *

The promise of dissolution and a certain spurious modesty can be combined, as follows: the endless investigations of the

* Cf. comments on this by Professor W. H. F. Barnes in *The Philosophical Predicament*, London 1950, p. 121.

nuances of usage can simply be indulged in, without it being made clear *why*. It may be because by such means all philoso-phical problems will be dissolved.

Or—whilst this indefinitely protracted investigation will not dissolve—it is at least a necessary preparation, a "begin-all".* (There are no signs of the end of the beginning, however.)

Or—the activity is just pursued for its own sake, as "pure research".

Whichever of these rationalisations is adopted—or rather when, more characteristically, each is invoked according to convenience—the effective result is a kind of indefinite filibuster. Criticisms are left unanswered, solutions are not presented, and the usage-observation goes on and on and on. Those who ask for some results are told they must wait.

But how long? Note that one form of the theory also says that boredom is a sign of that philosophical illumination which fol-lows on the observation of usage. This fits well with the general scheme, at any rate of what we have called crude Linguistic Philosophy: when we fully perceive the contexts and usages of an alleged problem, we see that there is nothing to puzzle about, nothing to answer.

There is a problem here however: how could one distinguish the boredom of attrition from the boredom of illumination?

6. THE RELUCTANT CENTIPEDE

The linguo-philosophic vision of the history of thought is—and has to be, given its diagnosis of what philosophy is—some-thing like this: there is a first stage of intellectual innocence and health, in which people just *use* language, without puzzling about it and hence without puzzling philosophically about the world. (Some people retain this innocence—for instance G. E. Moore, who did not puzzle about the world or science, and only entered philosophy because he was puzzled by what other philosophers said.) This stage can be compared to the happy stage in the life of a centipede when it just wanders about, using its legs but unworried by them.

The next stage is when it begins to puzzle about its own power of mobility.

To explain this, it postulates theories. Impelled by Occamist

* Professor J. L. Austin's phrase.

yearning for economy of hypothesis, it supposes that it has only one leg, or only two, or a small number, anyway. This corresponds to the stage in the history of thought when philosophical *theories* are postulated.* Now if a centipede equipped with hundreds of legs supposes it has but two—or if a language-user using language in hundreds of ways supposes he uses it in only one or two ways—then the centipede will sooner or later, probably sooner, find itself in trouble. Attempting to assimilate its many legs to one selected leg will lead it to fall over its legs.

But the cure is simple. The Wittgensteinian anti-Occamist discovery of polymorphism, of the large—indeed, infinite— number of language legs, liberates the hapless centipede from his self-imposed paralysis. Now all is clear. Each leg is recognised and allowed full scope, uninhibited by attempts to use it as though it were another. . . .

The cult of the idiosyncrasy of various kinds of use of language was of course anticipated by G. E. Moore when he chose as the motto of his *Principia Ethica* Bishop Butler's dictum that everything is what it is and not another thing. This alleged insight is so important in Linguistic Philosophy that Professor John Wisdom has given it a name, the "Idiosyncrasy Platitude".† The devotion to this insight accounts for why so much Linguistic Philosophy consists of explaining at great and tedious length that something or other is just what it is.

In Ignazio Silone's *School for Dictators*, there is a comic Professor whose contribution to the discussion takes exclusively a form something like this: "Democracy is Democracy and can be nothing but Democracy." "America is America and can be nothing but America." "Government is government, and can be nothing but Government."

It is doubtful whether Silone, in inventing the Professor, foresaw that he was describing an actually coming *Revolution in Philosophy*, an actually existing philosophic movement destined

* As late as 1956/57, Professor J. L. Austin used the term "tertiary stage" (of the philosophic disease) *ex cathedra* as President of the Aristotelian Society, to designate any theoretical or general attempt to deal with the problem of free will and determinism, as opposed to dissolving it by careful attention to how words are used. He has also claimed—remarkable achievement—not to understand what determinism means.

† *Philosophy and Psycho-Analysis*. Oxford 1953, p. 51.

to replace all past philosophy, cure mankind of the "tertiary stage" (Professor Austin's expression) of the intellectual disease, and set human thought right along the lines of the Professor.

7. THE WITHERING AWAY OF PHILOSOPHY

The doctrine that philosophy must wither away as we become acquainted with the patterns of our use of words is curiously reminiscent of the Marxist view that the *State* will wither away.

Just as the Soviet State has not withered away, so our major philosophical problems have not been dissolved to general satisfaction. The reasons underlying both these abortive hopes seem similar: an excessively monolithic diagnosis of evil. Marxism supposes that the State, coercion, has but one cause—class conflict. (Naturally, if this were so, the termination of class conflict should show itself by the withering away of the State.) Similarly, Linguistic Philosophy has a unique-cause theory of philosophy or philosophic error: namely, linguistic confusion, or the attempt at "transcending language", and variants of this attempt, such as misleading or *general* models of how words mean things.*

8. THE SPURIOUS FOX

This—an excessively homogeneous, unique model of how philosophy works—is a part of my diagnosis of Linguistic Philosophy. Many have noticed the triviality of linguo-philosophic practices: my concern is to diagnose the compulsiveness of that triviality and to show that the appearance is not deceptive. The movement itself *is* trivial. This diagnosis may seem surprising and paradoxical, for it is precisely in terms of this: of obsessional, over-general models that Linguistic Philosophy itself diagnoses *older* philosophies. Under various guises, the famous piecemeal approach, the ad hoc-ness, the disclaimers of general positions, are part of Linguistic Philosophy, of its famous *foxiness*.

Superficially, nothing indeed could seem more unjust than to accuse Linguistic Philosophy of excessive homogeneity, of being hypnotised by one model, etc. Willingness to try anything, the unpredictability of fly-releasing ploys, the variety of ways in which language is used, all these things are or were (until it

* *Philosophical Investigations*, Oxford, 1953, p. 47.

became quite tedious) much proclaimed, and in some measure
even practised.

But: what underlies this variety of doings and this interest in
the variety of uses of language is the unique picture of the situation when someone is philosophically puzzled—of something
having gone wrong with his view of how words are used. Words
are used in complex and manifold ways, and he is allegedly
interpreting the use of some words more simply than our actual
use warrants, or interpreting one kind of word as if it were
another, or—a further complication—he may be trying to say
something which could only be said if we could say things outside all rule-bound languages, outside language altogether. In
short, there is the hedgehog-like * conviction that foxiness is the
answer to everything. Note that faith in foxiness is one of which
we can never be disabused: if solutions are endlessly various, if
that very variety is the clue, we can never be sure we have tried
all the ways. One cannot be fully disabused, though one may
lose faith by having one's patience tried too hard. This has
presumably happened to those who no longer claim that "dissolutions" must come, and who are prepared to make do with
"pure research".

So that despite its seeming open-ness at *one* level, Linguistic
Philosophy is bound by an obsessional model at *another*.

9. TWO-TIER DOCTRINE AND
INVERTEBRATE PHILOSOPHY

By two-tier doctrine I mean this: Suppose a man says he
knows which horse will win the Derby, *and* that you can never
tell who will—he can hardly be wrong. The difficulty is in
combining the two assertions in one formula which sounds
appealing, and which seems to be one indivisible doctrine.
Dialectical Materialism is a classical case of a two-tier doctrine:
materialism makes certain claims, *dialectical* says, if it says anything, that all claims are liable to be reversed or limited by
opposite claims. You cannot lose on this.

Linguistic Philosophy is a *very* plausible two-tier doctrine,
thanks to its cult of the "*ad hoc*" which is "type-ambiguous", i.e.
there is nothing to indicate the level at which that *ad hoc*-ness is
to operate.

* "The hedgehog knows one big thing, the fox knows many things."

At the bottom level, the *ad hoc*-ness is plausible, attractive, and fits in with the general model used by Linguistic Philosophy. The general argument is roughly that philosophic illusions arise from the variety of uses of language—well, what follows is that we must see them in their great variety, and be *ad hoc* in our approach. This is reasonable enough.

But: if this model itself, or its relevance in some context, is challenged, the customary, but no longer apposite, *ad hoc*-ness can be invoked, as follows: "But you are misunderstanding us, you are making our practice into a rigid dogma, whereas our dearest tenet is, on the contrary, the need for an elastic *ad hoc* approach. And just because we are wedded to that elasticity, you cannot bind us to the rigid model you have drawn up for our benefit." (Re-employing the stress on diversity, it can be used to evade any objection.)

But: the need for elasticity in dealing with problems follows from the general model which cannot itself benefit from the same excuse.

Ad hoc-ism is a kind of attempt at having a totally invertebrate philosophy, in the image of an allegedly invertebrate language.

10. THE FULL CIRCLE

A device alternative to the use of the two-tier structure is what one may call the *Full Circle*, or *Me Too*. It is, really, the application of a general recipe for a successful revolution. The recipe runs: take a viable system (social, of beliefs, or philosophical, etc.) consisting of elements, a, b, c, etc. Abolish or invert a, b, c, eliminating traces of them and of their past presence. Of course the New System, consisting of not-a, not-b, etc., will be highly revolutionary, novel, etc., and give you the *réclame* of a great innovator, revolutionary, etc.

However, the trouble so far is that not-a, not-b, etc., may form a system which is not merely revolutionary, but also absurd. No matter. If you have followed the recipe correctly and eliminated traces and memories of a, b, c, etc. (at least from your own mind), you can now gradually reintroduce them, and slowly finish again with the original system a, b, c, etc. You now have *both* a viable system *and* the aura of a just innovator and revolutionary.

This is exactly what has happened to the "Revolution in

Philosophy". Consider the "discovery" that the APC and appeals to usage do not solve normative problems: who ever doubted that before the "Revolution"? It was, on the contrary, just the reason why people were not interested in usages. Linguistic philosophers have smuggled these double reversals into the Revolution, making it more viable, without, however, confessing that the wheel was turning full circle.

Other examples: Professor Austin's remark as President of the Aristotelian Society that just because things are the way they are words are used the way they are. Indeed—*just this* was the basis of the old philosophic practice of not banning inferences from the form of concepts to the nature of things—a practice whose undermining was such a vaunted feature of the "Revolution in Philosophy". Or: the recommendation that philosophers should explain why and how language works as it does, what general features of the world cause it to be as it is *—ideas which have their merit but which strike at the very heart of that "Revolution" to which they are now credited.

Or again—and this is an important example—Mr. Warnock's readmission † of "new visions" into philosophy. Linguistic Philosophy began as the doctrine that new visions were pathological, the by-products of a misuse of language. *This* was the justification of concentrating on the actual use of words. And now they are re-admitted—and it is even said that they are essential for philosophy!

11. SOLVITUR AMBULANDO

It is sometimes said (or more precisely, it is often said by Professor Ryle) that one should not meta-philosophise (i.e. talk *about* philosophy) so much, but rather get on with the job. Now the attraction of meta-philosophising, of talking *about* philosophy, seems to me not vicious or self-indulgent, but a *consequence* of Linguistic Philosophy. It is simultaneously a theory about the world, about language, and about philosophy. Its theory about the world, however, is very unexciting and shared with all unimaginative men: one fails to see its point unless one sees it in the context of its doctrine *about* philosophy. Similarly,

* Cf. Mr. P. F. Strawson, in *The Revolution in Philosophy*, ed. G. Ryle, London 1956, p. 107.
† *English Philosophy since 1900*, London 1958, Chapter XI.

its doctrine of language is too piecemeal or negative to be interesting as such; and in as far as it contains general claims, such as the need for contrast, it is something more accurately explored by the communication engineer. Its point only comes to light when seen in the context of its meta-philosophy.

Meta-philosophy is the kernel and most interesting part of Linguistic Philosophy, and we cannot but return to it. The only thing to do with *this* temptation is to give in to it. (The idea that only the applications count is a myth, like the alleged importance of the complexity of Wittgenstein's thought.)

For there is, as pointed out, a kind of complete circle between the theory of language (that it has rules, requires contrast, etc.), the unavowed naturalism acting as criterion of what is a problem and what a solution, the therapeutic approach which follows from that, and the polymorphic or *ad hoc* method of therapy which rightly follows from the theory of language. Even when bits of the circle are seen to be silly (the APG and its normative application, notably), there is a tendency to slip back, for all the other links push one back. Hence the general ideas, the system as a whole, *must* interest the critic—and the devotee, really—more than its detailed application.

There is of course a good deal of merit in the idea that one should not be too preoccupied with method, to the detriment of substance. But the moment when the principles of one's own method are being subjected to criticism is *not* the right one for invoking this idea.

In any case, the distinction between substantive *doing* and second-order reflection is inapplicable to philosophy. What seems substantive to Ryle—the examination of concepts through their verbal expression—would, just as naturally, be considered a second-order activity by others. What seems second-order to him—the question *whether* ordinary language is relevant—would as naturally seem a substantive philosophic issue to others. The distinction which he takes for granted is in fact *just* the kind of thing that is most controversial. By the time we are agreed where this line is to be drawn, most problems have been solved, or rather prejudged.

12. DIFFERENTIAL REALISM

This technique consists of misinterpreting other people's doctrines by systematically taking them at a different level from the one intended by their authors. The prototype of this technique can be found in the facetious remark we can make if somebody tells us "I have the same picture at home". We reply "If it is in your home then it can't be the same as the one here". In a sense we are right, but the joke is a feeble one.

Linguistic philosophers have employed this technique in all seriousness, treating it as if it were a genuine refutation, claiming that the opponents had themselves been misled into treating a doctrine true at one level as if it were also true at another. In part they have also been encouraged into this practice by the general outlook of Polymorphism. For instance, some linguistic philosophers have "refuted" the doctrine that the essence of moral statements is an attempt to persuade people into activities or attitudes, not by saying that the essence is something else, but simply by claiming, as indeed is true on one level, that there is no one single motive characterising all individual employments of any one kind of expression. Quite so: but people who defended the doctrine in question were under no misapprehension about this. The doctrine did not deny the variegation of human motives in asserting moral claims, or in anything else. It merely claimed that the general characteristic distinguishing ethical terms generally, after the particularities of the individual case had been quite justifiably left out, was persuasion. This may or may not be true, but it is beside the point to stress the undeniable but irrelevant fact that people have many additional specific motives in their daily life. One can see how, given the general polymorphic outlook and the view that philosophic theories are inspired by over-simplification and the presence of unique models, linguistic philosophers were led into supposing that they could cut short a problem in this way.

Another very important example of the application of this particular technique is the "refutation" of Bertrand Russell's "Theory of Descriptions". That theory offered a translation of expressions such as "the present King of France" or "The Golden Mountain". A translation was thought philosophically necessary, given the interesting question: "How do these expressions manage to be meaningful? They do not refer to something. There is no present king of France nor a gold mountain to which they could refer." The logical technicalities and merits of Russell's theory need not detain us here. Linguistic Philosophy has substituted no novel answer to Russell's famous theory: it has, on the contrary, supposed that it can undercut the whole problem by pointing out that expressions as such *never* refer to anything. Only *particular employments* in concrete contexts by individual people manage to refer to things.* This is so, in a sense. If we wish to be so utterly literal-minded, it is true: expressions in the abstract fail to "refer". But so what? The problem of how expressions of that kind manage to refer survives *even if restated in terms of particular utterances*. The old way of formulating it was perfectly legitimate, unmisleading and indeed avoided the confusions which result from the later way.

13. THE NEW KORAN

The (untrue) story is told that the Muslim conqueror of Alexandria ordered the burning of the books in the Library with the following argument: either the books say something other than the Koran—in which case they are false, or they say the same as the Koran—in which case they are redundant. In either case—burn them!

The argument is unanswerable, given that one possesses an exhaustive repository of truth such as the Koran. Linguistic Philosophy does of course conceive of itself as possessing such an exhaustive inventory of truth, at any rate as far as philosophical truth is concerned: namely, the Oxford English Dictionary. Philosophical questions are conceptual questions, and concepts are the uses of words. When all the uses are listed (and the OED is the nearest approximation to such a complete listing, though of course the linguistic philosopher may have to supply additional detail) what question could conceivably remain? None.

The linguistic philosopher in fact proceeds exactly in the manner of the conqueror in the story. All philosophic assertions are either true and reduplicated in the OED or usage, or not reduplicated there, and false. For a philosophic truth is the

---

* This point, buried under a characteristic fortification of scholastic distinctions, is found in Mr. P. F. Strawson's "On Referring", in *Essays in Conceptual Analysis*, ed. A. Flew, London 1956, p. 21.

account of the meaning of a term, that is, an account of its use and the claim that it has a use: an entry in the OED is adequate evidence that a term has a use and, usually, a specification of what that use is. (All the philosopher need do is, sometimes, to expand the account and to relate it to a problem.) But the OED not merely contains nothing but philosophic truth, it also contains all philosophic truth. A philosophic theory not reduplicated in the OED is, *ipso facto*, a false account of the meaning, of the use of some concept.

The treatment of the OED as a Holy Writ can be observed in the practice of linguistic philosophers, but it is also conveyed by certain celebrated slogans of linguistic philosophers, such as that "philosophy begins and *ends* in platitude"—that is, its conclusions are but the repetition of what we normally say (and what we normally say about concepts is recorded in good dictionaries)—or that "philosophy leaves everything as it is".

Some linguistic philosophers * have denied the applicability of the Koranic analogy: whilst admitting that, given the linguistic method, everything *in* the OED had a use and a meaning, they denied that it was a part of the method to exclude all additions to it. The Koran is true, it appears, but it does not exhaust truth.

It is impossible to square the asymmetry alleged by Pears, the view that the OED has Koranic status only in that everything in it has meaning, but not in the sense that everything *not* in it is excluded—with slogans such as that "philosophy begins and ends in platitude" or that ordinary language is perfectly in order as it is. The introduction of a new manner of speaking cannot be a platitude, and it would not be an improvement if everything in the OED is in order. Yet nonplatitudinous innovations which are improvements constitute the history of science and philosophy.

However, it is *perhaps* possible for these particular linguistic philosophers to dissociate † themselves from those doctrines (though it is hard to see how this can be done consistently, in view of the importance of those doctrines as justifications of the methods and practices of Linguistic Philosophy in general).

---

* Messrs. D. F. Pears and G. J. Warnock, in a discussion broadcast on the BBC's Third Programme in October 1957.

† But there is evidence that they *cannot*. Cf. G. J. Warnock, *Berkeley*, Penguin, London 1953, p. 239.

But, even if they do, they remain wedded to the Koranic Dictionary view, without asymmetry, as can be shown in connection with the next device.

14. SALADIN'S FORK

There is a mediaeval story about the King who convoked a rich Jew and bid him debate the relative merits of his own and of the King's religion. But the debate had to be carried out on the assumption that the King's religion was the true one, for indeed to suppose otherwise would be blasphemous. Needless to say, the Jew, if he did not succeed in avoiding the debate altogether, was bound to commit either blasphemy or self-contradiction. Lessing used this theme for his play *Nathan the Wise*: in the play, Nathan succeeds in evading the question put to him by Sultan Saladin with the intention that the answer, whatever it is, should be a pretext for the confiscation of Nathan's wealth.

No possibility of evading such a similarly loaded question is left to anyone wishing to dispute the validity of the linguistic approach. The simple-minded trick played by Saladin on Nathan is repeated, with the difference that the inescapable dilemma is between self-contradiction and unintelligibility. (The sin of nonsense replaces that of blasphemy.)

Though this is one trick amongst many in the equipment of Linguistic Philosophy, it is also the underlying essence of its method, whichever other trick happens to be employed. The essence of Linguistic Philosophy is the discussion of the rival merits of established ordinary usage and of some other manner of speaking, *on the assumption that the ordinary usage is the better*. The assumption is not always made clear, it is simply built into the rules of the discussion: Deviation from ordinary use is *ex officio* 'unintelligible', unless 'it is given a sense'. Thus, for instance, Messrs. Pears and Warnock attempt to rebut one half of the Koranic-Dictionary thesis (having conceded the other half), namely the allegation that all deviations from established usage are necessarily outlawed by Linguistic Philosophy, declaring in a rather starry-eyed manner that there is no objection to innovations provided that they "are given a use". Very well: but what counts as "giving a use" to a new way of speaking?

Note that any radical innovation is, *ex hypothesi*, a philosophical issue. (And, of course, non-categorial innovations are not concerned: no one denies, or credits Linguistic Philosophy with denying, that new names may be given to individual objects within hitherto recognised types.) But philosophical theses count as "odd", they are defined and identified as those which violate established use.* To "give them a use" is to describe some kind of behaviour and context in which they could play a part, and to describe that behaviour and context in the ordinary, Third Person terms. . . . (in other words, to show that it reduplicates something *in* the OED). There is no breaking out of this circle. The requirement is like saying—revolutions are all right, always provided they can be justified in terms of the existing constitutional practice.

This game is rigged, and doubly rigged. It is rigged in the first instance by the insistence on appealing to ordinary language, and in the second instance by the behaviourist theory which is incapsulated in the game model of language.†

The "proof" of the impossibility of a private language has a similar Saladin-esque logic: language being defined as a public game, it is shown that—as you might expect—a private language would not be a public game. Even more strangely, the proof makes use of the fact ‡ that the second-order concepts by means

* In the preceding discussion, Pears attempts to disprove the Koranic allegation by distinguishing between the drawing of limits of significance, and the limits of what is relevant for philosophic problems. But in view of the fact that conceptual innovations *are* philosophical, the consideration of this is absolutely essential for seeing the circle by means of which the Koranic dilemma excludes any categories *not* in the OED as much as it underwrites those which *are* in it.

The fact that there is no way of distinguishing, in general, categorial and intra-categorial concepts only strengthens the point.

† Cf. the version of it by Mr. A. MacIntyre, in *Universities and Left Review*, Summer 1958, p. 72.

‡ The "paradox of analysis", which postulates the dilemma that an analysis is either a mere synonym and hence trivial, or more than a synonym and hence false, has its equivalent in Linguistic Philosophy: a neologism can either be accounted for in existing terms, in which case it is redundant, or it cannot, in which case it has not "been given sense".

But in Linguistic Philosophy it is not recognised to be a paradox which damns the assumptions and procedures which lead to it. A generation ago, Frank Ramsay wittily described scholasticism as pretending that what is not clear is. A new species has emerged: pretending that what *is* clear is not.

of which we would distinguish a private language from a public one from the outside, concepts distinguishing sensations as such from public things as such, could not occur in the private language itself. Quite so: that is what makes it private.

Thus criteria which make a concept acceptable are not stated or avowed. The need for their specification has even been irritably denied or defined in terms of agreement by colleagues.* So what claims to be a neutral technique in fact turns out to be a selection procedure which awards certificates of clearance to concepts, or accounts of concepts, which fit a certain vision of the world.

15. THE INDIAN ROPE TRICK

This might also be called lifting oneself by one's own shoe-laces. The essence of this particular device is a kind of systematic inconsistency.

Now inconsistency is not a new phenomenon. All of us are guilty of it, and past thinkers have no doubt been guilty of it. It is often possible to discover the internal inconsistency of someone's thoughts by skilfully juxtaposing various beliefs of his that were not thought out jointly. What is new about Linguistic Philosophy is that when such inconsistencies occur within it, they are never discovered, noted or considered important. They are not supposed to require correction. This is where, once again, Polymorphism and the cult of the piecemeal approach comes in—the view that each problem calls for its own treatment. The idea that philosophy is *not* the building of a coherent world picture can be interpreted, and is interpreted, as implying that there is no need to be preoccupied with consistency in what one says at various times in dealing with various problems. Polymorphism and the myth of the piecemeal

---

* "A common demand on the part of the opponents of analytic philosophy is for some set of criteria by which one could judge a philosophic analysis of a concept. To this request Austin replied, somewhat sardonically, 'If you can make an analysis convince yourself, no matter how hard you try to overthrow it, and if you can get a lot of cantankerous colleagues to agree with it, that's a pretty good criterion that there is something in it.' " (*The Times*, 17.5.58.)

Professor Austin's colleagues may be cantankerous *within* the method, but they are conspicuously un-cantankerous *about* it. Given the method, all the rest follows, by devices that have been explored.

approach are used as an omnibus, blanket, protective measure, not merely against refutation but equally against inner consistency. It provides a general *carte blanche* for using mutually inconsistent arguments, and an encouragement to climb up the rope, when one has also removed any support for it.

To give an example: A philosopher will give an account of logical necessity in terms of human conventions, namely that necessity springs from the tacit conventions governing our use of language. At another time he will give a diagnosis of what underlies the problem of other minds (the difficulty we have in giving an account of how we can ever know what other people feel, as opposed to merely seeing the external manifestations of their feelings). He will stress the utter logical impossibility of feeling somebody else's feeling, with the innuendo that if we fully realise that we are dealing with a *logical* impossibility, and not a contingent one, we shall cease feeling that we are missing something. If, however, the two analyses made by the same philosopher are put together, the result is that the impossibility of feeling somebody else's feelings becomes a convention of language! On one actual occasion when the philosopher in question was asked to comment on the two analyses conjointly he bluntly refused, without explanation. A philosopher working in a tradition unequipped with Polymorphism and the other face-saving devices would feel that the situation presents a problem, and try to arrive at consistency in his own thinking. For a linguistic philosopher, there is no such need. On the contrary, it illustrates his own doctrine of Polymorphism and the need for an ad hoc approach.

The successive use of quite inconsistent ideas or principles, and the "polymorphic" and other devices which purport to justify it, may be called the Indian Rope Trick. The linguistic philosopher climbs up many ropes—but beware of trying to convince him that something must be supporting the rope.

16. PHILOSOPHY BY FRISSON

This method is complementary to philosophy by attrition (or by filibuster). Like these styles, *Philosophy by Frisson* is rendered necessary by the view that there is nothing that can be said in philosophy, either because there *is* nothing (to say), or because it cannot be said.

If there is no doctrine to be communicated, what is communicated must be an insight, an attitude, an illumination. This can be done either by the interminable retailing of specific information about usage, each individual item of which is trivial but which collectively somehow initiate one into the picture, the frame of mind, the perspective, or what not: or alternatively it can be done, less tediously, by some dramatic little argument, by a few well chosen words which illuminate us more quickly. Not all linguistic philosophers—happily—have the patience to wait for the release of the fly from the fly-bottle by an unselective trial-and-error retailing of usages. Some, knowing how to release the fly, are prepared to take a short cut. The sudden illumination—as opposed to the protracted one which is said to be heralded by boredom—can most appropriately be called the *frisson*. (Note that it *must* be something like this—for it cannot be a proposition, a statable discovery.)

Linguistic Philosophy communicates no doctrine, it illuminates, and linguistic philosophers are sometimes willing to help on the flash of illumination in the time-honoured manner of illuminators—the dark saying, the apparent paradox, the little argument with an unacceptable conclusion which is not to be taken literally, the seeming irrelevancy delivered with the air, "those who understand, see the point", etc. These are all to be found. Linguistic Philosophy is, in theory, supposed to start from the "cramp", the intellectual paralysis caused by inability to cope with some muddling group of notions. Linguistic philosophers are not beyond occasionally also inducing a little pre-illuminational experimental cramp.* The mastery of devices employed for producing these *frissons* can be acquired, and so can a sensitivity, a receptivity to them. I imagine devotees of these titillations can keep themselves in a state of pleasurable excitement for hours on end with such Intimations of Ineffability. Once one has learnt the techniques for inducing these emotional accompaniments of illumination, one may sometimes even induce them independently, without either cramp or illumination. . . . Crystallisations may be provoked with nothing to crystallise.

The dark sayings, the bewildering alternation of drawing attention to the obvious, to the overtly behavioural, of insisting

* Cf. Professor J. Wisdom: "Philosophers should be continually trying to say what cannot be said." *Philosophy and Psycho-Analysis*, p. 50.

that all is plain before us, with, on the other hand, hints at the most terrible difficulty, at inner torment, at ineffability (experimental neurosis can after all be produced by such methods!) are used not merely to produce titillations in the devotees, but also to cow the neophyte into submission. (I should add that, personally, I prefer philosophy-by-frisson to philosophy-by-attrition. But it should be noted that the latter can also be seen as a special, final refinement of the former. For the real connoisseur, the *subtlest* pleasure is the greatest. Any tyro can be titivated by dramatic paradox, but the refined palate can find finer pleasures in the slightest nuances of platitude.)

17. KEEP THEM GUESSING

The doctrine is never quite disclosed: not merely the ineffable items, but even the presumably sayable diagnoses of error are often just indicated, or it is just indicated, *ex cathedra*,* that there is one without precise specification. (The mode of communication is disclosure of a revelation rather than the presentation of an argument.) This makes sure that the disciple can never be certain of having got it right. *Comprendre c'est égaler*, and here there is no danger that one will understand.

No wonder that disciples who sell their souls to Masters of the movement—and not only to Wittgenstein—are liable, as one can observe, to feel *very* angry when they encounter, or cannot avoid encountering, an outside sceptic. *They* have had to suppress their doubts and uncertainties, which cannot be agreeable. To be reminded of them is not pleasant. One can defend a real certainty calmly: a forcibly self-imposed one, accompanied by fear of acknowledging one's own uncertainty to oneself, is hard to defend with equanimity.

The reader or pupil of the linguistic philosopher is thoroughly softened by a series of implicit threats. To begin with he is told that much or all of his ordinary thinking about general issues is in the sway of simple and misguided models from which it is hard to liberate himself (for although Linguistic Philosophy claims to be the philosophy of ordinary speech, it is by no means the philosophy of ordinary thought. On the contrary, it spurns

---

* As examples of disciples who have caught the Master's style one may take Mr. R. Rhees, in his Preface to Wittgenstein's *Blue and Brown Books* (Oxford 1958, esp. p. xi), or the works of Miss G. E. L. Anscombe.

ordinary thought, when it strays beyond the bounds of ordinary context, for then it is doomed to be mistaken.) There is an old definition of the philosopher as the man who speaks of important matters in such a way that one does not understand but feels that it is one's own fault. Linguistic Philosophy has certainly revolutionised the techniques for obtaining this last effect.

He is further softened up by the doctrine of ineffability, or of the need for some kind of oblique approach. It is all rather like those games in which the beginner cannot do right, all his natural reactions being just what he has to cure himself of. He soon cottons on to the view that it is all a matter of very strange and extremely elusive insights: for if philosophy merely confirms his own alleged unsophisticated platitudes, it must be something rather ethereal and very elusive, something or other intangible, that is present in the platitude, when a linguistic philosopher brings it out with repetitions and seemingly irrelevant detail.

Seeking this insight, the eye of faith sooner or later manages to catch it. Or rather not quite catch it, but grasp it sufficiently to provide some reward without actually giving security (security could only be had in a clear and explicit formulation, and that is, by definition, always misleading and a sign of lack of sophistication).

As truth cannot be had directly and explicitly, it can only be had in dark sayings or rather that linguo-philosophic speciality, the inverted dark saying, the opaque light saying, so to speak, the platitude used as an insinuation of deep insights.

It may seem strange that Linguistic Philosophy should be given to dark sayings, but this is so, and is of the essence of the thing. Wittgenstein treated the sense of mystery, and its objects, as natural processes (or by-products of such) in the world, and at the same time treated the natural way of looking at the world as a mystical illumination, something that cannot be said but can only be brought out. He uses all the paraphernalia of oblique and mystical communication on behalf of the natural vision of things, and all the sturdy extravert commonsensicality in the diagnosis and elimination of our older sense of mystery. This mystique of naturalism, fused with a naturalist view of mysticism, is what gives his philosophy its freshness and originality.

These insights of the mystically obvious, rather than of the mystically strange, sooner or later, given good will, produce the feeling of initiation and vision in the neophyte.

18. INSINUATION AND TABOO

This is a special and powerful application of Philosophy by Frisson. It is a very powerful technique.

Its essence is this: to begin with take some philosophic idea, for instance behaviourism, the doctrine that external behaviour or manifestations of feelings are all that inner feelings and thoughts amount to. Now an explicit *doctrine* of this kind is of course outlawed by linguistic philosophy. No practitioner or neophyte would be seen dead holding a doctrine of such generality, of such "septic", "cramp-producing" *intelligible* form. It is just the kind of thing that would ruin one's reputation and mark one indelibly as naïve. It is outlawed because it is para-doxical, it is inspired by some simple model (namely that all feeling-expressions have the role of designating overt behaviour); it is outlawed because it is philosophical and seems to imply that many people are mistaken in their daily beliefs, and so forth: above all, and this is what matters for the present argument, it is soon and powerfully impressed on anyone within the ambiance of Linguistic Philosophy that behaviourism is something unsay-able, technically and socially.

Once this is impressed, however, the technique of philosophis-ing by endless bringing up of examples and by numerous semi-lucid or plain dark arguments is brought into play; all these examples and suggestions and *reductiones ad adsurdum* insinuate one thing, namely the *idea* of behaviourism. They insinuate it but they do not *say* it. Of course this powerful barrage of in-sinuations is not ineffective. The listener or reader soon catches on to the conclusion that is being brought home to him, but he also knows from his previous conditioning that behaviourism is something that he must not say, that to say and believe it ex-plicitly would be the height of naïvety. He is, again, caught rather like an animal in an experimentally induced neurosis, or a man who falls in love because he is in the company of a woman he must not approach. If docile—and a remarkable number of pupils have been docile—he comes to see his own inner be-wilderment as a profound insight, an insight beyond words—which indeed in a sense it is. The required *frisson* has been induced in him and he gratefully sees it as a great illumination. What choice has he? To declare himself so imperceptive as not to see the implications of so many examples? Or, alternatively, to declare himself so naïve philosophically as actually to commit himself to an explicit doctrine? The only course open to him is to pretend to be illuminated, to be "no longer puzzled by the problem", and yet not to have any doctrine in which to express his illumination. The guilt which, with a part of himself, he cannot but feel for taking part in this fraud—though he does not dare declare it such to himself—binds him to his teacher. Perhaps, he feels, the teacher *really* sees the light, not in this rather dubious way in which he knows that he himself *half* sees it; but this hope is also a fear, for if so the teacher may one day discover that he—the pupil—hasn't had the full illumination after all. He has only had an inner fluttering bewilderment, which, in his more optimistic moments, he dares hope is the real thing. The teacher has everything, both ways. He claims to have solved the problem and yet has not chanced his arm by asserting something. He has merely brought in suggestions and examples, and if one day some brave child dares to cry that the Emperor is naked, there is *no* evidence that the teacher has *ever* claimed that the Emperor is clothed. This also is of the essence of Linguistic Philosophy.

19. WHO EVER SAID THIS?

This trick is not a very profound one, but it is one characteristic of certain linguistic philosophers and is amongst the least attractive. It consists in warding off criticisms by exclaiming with an air of seemingly total surprise—"Whoever said this?"—when their own doctrines are specified for criticism. (Note: it is important that he does not say "No one said this", for that would in turn commit him to a position which subsequent bibliographical research would show to be false. No—he merely *asks*, insinuating that no one said it, "Has anyone said it?" This at the very least has a filibuster effect by letting one in for prolonged discussions as to whether precisely the doctrine specified has been asserted in precisely those words by anyone. Even if it has, it is then possible to disown that particular, explicit linguistic philosopher as naïve or inadequately careful.)

A number of observers have shared my impression that however meticulous and careful a formulation of their doctrines is
presented to them, some linguistic philosophers pretend never
to have heard of it. Some achieve an amazing kind of skill in
the use of this device. Macavity is *never* there. Excluding conscious and deliberate dishonesty—how is it that they manage to
convince themselves that all statements of their own position,
notably when specified for purposes of criticism, are incorrect?

There are various answers: for one, the curious belief that the
least and ultimate nuances of expression are of the utmost—and
indeed, exclusive—importance. This seems to me false. Endless meticulousness in expression is important for legal purposes
and perhaps for accountants' purposes, but—as linguistic philosophers should be the first to realise in view of their insistence
that language is not a precise calculus—most ideas are something that we catch on to, and do not depend on the last
little comma and adjective for their communication. A further
reason why they believe that all statements of their own position
are incorrect is of course that, as they believe that they have no
position at all, the holding of positions is the prime philosophic
error. Philosophy records our concepts as embodied in speech,
and perhaps cures certain kinds of mistaken opinions, but it has
no opinions of its own to add. Hence *no* characterisation of their
own position can be correct.

20. OFFENSIVE AND DEFENSIVE POSITIONS

One of the most obvious sociological observations, concerning
movements in general and ideologies in particular, is that they
have to undergo modifications when they are successful. Ideas
and practices suitable for a revolutionary ideology, bent on
capturing positions of power, are not always suitable for the
same group or ideology when these positions are captured. The
responsibilities of power, the vested interests of success, call for
strategies quite different from those that were suitable when
there was still nothing to lose and everything to gain. Linguistic Philosophy had to promise much at the beginning—a radically new and exclusively correct way of doing philosophy, the
"dissolution" of all philosophic problems. Now that the practices are established, most of this risky ballast is being shed: for
although the intention is to give as few hostages to fortune as

possible, to be as modest as possible, to treat the linguistic approach as *given*, and to place the onus of proof on the critic—and, by claiming little, to make it as hard as possible for him to disprove the now diminished claims (which asymptotically approach zero in the case of some linguistic philosophers).

Consider, for instance, the vacillation between claims to determinateness and claims of neutrality. One of the strongest selling points of Linguistic Philosophy, when in the ascendant, was the promise (very commonly made by new philosophies) that at last the true path had been found, and that henceforth, instead of the interminable inconclusiveness of past thought, *determinate* answers (or "dissolutions") would be provided. Lately, however, it has been claimed, in answer to the charge that Linguistic Philosophy prejudges issues by its very method, that this philosophy is a *neutral* tool, that naturalists and transcendentalists, theists and atheists, etc., can all use it. Perhaps: but can the method have the virtues *both* of determinateness and of neutrality?

Or: In its earlier stages, it was claimed to be *revolutionary*; more recently, the stress has been on *continuity* with the past. Novel ideas had to be claimed to justify the introduction of such novel practices: continuity is now claimed mainly in order to avoid the drawing up of balance sheets of how much the revolution has achieved. If it is merely a continuation, it is at least no worse than philosophies which preceded it, it is claimed, and there is no call for abrogating it if it has failed—as it has—to deliver the promised goods.

21. A SENSE OF DECORUM

A particularly important consequence of success and establishment is that Linguistic Philosophy has acquired a fine and powerful sense of decorum. Any fundamental criticisms of it are ruled out as indecorous. . . . (Given the number and strength of all the defensive, evasive, delaying and smoke-screen-emitting defences, it is more than doubtful whether a decorous criticism would be even noticed.) This powerful sense of decorum is curious in a movement descended from the castigation of past thought as *nonsense*, and which itself described past thought as *pathological*.

22. COLLECTIVE SECURITY

The manner in which the whole inter-locking system of ideas, values, practices and assumptions provides support for each of the individual parts—and facility for temporary withdrawal—has been pointed out earlier. It also accounts for their Jack-in-the-box characteristic: any evacuated or modified position is so to speak pushed back to its original significance and extent by the rest of the system, irrespective of nominal qualifications or of the failure to re-affirm that position explicitly.

This accounts for one conspicuous feature of linguo-philosophic theses—*they all seem to say both more and less than they actually say*. Criticise one of them and, if you manage to get a confession that it is a part of the corpus at all, you will find that it evaporates in your hands into something quite innocuous: not merely because it has been qualified and watered down, but also because, in isolation, they very often really do say either very little, or something plainly true.

But at the same time, when in full *use*—amongst the faithful, rather than scrutinised by a critic—how deep and pregnant they are! The reason is, of course, that to anyone familiar with the system of which they form a part, any single constituent conveys the system as a whole, or those parts of it that suit him, and the whole complex of insights, valuations and ways of looking at things it contains. This sense of richness, obtained through a single move or assertion reminding one of a whole system of which it is a part, is something which also falls under the rubric of philosophy-by-frisson.

CHAPTER VII

ASSESSMENT

1. WHAT REMAINS?

THERE IS A SENSE in which, once Linguistic Philosophy is properly understood, further criticism is redundant. To see the particular syndrome of ideas, practices, presuppositions, expectations, values and tricks, and to see their interconnectedness in a kind of extended defensive system, is also to see its circularity and to be free of the temptation to adhere to it. Linguistic Philosophy maintains that to describe and see the mechanics of a problem is to be free from it, and to see the redundancy of attempts to answer it: ironically, just this applies to Linguistic Philosophy itself. Thus the "therapeutic" theory that a full description of the symptoms obviates them—holds in at least one case. Paraphrasing a remark of Karl Kraus about psycho-analysis, Linguistic Philosophy is the disease which it strives to cure.

Whilst it is easy to refute many points within the style of thought we call Linguistic Philosophy—and, indeed, to accept others—it is for various reasons doubtful whether the style as a whole can be refuted effectively in any technical sense. It is apposite at this point to quote an elegant, and true, passage from a linguistic philosopher, Mr. G. J. Warnock *

"... metaphysical systems do not yield, as a rule, to frontal attack. Their odd property of being demonstrable only, so to speak, from within confers on them also a high resistance to attack from outside. The onslaughts of critics to whom, as likely as not, their strange tenets are very nearly unintelligible are apt to seem, to those entrenched inside, misdirected and irrelevant. Such systems are more vulnerable to *ennui* than to disproof. They are citadels, much shot at perhaps but never taken by storm, which are quietly discovered one day to be no longer inhabited."

* *English Philosophy since 1900,* 1958, pp. 10 and 11.

There is no remark in this sociologically very perceptive passage which does not apply to the system of redoubts, underground passages, etc., etc., which constitute Linguistic Philosophy, except that the day of quiet abandon has not yet arrived (in part because no attractive new position, to which the tenants of Linguistic Philosophy could move, has been discovered). But before that day comes, it is perhaps worth having a record of the structure and defensive tactics of it. Once it ceases to be a living movement, its very strange habits and assumptions will become almost unintelligible.

If one gathers in all the particular concessions and modifications that have been made on its behalf, one can see that in a way the outlook has already received ample refutation, even by its own protagonists. It has failed by the pragmatic test of success—is anyone ready to claim that it has solved any major, hitherto intractable philosophic problem? It is no longer claimed to be the only way of looking at the world philosophically. It is no longer held that all extra-scientific and extra-logical problems must be "dissoluble", nor are many now willing to make the prediction that a significant number of problems *will* be dissolved in the appropriate manner. . . .

In *detail*, it is also conceded that arguments from the *de facto* use of words do not solve questions of value, and perhaps it would (and certainly should) be conceded that virtually all philosophic problems fall into this category. (The question is always about the legitimate manner of speaking, not about what we do happen to say. The two questions have only been confused because linguistic philosophers have supposed that the latter is the only possible evidence for the former, and this they have supposed because they thought it was entailed by the denial of an absolute language.)

Taking all these face-savers, tactical retreats, weak reformulations and so on *together*, what is left of the *Revolution in Philosophy* is either nothing at all, or something so feeble, so innocuous, so hedged, eclectic and qualified that one would not have the heart to disagree with it.

But it would be mistaken to infer from all this that a refutation of it is redundant, still less that it has really already been carried out by the protagonists of ex-protagonists of the doctrine itself. It has not. The movement is going strong, even if a little less confident, a little more bored. There is a world of difference between a presentation of a point as a refutation and its presentation as a minor concession or even as a new integral part of the doctrine and a new extension of its insight, even if *logically* it inevitably has the force of a refutation. By means of the Full Circle trick, the defects of Linguistic Philosophy have been generally claimed to its credit. Moreover, the various defects have not been so to speak read simultaneously: thanks to the Indian Rope trick and the polymorphist principle of the need of the piecemeal approach, the numerous defeats have not been allowed to add up, as in fact they do, to a debacle.

Linguistic Philosophy may *formally* allow—or even incorporate—any and all objections which amount to reducing it to an innocuous, all-embracing, naught-denying position, and yet *informally* and effectively it does not amount to such a position. A doctrine may formally allow of facts that are adduced against it as would-be objections; and yet informally, in the whole corpus of what it intimates, indicates, in the visions and activities it encourages, the vistas it opens—in all these, it may do its utmost to obscure them. In philosophy, and perhaps in other fields, such informal aspects of a doctrine are often far more important than the formal definition.

2. THE CIRCULARITY

Linguistic Philosophy, as an *activity* (of observing "how we use words"), whether therapeutic or pure, contains doctrines and criteria in a camouflaged form. It insinuates and presupposes those doctrines and the values on which the criteria are based. This is bad for a number of reasons: it makes against critical examination of those values and ideas and against critical examination in general; it inhibits thought and prejudges issues.

To "observe how we use words" is to make statements, in ordinary language, about the role, function, effects and context of expressions. But in doing this, the concepts and presuppositions of that ordinary language are taken for granted and insinuated as the only possible view. We smile at scholasticism which *had* to prove what Revelation supplied anyway. But Linguistic Philosophy *has* to prove, "make acceptable", what common sense or linguistic custom provide anyway. (Linguistic Philosophy is scholastic in this sense as well as in its pedantry.)

Given this, can Linguistic Philosophy be anything else than

a roundabout way of insinuating and presupposing the current ordinary view—and, in those many cases where the ordinary view is ambiguous, open, and in some historic mid-stream, can it be anything other than a technique, a kind of pseudo-spiritual exercise, for confirming oneself in the view one fancies, whilst giving oneself a spurious impression that one has found an additional argument, and indeed a most conclusive one, for that view? Metaphysics is said to have been about words when it claimed to be about things. Linguistic Philosophy is about the world when it claims to be about language. It starts from a new way of looking at things—through language seen as *doings in the ordinary world as ordinarily conceived*—and it implicitly returns to that world. One can only get out of a method what one puts into it: and what is put into the linguo-philosophic practices—and how—is by now obvious.

Which problems are odd and philosophical, which locutions need to be accounted for, what kind of accounts are allowed to stand as adequate? Linguistic philosophers talk as if the marks of oddity, puzzlesomeness, and clarity were obvious. But obviousness is not obvious. In fact, people in the main find odd and clear what they have been trained to regard as such, but the current Linguistic Philosophy, whilst claiming to make the puzzling clear, in fact consists of a training which teaches one to regard all ordinary locutions as *eo ipso* clear, and all philosophical ones as *ex officio* odd.

All this is doubly wrong: first, because the soundness of the ordinary view is an idea smuggled in by a trick, rather than fairly asserted and defended, and, secondly, because there is nothing sacrosanct or necessarily valuable about the ordinary view. Perhaps I should add that I have no temperamental or other hostility to either naturalism or common sense, as such. Metaphysical reverie plays a small part in my life. But I like my naturalism (or any other doctrine, for that matter) *clean*, rather than insinuated by confused and pretentious tricks setting up to be the last word on clarity and honesty.

It may be admitted that the third-person, naturalistic or conceptually-conservative view is *a* view of the world, but it is not one that has any pre-eminence or particular claims. It is true that certain things may be said in favour of ordinary language. It would not be in use, and it would not have survived were it wholly without merit. But this argument, as in politics where it is often used to buttress conservatism, proves fairly little. Very silly and undesirable things often survive, and neither society nor language is such a tightly integrated whole as would disastrously suffer from alteration of some one part. The feebleness of the argument from longevity is particularly marked in times when rapid and fundamental change is taking place anyway, when past fitness to survive may even be an index of present *un*fitness—and we are conceptually, as well as in other ways, living in such a time.

The second thing that may be said in favour of according special status to ordinary speech as the fundamental form of our thought is that after all we always have to start from it. Our first formulations of our problems have to be in terms of it. This again shows far less than is often supposed. Even if we have to employ ordinary concepts in our formulation of new criteria or notions, there is nothing to stop us, once the new notions are in use, from rejecting the old ones which had helped us to construct them. *That* kind of ladder can be, and often is, thrown away once we have climbed up it.

It is in any case false to suppose that new ideas—and their expression—always arrive by so to speak climbing on the backs of previously established ones. What characteristically happens is that a new thought, a new way of looking at things, a new style of expression starts its life as an inchoate, semi-articulate feeling, proceeds as a new manner of expression whose relation to the old is unclear and turbulent, and only has its relation to the old clarified and stabilised some considerable time after its use has become well established. It cannot at once—or ever— be shown to have been "given sense" by the old criterion! The exploration of the "logical liaison" or "logical geography" of a concept, old *or* new, is a long and difficult business—as linguistic philosophers are themselves the first to point out—and if it had to be done *first*, we should very seldom have any conceptual innovations. New-born concepts are not in general strong enough to stand it. And yet, linguistic philosophers do claim that such stringent tests must come first, when they maintain, as Professor Austin does, that linguistic analysis is the begin-*all* of philosophy.

3. TRAVESTY OF THOUGHT

Another way of formulating the criticism of Linguistic Philosophy is to say that it travesties thought, and above all that it fails to cope with all manifestations of creativity and originality in it. The picture which is inescapably and pervasively suggested by the procedures and ideas of Linguistic Philosophy is that thought is a move *within* a language game—whilst thinking about and outside such "games" is intellectually pathological, or at best very exceptional. This is wholly false. Important ideas and intellectual progress consist generally not of making a clever move *within* an existing game, but of a change in a "game"—that is, a system of concepts—a change which improves it. The static picture is not even true about the daily use of speech, in which new locutions are appreciated, recognised and understood.

Thus what Linguistic Philosophy considers to be the essence of the pathology of thought—namely, shifts in meaning—is, on the contrary, the essence of genuine thought. Moves within established games are the dead, ritualised aspect of thinking. It is of course necessary that there should be such frameworks, but *thinking* of the important kind is the alteration or comparative assessment of them, not the carrying out of the prescribed ritual inside. Linguistic Philosophy ignores and denies this.* Indeed it has an inverted vision which treats genuine thought as disease, and dead thought as the paradigm of health.

The general public often supposes that Linguistic Philosophy is an attack on *metaphysics*. But metaphysics is a red herring. In reality, it is simply an attack on *thought*.

It is worth noting an important but misplaced insight of Linguistic Philosophy, especially as expounded by Wittgenstein and John Wisdom, namely the importance of the emotional concomitants of thought. These philosophers have stressed, as previous ones have not, the fact that some of our thinking is accompanied by things such as perplexity, a feeling of cramp, that certain positions are asserted only with bravado, etc. Earlier philosophers would have supposed such psychological back-

---

* Cf. G. Warnock, *Berkeley*, 1953, pp. 240 and 241. Warnock argues, in effect, that statements within a system of concepts may be true or false, but that one cannot compare one way of speaking with another and say it is truer. This error is at the root of Linguistic Philosophy.

ground to be logically irrelevant. Linguistic philosophers are right in noting and stressing it, but quite wrong in diagnosing its source. They suppose it arises from the fact that in dealing with *philosophic* issues, in which our thought has unhinged itself from the customary rules and habits of the language games of which the relevant concepts are part, and that this is responsible for the perplexity accompanying the question, the bravado accompanying its answer, etc.: they have supposed that these emotions are somehow essentially connected with philosophical (formal, or confused) thinking.

On the contrary, it seems to me that such psychological stresses accompany all or most important thought, and indeed that all or most important thought is a matter of groping amongst "language games", ways of thinking and looking at things, and not a matter of making moves within them. Thinking is seldom a matter of proceeding from premiss or evidence to conclusion but from a sense of bewilderment or confusion to the establishment of some kind of order. What linguistic philosophers suppose to be characteristic, logically and emotionally, of categorial confusion is in fact the general characteristic of thought, other than dead, repetitive, ritualised "thinking", which we hardly call by that name.

There is another respect in which Linguistic Philosophy is a total and harmful travesty of thought and of the manner in which thought progresses: through its *Polymorphism*. The exaggeration of the truth that things, and in particular types of use of expressions, cannot all be alike leads to another mistake, and one more serious. It leads to the neglect and underrating of the extent to which thought *is* the introduction of homogeneity and order into things previously diverse. To understand something is, in general, to see it as a case of something more general. Both intellectual and moral progress depends on the discovery and employment of conceptual devices that *unify*. "Only connect." Wittgenstein's belief that it is more important to see differences than resemblances, that we are more often misled by exaggerating the similarity rather than by overestimating the differences between things, is wrong and harmful. His attitude and philosophy might be summed up by the inversion of E. M. Forster's dictum: in effect, Wittgenstein recommended "Only disconnect". This would lead to the paralysis both of science and of moral progress, which consists, essentially, of unification, of the elimination of arbitrary and unnecessary distinctions. (This cult of diversity and idiosyncrasy is particularly harmful when combined with the uncritical, substantive use of linguistic functionalism, the view that there is a strong presumption in favour of the usefulness of any existing ways of speaking, distinguishing, etc. This then amounts simply to an apotheosis of the *status quo*, of existing prejudice.)

The anti-scientific, polymorphic activity invented by Linguistic Philosophy is sometimes defended by the contention that it only applies to philosophy, not to science: to the second-order study of our concepts, not to the first-order study of things.* The need for abstraction, generality and ideas is then conceded for *science* and the study of the world, but it is maintained that, in studying our own concepts, either the nature of the material or the purposes and angle of the enquiry require a non-abstractive, minute, case-by-case investigation. (The *special* case for Polymorphism in philosophy can of course be reinforced further if one still believes that philosophy is therapeutic. Therapy is by its very nature geared to the individual case.)

But this defence depends for its validity on the first-order/second-order distinction and the idea that quite different types of thinking are relevant to each. But this is a fallacy, deriving from the notion that ordinary, substantive thinking is just the carrying out of moves *within* a conceptual system, quite unlike the investigation *of* a conceptual system and that the system can be simply "exhibited". But this is doubly wrong: thinking about things is not just the use of a pre-existent system of concepts. And it is equally absurd to imagine the second-order knowledge of our concepts, our language games, as free from the normal conditions of knowledge—namely the reliance on abstract concepts, with their systems of which they form integral parts. Wittgenstein and linguistic philosophers talk as if we could *touch*, know by a kind of direct contact, by exemplification, the uses of language and their contexts: and they seem to suppose this can be done, because one can *exhibit* them, and that this exhibiting, the adducing of examples, provides knowledge without the intermediary of a conceptual frame. . . . But this is a myth: *examples insinuate*, and the insinuated generalisation is there, even if not articulated. One cannot describe

* For instance, this is suggested by Professor S. Toulmin in his Inaugural Lecture published in *The Universities Quarterly*, August 1957.

the use-in-the-world of an expression, without having a picture of that world first.

This is, in fact, one of the ways of seeing the essence, and the fallaciousness, of Linguistic Philosophy: it has invented a special realm of "language uses", a realm free from science and its methods, safe for the philosopher, secure and stable, without the embarrassment of being, like the earlier retreats of philosophers in face of the advance of science, transcendental. . . . But, absurdly, one has to claim, by implication, to know this realm in a curious ideographic way, by exhibiting, cottoning-on, insights . . . without anything tangible, sayable, ever emerging. This myth would be convenient if it were true.

4. FAILURE OF NORMATIVENESS

The educated reader who has no specialised training and initiation into modern philosophy tends generally to have the following reaction when faced with Linguistic Philosophy: this kind of stuff, apart from being extremely dull, fails to provide any illumination or guidance. What is conspicuous about Linguistic Philosophy is its abdication of any kind of *normative* role, both in its practice and in its programmatic announcements.

The uninitiated outsider feels this, but, unfamiliar with the complicated lay-out of the immense defensive works of Linguistic Philosophy, he is unable to make the charge *stick*. He is assured that he is requesting something which philosophy does not, cannot, or should not provide; that his requests for illumination and guidance are grounded in confusion and really call for cure and not gratification, and so forth.

It is the purpose of this section to show that the outside critic is *right*.

To do this, one must first of all indulge in a sketch of the place of normativeness, of guidance and evaluation, in philosophy in general.

A certain rough law holds for the history of philosophy, namely: P equals $1/p$, where P is Platonism and p psychologism. By Platonism I mean here the setting up of ideals, claimed to be demonstratively or rationally known and independently existing. By psychologism I mean the causal, psychological account of cognitive, evaluative processes as natural processes, seen in the Third Person. In other words, the law says: the more we give natural accounts of knowledge, valuation and so on, the less we can at the same time claim independent validity for the criteria of things such as truth, rightness, beauty; and, conversely, the more we attempt to see those criteria as *valid*, the less we can look at their application as natural, contingent processes which just *happen* to be as they are.

Platonistic theories are hard to believe: psychologistic ones make it hard to believe in what we need to believe, namely our values. Thus one can easily see why the reciprocal law must hold.

Philosophers generally face the dilemma of either giving an account which *validates* some value or criterion or practice (but to do so they have to invoke something more than the activity in which that value is applied), or, alternatively, choosing in a hard-headed way simply to give an account of that activity without going beyond it, in which case they do not strain one's credulity, but at the same time fail to provide reasons why that activity should be pursued in its usual way, or at all.

A clear and simple example of this dilemma is, for instance, the dispute between Natural Law theory and legal positivism. Natural Law theory provides a moral validation for actual law, but it is hard to believe. Legal positivism restricts the study of law to law as actually enforced, but it fails to give any justification for changing or, occasionally, resisting positive law, or indeed any explanation of how what we call improvements in a legal system could be other than arbitrary.

The dilemma is harder to face with regard to some kinds of thinking than others. For instance, there are descriptive, or rather Third Person, accounts of deductive thinking which at the same time give a justification of it: by saying that deduction is, in essence, mere repetition which does not *add* anything, it also explains why it is valid. The validation of deductive thought (if this kind of theory is true) either involves no normative thinking of a Platonic kind, or only the invocation of a very weak and hardly controversial additional premiss, namely that repetition leads to a truth if the repeated statement is true.

On the other hand, the dilemma becomes much sharper with regard to non-deductive scientific inference, and is probably at its sharpest in the field of ethics. It is the essence of Linguistic Philosophy that it considers itself to be the overcoming of the dilemma described. It sees itself as the termination of what one might call evaluative epistemology, of asking whether we "really know", of discussions which assess whether we are entitled to the general categories of knowledge or discrimination (scientific, religious, ethical and so forth) that we, or some of us, normally claim. It prides itself on neither trespassing on the scientist's realm and investigating the empirically observable process involved in knowing, valuing, etc., nor inventing special realms in order to validate or support those activities.

It holds that the switch in the angle of vision, the switch to a Third Person observation of the actual interrelation of *expressions*, obviates both the need and the temptation to indulge in those activities.

But of course this alleged overcoming of the need to validate is merely a camouflaged validation. Linguistic Philosophy is simply the systematic indulgence in the generalised form of the Naturalistic Fallacy, the inference from the *actual* to the *valid*.

The standards actually operative in the use of language are dressed up, or rather smuggled in, as *the* only possible answers,* as validated or rather not requiring validation, simply in virtue of being used. Their criticism, or attempts at their assessment, is ruled out either as meaningless and metaphysical (because, allegedly, inspired by some notion of an absolute language), or as extraphilosophical, or as something to be postponed *sine die* until the interminable preliminary word-picking is done. . . . Again, we can observe the drift from an interesting thesis (which *did* commit the fallacy) to a re-definition of philosophy, which avoids error but is simply trivial.

Epistemology, the questioning whether and what and how

---

* The smuggling in of values and criteria can be done in (at least) two ways: the more customary one is through "examining how words *are* used" and ruling out any standard by which that use could be judged as a "metaphysical model". But it can also be done directly from the Activity theory of mind, as follows: "knowing how" precedes "knowing that", yet all criteria are of course formulated—*ex hypothesi*—as pieces of explicit "knowing that". But "knowing that" being derivative from the activity, from "knowing how", it cannot be used to judge it. Judgment is irrelevant, and the term "validity" itself only cherished by confused philosophers.

This way was tried by Professor Ryle in his Presidential Address to the Aristotelian Society, 1945.

we know, may perhaps in the past have been formulated in misleading pseudo-psychological language, but it was, in substance,
an attempt to do something that has to be done, namely, evaluate and delimit our activities.

Linguistic Philosophy does not overcome such epistemology,
it prejudges it and substitutes a trivial enquiry for it. It does not
escape the Inverse law, it is merely subject, without noticing it,
to a special version of it, namely:

L equals $1/l$ where L stands for language (or features of it)
interpreted as necessary and l for language or features of it seen
as contingent.

Linguisticism is no better than psychologism.*

Crude Linguistic Philosophy is simply the expansion of l to
such an extent that capital L in effect disappears. Everything
becomes absorbed into how we in fact happen to use language.
This is merely another way of saying that Linguistic Philosophy
is but a camouflaged naturalism. The camouflage is provided
by the insistence on the fact that after all language is a natural
process (which in some sense indeed it is) and that this is the
correct way of looking at it and at philosophical problems.
Alternatively, the insistence appears as a denial of any possible
standards of appeal outside *de facto* language as employed, for
"words have the meanings we give them", it makes no sense to
ask what they *really* mean.† One might indeed call Linguistic
Philosophy "linguistic positivism", not so much on the analogy
with Logical Positivism as with *legal* positivism, the denial of
a perfect language resembling the denial of Natural Law.‡

* Mr. W. Kneale makes a similar point. Cf. his contribution to *The
Revolution in Philosophy*, p. 31. Though a contributor to that volume, which
is mainly a linguo-philosophic tract, Mr. Kneale is *not* a linguistic philosopher. Wittgenstein himself foresaw the danger of linguisticism (cf.
Tractatus 4.1121), though he did not avert it.

† Cf. Mr. R. Rhees' Preface to *The Blue and Brown Books*, p. xi.

‡ The *Tractatus* was a system where L was so large as to make l disappear
(*apparently* contingent language was but a cloak for thought which could not
but be formally correct; *in a sense*, Russell was wrong in interpreting the
book as an account of an *ideal*, perfect language. It was an account of an
ideal which actually existed hidden under actual language.) There was no
invalid thinking (5.4731 and 5.4732), all actual thinking being either the
camouflage of a kind of transcendental thinking, or *non*-thinking, *non*sense.
If one thought confusedly, one was *not*-thinking.

This is like saying that there are *no* bad sculptures: only good ones with
redundant bits stuck on. (The good ones are as it were latent underneath.

There are, of course, the non-crude versions of Linguistic Philosophy. They correspond in terms of our present scheme, to the situation arising if capital L is allowed to have a significant value. There are arguments within Linguistic Philosophy interpretable as claims that language *must* be of a certain kind. This type of argument can no longer be assimilated to the crude version of the philosophy.*

But these ideas, whatever they are, which are to hold *necessarily* about language, can hardly be simply ideas "about language". The whole appeal of Linguistic Philosophy, in removing mystery and claiming to throw light on hitherto dark places, lay in claiming that philosophy was "about language", in some sense of "about language" which would have removed philosophy from intangible, mental, transcendental, atomic or other realms, and made its field instead something that can be observed and straightforwardly investigated.

The truth is, of course, that these subtle, sophisticated, Triple Star versions of Linguistic Philosophy are parasitic on the crude kind. They survive thanks to the failure to distinguish the two species, and flourish in the ambiguity thus generated.

5. THE PARADOX OF PASSIVITY

The absurdity and question-begging nature of the neutralist, so to speak *passivist*, position of Linguistic Philosophy can be brought out by carefully considering the slogan, "Philosophy leaves everything as it is." (The crucial question will be—just what is *everything*?)

This claim corresponds in the pre-linguistic formulations to the thesis that consciousness does not affect its objects even when those objects are themselves aspects of consciousness. In this form, the "realist" insight is no longer so obvious or compulsive! On the contrary, it is notorious that self-consciousness generally modifies the self-conscious mind.

. . .) The specification of the latent forms "underneath" can very naturally be described as a specification of the *ideal* sculpture (or language), as Russell in effect did. This was less a misinterpretation than a more natural formulation.

The language described in the *Tractatus* was in effect to ordinary language as Natural Law was once meant to be to positive law.

* Cf. our discussion above, of Triple Star Linguistic Philosophy.

But we need not pursue that theme at the elusive level of "consciousness", mind, etc. We can instead reconsider it in its more concrete, tangible, linguistic formulation. It is far from obvious—indeed, it is extremely unlikely—that awareness of the working of a language game, of a type of discourse, does not affect it. For one thing, such an awareness makes it possible to alter the game, and by high-lighting such defects as it may have, may make changes both feasible and attractive. (This much might perhaps be squared with the passivism of Linguistic Philosophy by the trivial redefinition, which would restrict the appellation "philosophy" to the clarification of the game, and rule out its reform as extra-philosophical. This is the standard *later*, watered-down form of Linguistic Philosophy: the original form insisted that reform was impossible or redundant.)

But more than this: there are many language games which become unworkable when properly understood: where self-consciousness not merely does not "leave everything as it is" but simply *necessitates* change. Many "conceptual systems", in primitive societies and in advanced ones, contain confusions and absurdities which are essential for their functioning. To lay them bare is to make such a framework unworkable.

Linguistic Philosophy is absurd in that by implication it rules out this possibility—the existence of a socially, conceptually pervasive error, of myth. Its passivism—its acceptance of all operative language games as *ipso facto* valid, and as the ultimate authority on the meaningfulness of the concepts, the moves, occurring within them—commits Linguistic Philosophy to an absurd substantive sociological thesis: namely, that no society has ever had a Golden Myth, or an Evil one for that matter.*

* Professor Austin, however, notices this ("Presidential Address to the Aristotelian Society", 1956/57, p. 11): ". . . superstition and error and fantasy of all kinds do become incorporated in ordinary language and even sometimes stand up to the survival test (only, when they do, why should we not detect it?)" This calls for some comment.

(1) How does this possibility square with the paean to ordinary language earlier (p. 8) ". . . our common stock of words embodies all the distinctions men have found worth drawing . . . these surely are . . . more sound . . . than any you or I . . . think up."

(2) "*even sometimes* stand up to the survival test"? Is it so rare?

(3) "Why should we not detect it?" We can hardly detect it if, for examining those locutions, we are only allowed to use some others from the same stables, and if what counts as "clarification" is an account of the relation of some of them to others in the same system. And is it so easy to

The supposition of passivity and neutrality is wrongly taken over from the earlier, Logical Atomist search for very general and totally all-embracing logical *forms* (neutral *vis-à-vis* content). But the dogma of the *apartheid* of form and content, of the conceptual and substantive issues in given fields is mistaken. (Anyone involved in actually working in a substantive field knows that the main issues often are conceptual ones. It made sense to separate them, perhaps, for the *very* abstract "formal concepts" of the *Tractatus*: it makes no sense now.)

But let us return to the slogan, "Philosophy leaves everything as it is." As indicated, its interpretation depends on what is covered by "everything".

Does "everything" include the language game known as *philosophy*? If "everything" means *everything*, then it should: and then, indeed, in a most left-handed sense, Linguistic Philosophy leaves everything, *everything* as it is, including past philosophy: in which case we might as well get on with past philosophy (which has been left "as it is") and happily disregard anything so totally inert, totally, generally and indiscriminately passive— on its own account—as Linguistic Philosophy.*

Alternatively, "everything" does not mean *quite* everything. It excludes (old) philosophy, the disease of language. But how is one to identify "philosophical", diseased uses of language, uses without a use? That they *call* themselves "philosophical" obviously is not sufficient—not all philosophical paradoxes are prefaced by a warning that they are philosophical, and some work which *is* so prefaced may be good Wittgensteinian philosophy before its time. The answers that are given to this question—that expressions are in order if they "have a use", etc., etc., etc., are of course circular: a vision of the world is incap-

---

detect superstition, error and fantasy? This would be good news if true, but it cannot be proven so easily. In fact, being false, it cannot be proven at all.

At least one linguistic philosopher has in fact extracted this substantive sociological conclusion from his own premisses, in the form that there is no inter-action between people's concepts, or views of concepts, and their religious behaviour. Honestly noting this odd consequence, he made somewhat unconvincing attempts at evading it. Cf. Mr. A. Quinton's remarks in "Philosophy and Belief" in *The Twentieth Century*, June 1955, p. 519.

* A similar point was forcefully made against the attempt to apply Wittgensteinian ideas to the philosophy of science by Dr. J. Agassi in a paper delivered to the Philosophy of Science Conference held at Oxford in September 1958. Cf. *The British Journal for the Philosophy of Science*, 1959.

sulated in the criteria of what it is to "have a use", or what kind
of vocabulary is permissible in describing "uses", and so on.

The type of criterion that is tacitly used has been described
earlier. Let it be added that the precise criterion that is
smuggled in and insinuated may and does vary from one linguistic philosopher to another. One of them may class religious
claims amongst those mis-uses of language which are pathological and which are *not* "left as they are", but shown to be
useless; * others, just as plausibly, and basing themselves on the
widespread "use" of religious utterances, include them amongst
the many natural categories of species of employment of language which *are* "left as they are", and only demolish rationalis-
tic attempts at criticising religion.† The situation is completely
indeterminate. The only rational approach is to discuss what
kinds of uses are legitimate, and this kind of general philosophy
which judges usages rather than submitting to them, is precisely
the kind of thing that Linguistic Philosophy prides itself on
supplanting and outlawing.

In brief: if "everything" does not mean *everything*, Linguistic
Philosophy must abandon its self-ascribed pedestal of neutrality,
and condescend to argue in defence of its tacit and insinuated
criteria of linguistic health and disease. It would then become
interesting—and incidentally cease to have the characteristics
which define "Linguistic Philosophy" as it now is.

But if "everything" *does* mean *everything* (which in practice it
seldom does), then Linguistic Philosophy really does leave everything as it is, and is of no interest whatever. It does fall back on
this position, which amounts to saying nothing whatever, when
under pressure. That this is one of its possible interpretations
helps to account for its compulsiveness, the fact that its devotees
feel irresistibly that it *must* be true. On this interpretation, indeed it must. Paraphrasing an early aphorism of Wittgenstein:
it is true because it says nothing.

* This is, I think, the attitude of Professor A. G. N. Flew to some theological doctrines, especially those which attempt to square the doctrine of
divine benevolence with the many obvious features of this world.

† Cf. Mr. A. Quinton's remarks in "Philosophy and Belief", *The Twentieth Century*, June 1955.

6. THE DIMENSIONS OF CAUTION

One of the characteristic *late* defences of the linguistic procedures, an alternative to the therapeutic promise or to the insistence that this alone is an intelligible way of looking at things, is in terms of *caution*. The attitude is something like this: we claim nothing about the world or language or philosophy, and we promise nothing. All we do is to proceed very very carefully, with just a touch of the suggestion that both the problems and the solutions of past philosophers arose only through rashness and carelessness. (In as far as there is a suggestion that carefulness will obviate them, this approach has an obvious affinity with the promise of therapy: but no cure is guaranteed.)

This attitude generates its own atmosphere and set of pervasive values; that it is apparently far, *far* better never to have loved at all, than ever to have loved and lost. It is a rather unattractive atmosphere: just as some societies or milieux become sartorially obsessional and ritualistic, with individual damnation following the least lapse from the norm, but without positive ways to salvation—similarly, this world is one where no positive achievement can make a man, but a slip can unmake him. This curious but characteristic atmosphere is in part the corollary of the view that philosophy cannot have anything positive to say of the world. In part it is perhaps an inherent feature of the rather orchidical and precious milieu in which Linguistic Philosophy came to flourish after the war. This is really quite independent of Wittgensteinian ideas, and perhaps merely found a rationalisation in them.

The cult of caution is either a lukewarm version of the therapeutic theory, or a facet of a rather curious theory of knowledge. The merits of the former have already been discussed. The second alternative manifests itself in slogans such as the careful, indeed minute examination of our concepts—by means of a study of their verbal manifestation—as the *begin-all* though not necessarily the end-all, of philosophy. This idea is supported by the seemingly plausible contention that questions can be answered better if clearly stated. Certainly: but much depends on the local criteria of clarity, and on what counts as a termination of the process of clarification.

The effect of the application of the Austinian *begin-all* theory would be to destroy all new ideas. It strives to *look* like a severe but just examination that *would* let through a truly deserving candidate: but the rules are such that no-one *could* qualify. Its idea of a truly deserving candidate to conceptual innovation is one that combines incompatible characteristics— novelty *and* intelligibility in terms of the previously customary notions. . . .

The point can be illustrated from the emergence of Linguistic Philosophy itself. Its protagonists wish to see it judged on its qualified present formulation, not the exaggerated claims which clothed the first statements of it—such as the promised cure of all philosophic puzzlement, or the systematic indulgence in "solving" problems of value by reference to the actual use of words. . . . But the begin-all technique does not allow any new set of ideas the time to shake itself down, to trim itself: it kills them at the start. (One leading figure is most plausibly credited with the remark that he conceives his task as seeing to it that young men do not have any ideas.)

Caution is not new: Descartes was being cautious when he tried to doubt everything, so as not to be caught by any error. The new and interesting thing about the contemporary cult of caution is that it has performed a kind of half-turn on Cartesian caution. The modern cagey philosopher would consider *doubting everything* to be the height of *un*-caution—for it presupposes that it makes sense to doubt everything, to suppose that all ideas are false. But this is a very strong assumption!—so the argument runs. In other words, the new doubt is directed towards suppositions of significance and not suppositions of truth. (The meaningfulness of a doubt, and not the truth of a belief, is questioned.) It finds its security not in total disbelief but in refusing to budge from normal assumptions. Its security and ultimate bed-rock is not scepticism, but ordinary discourse, and from this it will depart only when each departure is fully guaranteed to remain meaningful. (In other words, never, or only in trivial cases.)

It was indeed a weakness of Cartesian doubt that in doubting the truth of everything, it would not doubt the *significance* of seemingly meaningful suppositions. The corresponding weakness of the linguo-philosophic attitude is that, in displaying the utmost caginess towards any claims of meaningfulness outside utterances hallowed by use, it fails to be sceptical about the truth of the presuppositions of ordinary discourse, and indeed

underwrites them in a curious kind of way (by outlawing as
meaningless all general doubt about them). Whilst it is an
advance to become sophisticated and critical of claims to meaning as well as of claims to truth, this critical attitude in one direction should not be a cloak for dogmatism in another. The new
style of caution is liable to be but a camouflaged credulity. And,
as Thurber says, there is no safety in numbers or in anything
else—certainly not in sticking to usage.

7. THE DIMENSIONS OF EMPIRICISM

A similar ambiguity to that found within the notion of
"caution" can also be found within "empiricism". Once again,
the key idea of Linguistic Philosophy can be conveyed in terms
of the shift from one aspect of it to another. Is Linguistic Philosophy a form of Empiricism?—one may ask. One insistent
answer is *Yes*—for does it not consist in looking at language as
it is, rather than deducing what it is from what it is mistakenly
supposed it must be on the strength of some *a priori* model?

But as insistently comes the answer *No*—for is not the chief
achievement of Linguistic Philosophy the overcoming of the
empiricist world-picture which derives everything from bits of
sensing? *

Each answer is correct in its appropriate context. The interesting thing is to observe how those two contexts are related.

Linguistic Philosophy consists in seeing language as it is. as
employed, in action and not forced into the mould of a preconceived schema deduced from assumptions about how meaning is possible: but to see it in this way, one has to take for
granted the world *in* which the activities, the contexts, the concrete doings and purposes which *are* language are to be found.
In other words, an empirical approach to language presupposes an un-empirical, uncritical approach to the world.

Conversely, an empiricist (old sense) critique of our vision of
the *world*, cannot employ and accept the whole of our existing
inherited vocabulary, for of course that vocabulary incorporates
all those possible prejudices that are to be subjected to criticism.
Note that empiricism (old sense), the historically older form,
has played an immense and, on the whole, beneficent role in
the history of thought, in sifting out usable from vacuous or

* Cf. A. MacIntyre, *Universities and Left Review*, Summer 1958.

redundant concepts. Its beneficent impact has ranged from politics to physics, and the valuable work done by it is presumably not ended. Admittedly its application is no simple matter, and there are great difficulties connected with its correct formulation.

Linguistic Philosophy is only "empirical" in another sense. Its empiricism has achieved nothing except the eradication of one or two misunderstandings—the view that there is a rigid logical skeleton underlying our discourse, and the theory that our knowledge is literally built up from little atoms. How many people have seriously suffered from these misunderstandings? For those who have, the cure is now available. And for this achievement, the price is the abandonment of empiricism proper!

8. LINGUISTIC PHILOSOPHY AS AN ORIENTATION AND A STYLE OF THOUGHT

The preceding sections have concerned themselves with the defects of Linguistic Philosophy, taken seriously and literally as a doctrine. The most important criticisms that can be made of it however are perhaps not the careful ones directed at the formulated doctrine, but, on the contrary, those directed at the defects of Linguistic Philosophy seen as an outlook, a style of thought and argument, an orientation.

The reason why the so to speak informal defects are very important is that, after all, the majority of people who come into contact with philosophy are not professional teachers of the subject. Such people are then influenced by the general ethos of the teaching, rather than by nuances and subtleties within it. This shows that the general, informal impression would be of importance, *even if* it were really different from the fuller, esoteric understanding—which, in fact, it is *not*. And remember the double bluff: Linguistic Philosophy looks like saying that the world is a very ordinary place, as seen on a very dull morning—all else is confusion. A fuller understanding of Linguistic Philosophy shows that this is indeed just what it *does* say.

The worst harm it does is in discouraging thought by promising that it will be dull, must be dull, unless confused and "paradoxical". It has managed to create an intellectual atmosphere where this is more or less taken for granted.

The central objection to Linguistic Philosophy lies perhaps in the vistas and ranges of interest which it suggests (and make no mistake about it, anything outside them is in effect treated as *passé*, and fit only for the intellectually second-rate). Its range in effect excludes almost everything that is of genuine interest and that properly should be the starting-point of thought: science, and the social and intellectual transformation which humanity is undergoing. (Preoccupation with these is treated with derision, as a pathetic survival from the period prior to the professionalisation of philosophy. . . .) In brief, the triviality of Linguistic Philosophy resides not merely in what it does, but in what it discourages. It opens up the blind alleys of verbal "therapy", and tends to close all others.

The origins of the Higher Triviality lie in Wittgenstein's preoccupation with a range of problems which were, though perhaps comparatively narrow, by no means trivial: the nature of mathematics and language. But his ineffable or polymorphic ultimate answers to these problems, whilst themselves again not trivial, implied that only certain trivial activities were possible in philosophy. The generalisation of Wittgenstein's solutions and their unhinging from his particular problems are what account for the current practices. Even here, not all the initial questions and answers were trivial. (The relation of mind to body clearly is not.) It was the strange answers, methods and presuppositions connected with the initial questions which led to regions where both question and answer *are* trivial. The vistas are now such that no significant question could emerge—and, if it did, the methods would prevent a significant answer.

To paraphrase an old joke, Linguistic Philosophy allows thought to run the gamut of experiences from A to B; either ineffable mysticism, or dreary exegesis of the nuances of usage.

9. A COLLECTOR'S PIECE

It is sometimes claimed on behalf of Linguistic Philosophy, and in particular of its Wittgensteinian form, that its achievement is the introduction of a philosophically interesting new way of looking at things. This claim is made even by those who are not committed to the view that it is the only or best way of looking at them.*

* Cf. D. Pole, *The Later Philosophy of Wittgenstein*, London 1958, p. 79.

This claim is perhaps valid. The question arises—is this new vision in the front rank amongst philosophies? I think not. Philosophies such as Absolute Idealism or Logical Positivism proper are in that category, or, rather, they are local-temporary versions of what are perhaps archetypal attitudes of the human spirit. The idea that all things are connected and form a Whole, and that to understand things is to see them as partial aspects of that Whole—it seems to me inconceivable that men should *think* without some of them making this the centre of their thought. Similarly, the view that anything we claim to know must be either something that we have experienced or something that we have ourselves made up, is again an idea that must ever remain a possible starting point for the evaluation of human knowledge. (*Au fond*, Logical Positivism maintains that there are two activities by means of which anything is classed as true—verification and convention—and from the nature of these activities, something can be concluded formally about that which is known.)

Linguistic Philosophy is not in the same class. Its emergence, its compulsiveness, its power to seem a great illumination, to appear to throw light on what had hitherto been obscure—all this depends on too complex a set of conditions, which are unlikely to be repeated frequently in the history of thought. Its emergence and success presupposes too many factors: an epistemological orientation in philosophy; a predisposition to see problems in terms of logic and language; an exclusion of transcendental possibilities; a conservative and formalist spirit amongst philosophers, springing from a deep alienation from substantive and committed thinking; an organisation and ethos in teaching institutions favouring a lack of historical and social awareness;* the existence in sufficient numbers of philosophers, favourable to scholastic, minute and idiographic studies. These factors—plus, of course, the kind of spark, crystallisation, provided by Wittgenstein—were all required before the great linguistic illumination could emerge, and be diffused and accepted.

* For examples of the linguo-philosophic picture of the historic role of thought, see J. Wisdom's review of Bertrand Russell's *History of Western Philosophy* (republished in J. Wisdom's *Philosophy and Psycho-Analysis*) or Mr. A. Quinton's remarks in *The Twentieth Century*, June 1955, or Professor Austin's view on what alternatives exist to his method, in his Presidential Address to the Aristotelian Society.

It is unlikely that, in finite time, this propitious concatenation of circumstances will repeat itself. (Although, once successful, it is liable to be emulated in quite different milieus, simply in virtue of having been successful in a prestigious centre.)

Each of its ingredients has been here before: the Heraclitean insistence on diversity and the inapplicability of generalisations, the cult of common sense, the a-historism, the doctrine of the functional adjustment of cognitive and other human activities, the behaviourism, the formalism, scholasticism, conservatism, and so on. But their conjunction in a non-eclectic system, one endowed with genuine vitality, organic unity and a kind of *feel* of necessity, is something which is probably unique.

10. ORIGINALITY

How *original* is this outlook?

It may even be claimed that the ideas comprising Linguistic Philosophy are not even original. The only thing that is new is that the fallacies contained in them should have been *embraced*; but not that they should be *thought* of.

David Hume contemplated the possibility of embracing them, from roughly the same motives as those which led the linguistic philosophers to do so, and rejected them. Oppressed, as they were, by the counter-commonsensical conclusions of philosophic reasoning (*Treatise*, Book I, Part IV, Section 7) he wondered:

> "Shall we, then, establish it for a general maxim, that no refined or elaborate reasoning is ever to be received? Consider well the consequences of such a principle. By this means you cut off entirely all science and philosophy: you proceed upon one single quality of the imagination, *and by a parity of reasoning must embrace all of them*: and you expressly contradict yourself; since this maxim must be built on the preceding reasoning, which will be allowed to be sufficiently refined and metaphysical." (Italics mine.)

In other words, he rejected the view that philosophy must end in platitude, that it can leave everything as it is; and he did so because he foresaw the Paradox of Passivity, the "parity of reasoning" which would lead one to embrace too much. (He called the origin of ordinary ideas "imagination" rather than language, but that is a detail.) He also foresaw that such an attitude would merely consist in relying on, and incapsulating, one *further* philosophic theory: and thus no true neutrality would be attained. The idea that this might be avoided by Wittgensteinian double-think, by throwing away the ladder, did not occur to him—to his credit.

He well describes the condition which led him to consider the possibility of this solution:

> "Most fortunately it happens, that since reason is incapable of dispelling these clouds, Nature herself suffices . . . I dine, I play a game of backgammon . . . and when . . . I would return to these speculations, they appear so cold, so strained, and ridiculous, that I cannot . . . enter into them any further."

The linguo-philosophic cult of common sense and ordinary language is but an attempt to erect the effects of backgammon into a permanent system. Hume did not want that effect to be permanent: when

> "tired with amusement and company . . . I feel my mind all collected within itself . . . I cannot forbear having a curiosity to be acquainted with the principles of moral good and evil, the nature and foundation of government, and the cause of those several passions and inclinations which actuate and govern me. I am uneasy to think I approve of one object, and disapprove of another: call one thing beautiful, and another deformed; decide concerning truth and falsehood, reason and folly, without knowing upon what principles I proceed. I am concerned for the condition of the learned world, which lies under such a deplorable ignorance in all these particulars."

In other words, he did feel curiosity ("puzzlement" in the modern, question-begging jargon) where Moore did not, and where Wittgenstein tried to convince himself and us that there was no room for it. (No wonder Wittgenstein refused to read Hume on the grounds that he could not bear it.)

Hume in at least two places considers the possibility of Polymorphism, of abandoning the quest on the grounds that no general ideas are possible, that nothing is reducible to anything else and that everything is what it is and not another thing. (Book II, Part I, Section 3, and Book III, Part I, Section 2):

"Besides, we find in the course of nature, that though the effects be many, the principles from which they arise are commonly but few and simple. . . . How much more must this be true with regard to the human mind, which . . . *may justly be thought incapable of containing such a monstrous heap of principles* . . . were each distinct cause adapted . . . by a distinct set of principles!" (Italics mine.)

For "mind" read "language" in the modern jargon. So much for the possibility of there being *countless* kinds of proposition!

And one should add that there is a further difference between Hume's use of backgammon, and the use of language-analysis to cure philosophic perplexity: backgammon works.

11. THE CORRUPTION OF YOUTH

It is sometimes supposed that Linguistic Philosophy corrupts the young. This belief probably arises from the confusion of this movement with Logical Positivism proper.*

On the contrary, one can categorically assure anxious parents, headmasters, etc., that nothing could be further from the truth. Anyone who goes to the centres of teaching of this philosophy expecting epidemics of suicide, licence, nihilism, *actes gratuits*, drug-taking, fast driving as the only escape from a meaningless world whose values are backed by nothing but the custom and accident of language, is due for a big surprise. Nothing of the kind is concluded from the premises. Doctrines such as that there are performative sentences, or that "uses but not sentences refer" (I have a terrible feeling I may have got the phrasing of this latter idea wrong)—to mention two discoveries that were claimed to me to be the most important fruits of the post-war period—do not appear to have such dramatic effects.

On the contrary, at least one linguistic moral philosopher claims to have cured a young man's nihilism by pointing out to him that the logic of the expression "nothing matters" is different from that of "nothing chatters".† Weltschmerz is but

* Though I do not wish to suggest that Logical Positivism proper in fact corrupted anyone.

† Cf. Professor Hare's paper delivered at the Royaumont conference in 1958, published in *La Philosophie Analytique*, Les Editions de Minuit, Paris 1962.

Wortschmerz, it appears. The moral experiences of linguistic philosophers and their pupils are not of that kind. Not that they are devoid of other forms of it:

"I am very partial to ice cream, and a *bombe* is served divided into segments corresponding one to one with the persons at High Table: I am tempted to help myself to two segments and do so, thus succumbing to temptation. . . . But do I lose control of myself? . . . Not a bit of it. We often succumb to temptation with calm and even with finesse." (Professor J. L. Austin, Presidential Address to the Aristotelian Society, 1956, p. 24f.)

The argument is meant to show that succumbing to temptation does not necessarily involve loss of self-control—which, incidentally, it fails to do. (The fact that we give in to temptation in one direction does not imply that we lose self-control in others—that, for instance, we *also* abandon other rules of decorum: thus our maintenance of self-control in those other directions fails to show that we have *not* lost it with regard to the temptation to which we do succumb.)

The high drama of the occasion shows how far Oxford moral philosophy has progressed since the days when it was concerned with replacing books lost in the mail.

So parents may relax. Linguistic Philosophy corrupts no one. What it does do is bore them.

This boredom is the really harmful and dangerous consequence of Linguistic Philosophy. It kills curiosity, it insinuates the view that everything is as it seems,* or as you wish it

---

* The kind of analysis you give depends on the kind of world you believe in. This is particularly true if you think of language as an activity, a game *in* the world. (Especially if the analysis has to be minute, it cannot contradict that picture of the world, but must consist of an account of how the minute thing analysed fits into it.)

Even Mr. G. J. Warnock sees the fact that an "analysis" of a statement is but another version of the ontology to which one is committed—or rather, he is able to see it with regard to other philosophers. Cf. his *Berkeley*, p. 245: "This belief [that Berkeley's analysis had ontological backing] was . . . illusory; [the ontological statements] were in fact disguised assertions of that analysis itself."

The same is of course true, and cannot but be true, of Linguistic Philosophy itself. The difference is that the background ontology is pliable, unsystematic, and absolutises an unspecified set of uncoordinated assumptions of common language.

to seem. It treats ideas, which it calls paradoxes, and wonderment, which it calls perplexity, as pathological, and as an index of muddle. (And let it not be said that it only does so in philosophy but not outside it, for this distinction is based on the formalist confusion.) It attempts to complete the *Entzauberung der Welt*. Philosophy and thought began in wonder: Linguistic Philosophy tries to turn wonder into an index of confusion.

CHAPTER VIII

IMPLICATIONS

I. RELIGION

WHAT IS THE relation of Linguistic Philosophy to religion? The answer is not, as it was in the case of Logical Positivism, a simple one. Logical Positivism was, inevitably, anti-religious. Proceeding from the simple model of two kinds of meaning, there was no room in the realm of meaningful discourse for the transcendental, or mystical, or avowedly unintelligible, or *absolutely* evaluative, prohibitive, etc., assertions which characterise so many religions. For the Logical Positivist proper, religious doctrines had to be ruled out.

Whereas Logical Positivism is necessarily the denial of religion, the matter is quite different with regard to Linguistic Philosophy. The general, semi-initiated public which tends to lump Logical Positivism and Linguistic Philosophy together tends, mistakenly, to attribute the inherent anti-religiosity of the former to the latter. Anyone doing this will be surprised to find religious believers among the linguistic philosophers. Yet there is no contradiction. The first connection is this: Linguistic Philosophy by demolishing reason makes room—not only for faith, but also for Faith. It demolishes reason in philosophy by depriving sustained reasoning not merely of any ontological, but also of all informative, critical and evaluative functions. Its job, it says, is to describe how language works, and not to prescribe, judge, or inform. It may indicate the limits of a kind of discourse, indicate the rules operative within it, indicate the concepts occurring in it and so on—but actually to pass judgments is something extra-philosophical. Still less may it abrogate a whole species of discourse.

This being so—philosophy being but a study of language which "leaves everything as it is"—the stage is set for him who places his religion at an altogether different and more fundamental level. A philosophy so emasculated and harmless can be no danger to it. Religion is safe in the background, for in the foreground an innocuous philosophy "analyses concepts" within the safe convention that *de facto* use alone counts, and that to transcend it, for instance by the setting up of a world-picture which might conflict with the religious one, or with anything else, is philosophically always mistaken. This is not an uncommon attitude. This not merely leaves religion safe in the background, it also relegates to it all the needs which may exist—such as for some kind of unifying or consoling or directing ideas—by implying both that such needs cannot be met by philosophy and that there is nothing in philosophy which could undermine the religion which does meet them.

Given these premises, the validity of religion can in a sense be made to follow. For, after all, the religious use of language is one system of use amongst others, with its own rules, criteria, etc. If "meaning is use", then, most certainly, religious assertions have meaning, for are they not used, do they not have some use or function? The job of the philosopher is to locate and specify what that use is, but not to sit in judgment upon it. The denial of religion, one might go on to say, is merely another example of that fallacy which led past philosophers to deny what existed, and to assert what was false, simply because of preconceived criteria of meaning which failed to notice the actual use of words.*

The argument is in a sense valid, given the premises. One might indeed quibble in connection with the ambiguities of the

---

* The briefest formulation of this position is by Mr. Quinton: "I don't decide whether a man is my co-religionist by seeing how he argues, but by whether I find him kneeling beside me at church." (*The Twentieth Century*, June 1955, p. 519.) *Manners makyth faith*, it appears, *and not convictions*. Other, longer formulations of the position exist, but they boil down to this idea. And indeed, given the activity theory of mind, one can see how Quinton and others have been tempted to give an account of conviction in terms of kneeling, etc., and not of believing (partly, of course, because *believing* itself is turned into a kind of doing). It does not appear to have occurred to Quinton that the inability to tell a man's nominal faith from the way he *argues* is only possible in an age when nominal faith has indeed become nominal.

Of course, Linguistic Philosophy can equally be used to attack religion. It all depends on whether religion is included in the "everything" which is left as it is, or in the "philosophy" that is to be exorcised. If the latter, it can be attacked by the usual methods. There is *no* possible rational choice within Linguistic Philosophy between the two approaches. This illustrates the "magic mirror" theme—one can see just what one pleases.

word "use": it can mean "is employed" or "serves some valid function". The former can hardly be denied to religious discourse, by anyone, whilst the latter is denied by unbelievers. But this distinction is difficult or impossible for the linguistic philosopher to admit. Once drawn—once you allow that over and above *de facto* uses, over and above concrete language-systems, there are criteria of what uses may or may not occur, the whole structure of Linguistic Philosophy crumbles. (Some linguistic philosophers *have* gone through the Whole Circle, have gone this far, without noticing how much this undermines the justification of their normal practice.)

But, though valid within its premises, the argument is disastrous. For it proves the validity not of any one religion, but of all of them, and of all denials of any one of them, and indeed of *any* actually employed system of expressions (and is not the discussion of the relative merits of religion and atheism *also* a "use" of language?). The trouble with Linguistic Philosophy is not, as is often supposed, that it is too restrictive, but on the contrary that it is far too permissive. It issues blank cheques all round. It allows everything that "has a use", except, perhaps, philosophy proper.

The strange conclusion, the omni-tolerance, the all-pervasiveness of truth, is in fact something which Linguistic Philosophy shares, curiously enough, with Hegelianism. There are indeed differences between the two functionalisms—Linguistic Philosophy is fragmentary in approach, naturalistic, fails to integrate its functional interpretations in a whole, concentrates on the linguistic expression—but nevertheless they are fundamentally similar. "Do not ask for the meaning, ask for the use," says Wittgenstein; do not ask for the doctrine, as such, ask for the historic role, Hegelianism in effect claims. But the trouble with ascribing *uses* to all kinds of expression, or historic roles to all participants in historic dramas, is that from the viewpoint of such philosophy it is impossible to evaluate or take sides in conflicts.

So, the linguistic re-interpretation of religious conviction—and of doubt—is a travesty of both. It also makes nonsense of all historical or individual change of ideas or conversion. And this absurdity follows necessarily from the premises of Linguistic Philosophy, and can only be avoided by denying them.

2. POLITICS

The implications of Linguistic Philosophy for politics can be described as either neutralist, or conservative, or irrationalist. The neutralism is admitted and indeed often acclaimed by linguistic philosophers, whilst the irrationalism is indignantly denied.

The neutralism follows from the general conception Linguistic Philosophy has of itself and of thinking in general. Philosophy is the clarification of concepts, the elucidation of meaning: such clarification, such elucidation does not determine the truth or validity of the concepts or propositions analysed. "Philosophy leaves everything as it is." To specify the general rules of the game describable as "political thinking" is not to take sides in it or to make moves within it: to specify the rules of chess is not to play chess.*

Here, as elsewhere, the fallacy committed by the linguistic approach is the notion of an implicitly determinate game of which it can be said either that the rules cannot or need not or should not be changed, or that to change or to specify them is not a move within the game, or that to change them is extra-philosophical or extra-political. (But, of course, political conflicts have for centuries been *about* and not *within* the general conceptual "game".)

The linguo-philosophic approach is absurd, for a variety of reasons.

It presupposes a pristine logical purity in the existing political ideologies, a logical purity that would make them consist exclusively of "first order" valuations and "first order" factual judgments and not theories *about* them. But if they do not have this purity, and indeed they do not, those parts of them which are not logically simple and "first-order" are liable to come into conflict with philosophical analyses, and indeed they generally do.

Linguistic philosophers claim a political and ethical neutrality, and in particular they are anxious to clear themselves of the charge that they advocate or imply irrationalism.† In so

---

* Cf. *Philosophy, Politics and Society*, ed. P. Laslett, Oxford 1956, esp. Mr. Weldon's contribution.

† Cf. for instance Mr. R. Wollheim, "Modern Philosophy and Unreason", *The Political Quarterly*, July–September 1955.

far as they grant themselves a clearance of this accusation simply by deducing their innocence from the thesis of their neutrality, this has already been dealt with; in as far as they have more specific reasons for granting themselves absolution from this particular offence, they employ thoroughly fallacious arguments consisting in a misunderstanding of what irrationalism is and amounts to. *If* irrationalism consisted in some specific set of injunctions, for instance to indulge one's most violent emotions or to commit as many *actes gratuits* as possible, then indeed it would be true that Linguistic Philosophy enjoins nothing of the kind. But irrationalism does not consist of this. It is itself a "second-order" doctrine to the effect that choice between aims or injunctions is arbitrary, and in this sense it is indeed entailed by one of the central themes of Linguistic Philosophy. (But be it noted that this is one of the points on which Linguistic Philosophy is not merely unacceptable but also inherently inconsistent: in as far as it maintains that no criteria outside the actual use of language can be found for that use, it thereby entails irrationalism as defined: but in as far as this doctrine can also be read as maintaining "that all propositions are perfectly in order as they are", it can also be shown to entail a conservatism. Either of the two conclusions can be validly deduced.)

The claim to ethical, political neutrality was made not only by Linguistic Philosophy proper, but also by the philosophies which preceded it, such as Logical Positivism. The claim is equally invalid and for similar reasons. But the actual valuations which in fact seep through from these philosophies, despite their unwillingness to allow that they do, are quite different.

Logical Positivism was a revolutionary doctrine which, by exiling the many socially important kinds of discourse from the region of meaning, undermined many of the traditional ideologies; if it also undermined some revolutionary ones this was less perceptible. Even if it itself indicated no particular direction, by undermining and ridiculing all traditional values through ridiculing their support, it favoured fundamental change, at least conceptually. Later Linguistic Philosophy, on the other hand, is conservative in the values which it in fact insinuates. Again it is not specifically conservative, not given to indicating the needs to conserve this or that in particular, but conservative in a general, unspecific way. It refuses to undermine any accepted habits, but, on the contrary, concentrates on showing that the *reasons underlying criticisms* of accepted habits are in general mistaken.*

By stressing the impossibility of justification, and the fallaciousness of criticism from general premises, it is irrationalistic.

Thus linguistic philosophers have shown that, contrary to what Orwell thought, a cult of *oldspeak* can muzzle thought at least as much as an invented *newspeak*.

3. THE THREE STAGES OF WELTANSCHAUUNG

Linguistic Philosophy has passed through three stages: in the first, it saw itself as the one and only true *weltanschauung*, world-view. In the *Tractatus*, Wittgenstein in effect provides a recipe for how to *see the world rightly*. (Cf Proposition 6.54). Admittedly, this correct vision of the world was strange—and it was ineffable and based on a theory of language. But, indisputably, it *was* a vision of the world, and it even entailed or incorporated, as *weltanschauungen* do, views on ethics, values, aesthetics and the mystical.

The second stage was that of Wittgenstein's later views, the demolition of the theory of the one pre-eminent and fundamental language—with *its* associated "seeing of the world rightly"—and its replacement by the doctrine that there are innumerable kinds of languages, all enmeshed in the practice of living and in the world, each consisting of activities in the world.

This stage had two quite different implications for *weltanschauung*: (1) The view that *all* world-pictures were confusions, by-products of just the kind of fallacy which had led to the seeing-the-world-rightly, the illegitimate generalisation and absolutising of some kind of model of the use of words. The mistaken view of the *Tractatus* was taken as the very paradigm of metaphysics, of philosophical world-views—in fact, *weltanschauungen*, and they would *all* be dissolved by careful attention to how we use words in their various ways: the result being that we should then see the world rightly by seeing it in the unsophisticated, pre-philosophical way. In brief, all world-views were to go, to be cured: this is indeed characteristic of the

---

* For a fuller discussion of specific attempts by linguistic philosophers to deal with politics, see "Contemporary Thought & Politics", *Philosophy*, October 1957.

world-view of Linguistic Philosophy. (2) Another consequence could also be drawn: the world-view activities of men, notably religion, could themselves be seen as one example amongst others of the functioning language-uses, to be noted and accepted like all others.

The fact that both (1) and (2) follow from the second stage, the characteristic linguo-philosophic position, is what gives Linguistic Philosophy its marvellous elasticity. This is a magic mirror which allows everyone to see exactly what he pleases. For procedure (1) is applied to world-views one dislikes, procedure (2) to those one likes. Nothing could be simpler.

For the past few years some linguistic philosophers have reached a third stage, without necessarily abandoning the use of the two procedures of the second stage. The third stage consists not of condemning *weltanschauungen,* nor openly underwriting them, but of claiming that there is a separation between the field of philosophy proper and that of belief or *weltanschauung.** This is of course merely the application of the absurd theses of neutrality and formality to this problem. The picture is this: There is a technical, reasonably rigorous field called philosophy proper, as practised by linguistic philosophers (and earlier ones at their best), and there is a field of beliefs, unaffected by the former and not affecting it. This realm of beliefs is not the professional concern of philosophers.

This theory is really very strange. No one would ever have reached such a position except as a consequence of trying to wriggle out of the difficulties of the earlier stages. The cause of reaching this position is mainly the fact that neither of the programmes implicit in the second stage actually worked: it is neither the case that any world views have been dissolved by attending to how we use words, nor that world views can be legitimated by similar procedures.

This position can claim the achievement, rare even in philosophy, of being *both* false *and* trivial. It is trivial because it is simply the corollary of an arbitrary definition, drawing the line between allegedly technical issues of philosophy proper, and the unprofessional issues of belief. It is false because this distinction is a totally unworkable one. It could only work if it were the case—which, patently, it is not—that world-views did

---

* Prof. J. Wisdom, *Philosophy and Psycho-Analysis,* p. 196; A. Quinton, *The Twentieth Century,* June 1955; G. J. Warnock, *English Philosophy since 1900.*

not already contain ample commitments on the so-called technical issues of philosophy. Also: either the choice between world views is not arbitrary—and then, the application, choice and discussion of the criteria *is* philosophy—or, alternatively, the choice between them is arbitrary, and that itself *is* a world view, known as relativism or subjectivism; and if it is a correct one, then we should like to know it.

Some additional silly doctrines are associated with this. One is the attempt to show * that Linguistic Philosophy is not, after all, and earlier claims notwithstanding, a revolution, but merely a restoration after the excesses of Idealism. The picture is that earlier, pre-hubristic philosophers also soberly discussed technical issues, and that the apparent innovations introduced by linguistic philosophers are but a return to modest sanity. This retrojects the separation of philosophy and belief into the past and thus attempts to give it a certain respectability. Also, if the great revolution is nothing but the restoration of habitual procedures after a period of Idealist or hubristic excesses, then the revolutionaries are not called upon to justify their innovations by successes, which no longer constitute changes in what is the fundamental *status quo* and which thus do not have to prove their worth. This point is very important, for the *revolution* initially made great promises. If however it is but a restoration, such a reckoning is not necessary. . . .

The idea that the revolution is after all a restoration is absurd. In *some* ways it may be true that it has greater affinities with pre-Idealist styles of thought than it has with Idealism. But pre-Idealist styles of thought never separated themselves from issues of belief: such a separation had seldom occurred to anyone, except perhaps to people wishing to use it to avoid persecution by the authorities on belief, and indeed it is absurd. A possible exception to this is the kind of scholasticism which left belief to Revelation. And, indeed, Linguistic Philosophy has affinities with such scholasticism not merely in the triviality, cultivated pedantry and irrelevance of its labours, but also in this feature —the attempt to hand over crucial issues to some other source, which is then allowed to predetermine the conclusions which thought may reach. We smile at scholastics having to reach by reasoning conclusions prescribed by Revelation: but linguistic

* Cf. G. J. Warnock, *English Philosophy since 1900*, and S. Toulmin, in *The Universities Quarterly*. August 1957.

philosophers similarly *have* to reach conclusions predetermined by the Oxford English Dictionary or by common sense. Scholasticism has been secularised, that is all.

The claim that Linguistic Philosophy is a kind of restoration is absurd, because its characteristic feature, the discussion and determination of issues in terms of what we normally say, the treating of past and customary speech habits as authoritative, distinguishes it at least as sharply from past empiricist and any other kind of thought, as it does from Idealism. Idealism was killed by cruder weapons. The claim of Linguistic Philosophy was, after all, the overcoming of *empiricism*.

CHAPTER IX

SOCIOLOGY

I. PHILOSOPHY AND SOCIOLOGY

It is unfortunately not customary to include sketches of the social background and consequences of philosophies in expositions of them. This is deplorable, because their social role is frequently an essential clue to understanding them. People do not think in a vacuum, and even if the content and direction of their thought is in part determined by rational considerations, by where the wind of argument and the force of reasons and evidence drive them, these factors never uniquely determine what people think. By this I mean not that people are incapable of overcoming their emotional, non-rational inclinations (this may or may not be true as well), but that it is in the very nature of thought that its course is not rigidly dictated by some inherent rules. Some evidence may be incontrovertible and inescapable, some inferences cannot be resisted, and in those cases "we can no other". But the choice of problems, the choice of criteria of solutions, of rigour, of permissible evidence, the selection of hunches to be followed up and of those to be ignored, the choice of the "language game" or of the "form of life", if you like—all these matters which make up a *style* of thought or the spirit of the times, are not dictated by an immovable reason, and they are at the very least influenced by the social and institutional milieu of the thinker.

Any sociologist of knowledge, wishing to trace the mechanism of the institutional and social influence on thought, could hardly do better than choose modern philosophy as his field of enquiry. It provides him with an area of thought where the social factors —the tacit choice of criteria of acceptability, for instance— operate, if not in an experimentally ideal state of isolation, at least in greater purity than they generally do in other fields. Philosophy, quite patently and also self-confessedly, is not a kind of thought which stands or falls with factual evidence; nor is it a matter of operating (or ingeniously constructing *within*) a formal calculus with clear and agreed criteria of validity. (I am *not* saying that philosophy is arbitrary.) Philosophy is in large part a matter of explicating—and *choosing*—our concepts, and, incidentally, *of choosing what kinds of explications we find acceptable* (which amounts to: how in general we view the world and ideas, and what kind of role, say passive or active, we are willing to see them play in our life and society. The curious, and logically quite indefensible, insistence on the neutrality of concepts and on the passivity of accounts of concepts, which is such a striking and self-advertised feature of Linguistic Philosophy, is also profoundly revealing.)

The kind of concepts we choose (and the *kind of explication of concepts*) is perhaps more intimately and more directly connected with what we are, and what our institutions and values are, than, say, current chemical theory. Given this, the sociology of philosophy may be a more revealing, as well as a more manageable, field.

For some curious reason, itself not clearly connected with the logic of its ideas, but closely tied to its social background, the syndrome of attitudes describable as Linguistic Philosophy also frequently includes a hostility—verging on contempt—to sociology. This widespread and marked attitude is not based—to put it mildly—on any accurate, close or up-to-date acquaintance with the actual working of social studies.* There are exceptions to this, but they certainly are exceptions.†

It is ironical that this should be so, for a number of reasons. Linguistic Philosophy is itself a pseudo-sociology, just as it is a pseudo-metaphysics. Secondly, some of its insights logically call for sociological enquiry, if indeed they do not imply that sociology should replace philosophy. Thirdly, social factors which affected the nature of Linguistic Philosophy are themselves rather conspicuous.

Just as Linguistic Philosophy contains a metaphysic incapsulated in its rules of procedure—in insisting on minute investigations of the behavioural context of speech—so it also implicitly insinuates a sociology.

Professor Austin and Mr. Warnock have resuscitated the Survival of the Fittest—or, at any rate, of the pretty fit—in con-

---

* See for example Sir Isaiah Berlin's *Historical Inevitability*, London 1954.

† I have in mind Mr. P. Gardiner or Mr. P. Winch, or indeed Mr. A. Quinton's programmatic remarks in *The Nature of Metaphysics*, p. 161.

junction with the theory of the functional adjustment of institutions, both of which ideas they apply to language.* (Why only to language?) Must one really go through all this again? †

Or consider Austin's suggestion, in the same Address, to the effect that it should not be difficult to notice superstitions that are built into the use of words. Professor Austin must have a very strange vision of human history and society. Not only is it rather difficult, but the kind of method he favours—very minute, detailed investigations of the nuances of usage—could never lead to such a discovery. A "superstition" is such in virtue of violating some *standard* of rationality, and of course the minuteness of the enquiry would preclude the formulation of standards.

This kind of sociology, even though overtly formulated, is particularly harmful, like the insinuated kind, because it is only stated *en passant*, taken for granted, presupposed, treated as more or less uncontroversial in the course of seriously discussing only minor points about usage. . . .

In fact, Linguistic Philosophy calls for sociology. If the meaning of terms is their use and context, then those contexts and the activities therein should be investigated seriously—and *without* making the mistaken assumption that we already know enough about the world and about society to identify the actual functioning of our use of words.

2. AN IDEOLOGY

Linguistic Philosophy is an ideology. I use the term "ideology" in a non-pejorative and very general sense. Linguistic Philosophy happens to be *bad* ideology, but that is not a pleonasm.

An ideology manifests itself simultaneously as a set of ideas or

* Presidential Address to the Aristotelian Society, *Proceedings*, 1956, and *English Philosophy since 1900*.

† The argument fails through the inapplicability of the selection argument to small populations and short runs in unstable environments—languages have short lives compared with species—and the illegitimacy of the transitions from survival to fit or from fit to good. A linguistic philosopher once defined Existentialism as systematic misuse of the verb "to be". Linguistic Philosophy is the systematic misuse of the verb "to use"—and this argument hinges on that. Note that linguistic philosophers are perfectly familiar with the defects of natural selection and functional adjustment arguments in their habitual contexts—but when they are formulated in terms of or about *language*, they apparently fail to see their defectiveness.

doctrines, a set of practices, and a more or less closely organised, more or less institutionalised social group. The ideas form a reasonably connected system, related in part by mutual entailment such that if key ideas are understood, the others follow, and in part by weaker relationships of similarity and mutual suggestiveness.

There can be no doubt that ideologies in this sense exist "in the air", as general ways of going about things, suggesting approaches, facilitating interpretation and communication, whilst blocking alternative approaches or interpretations.

So far, in talking of "ideology", I have in effect been defining my use of the term. I now wish to specify some important characteristics which are, I think, often displayed by successful ideologies:

(1) A great plausibility, a powerful *click* at some one or more points which gives it a compulsiveness of a kind.

(2) A great absurdity, a violent intellectual resistance-generating offensiveness at some one or more other points.

The first of these is a kind of bait. An appealing outlook must somehow account for some striking features of our experience which otherwise remain unaccounted for, or are otherwise less well explained. The second feature, though initially repellent, is what binds the group, what singles out the cluster of ideas from the general realm of true ideas. The swallowing of an absurdity is, in the acceptance of an ideology, what a painful *rite de passage* is in joining a tribal group—the act of commitment, the investment of emotional capital which ensures that one does not leave it too easily. The intellectually offensive characteristics may even be objectively valid: it is only essential that, at the beginning, and perhaps in some measure always, they should be difficult to accept.

The plausibilities of Linguistic Philosophy are numerous and striking. It seems to account for the sterility of past philosophy, for how philosophy is possible despite the lack of experimentation, etc., on the part of philosophers. It appears to follow from the obvious, but nevertheless striking and often neglected, insight that there is such a thing as language, that it has rules like any other non-random activity, that words have meanings which must not be violated if one is to talk sense: it explains why common sense is so often right and justifies our daily reliance on it: it unmasks pretentiousness and vacuity, and diagnoses it. It fits in with the general naturalistic, anti-doctrinaire temper of the time.

Its intellectual offensiveness on the other hand resides in its claim that it denies legitimacy to certain questions, doubts, and a certain kind of ignorance, which in our hearts we know full well to be legitimate: we do *not* know whether others see the same colours as we do, whether other people have feelings, whether we are free to choose our aims, whether induction is legitimate, whether morality is truly binding or merely an illusion, etc. Many or all of these doubts and questions, which Linguistic Philosophy characteristically "cures" as misunderstandings of language, are in fact genuine. Their suppression without real conviction is the acceptance of an absurdity which binds the adherent to the movement. (This is also what is liable to produce such anger in him when he encounters a doubter of the movement.)

Of its plausibilities, the most important perhaps is that it is positivist—in the sense of allocating the exploration and understanding of nature and things in general to experimental science (whilst nevertheless reserving other functions for itself). It is doubtful whether ideologies which are not positivist in some sense have much chance of success in the modern world. This is due not so much to the existence of plausible epistemological models showing that only experimental science *can* explore the world—such models have always been available, almost since the beginning of thought, and they have not always been felt to be cogent—as to the conjunction of these models with the overwhelming, manifest success of natural science, contrasted with the unprogressive and woolly squabbling in non-scientific fields such as philosophy or theology. This makes some recognition of the place of science essential to an ideology if it is to appeal to modern man. Pure positivism, in the traditional sense, consists *au fond* of recommending that all thinking should emulate the ways of science, whatever they be, or pack up. This particular way out has certain disadvantages, notably that the ways of science (whatever they be) do not provide answers to some pressing questions, or fail to provide definite or intelligible answers, or provide uncomfortable ones. This being so, modern ideologies must, on the one hand, supplement science, and, on the other, make sure that they do not conflict with it and do not appear to trespass on its domain.

Contemporary theological doctrines, for instance, tend to take care to convey by their very tone and style that they are somehow at an altogether different level from scientific or ordinary thinking: gone are the days when the existence of God, the creation of the world and so on were debated between pro-religious and pro-scientific parties on the assumption that the meaning of the issue was clear but its truth was in dispute. In its own domain, the greater reliability of science is no longer seriously in doubt: the question is now how to delimit what its domain is and discover or establish whether other domains exist; and, if so, to indicate their features and the truths to be found in them. (Modern theologians no longer explain strange Revelations about the ordinary world, but tend to seek strange realms in which those Revelations will be ordinary truths.)

But what is true of the adjustment of theology to the hegemony of science is doubly true of those ideologies which actually emerged in the modern world.

3. SOME COMPARISONS

The striking examples, with which it is illuminating to compare the linguistic tradition in philosophy, are Marxism, psychoanalysis and Existentialism. Of these, the first two claim to be parts of science, but, unlike the big bulk of science, they provide suggestive, all-embracing and immediately striking systems of concepts, implicit guidance and so forth, which fit them, if true, to be orientations for life. The last does not claim to be part of science, but abstains from trespassing on it and contains an implicit explanation of why there is room for Existentialism in a region not open to science. Marxism resembles Linguistic Philosophy in possessing a monolithic theory of error: intellectual delusion will wither away with the State when the class struggle, which is responsible for their emergence, ceases. There are positive affinities in doctrine—the naturalistic view of man, the Third Person view of knowledge *—and in type of ideological device, notably the Two-Tier trick (see above), the custom of explaining away opposition and the associated Revelation complex. There are, of course, far more important and profound differences between the two outlooks, and it is in a way offensive to Marxism to compare the two. Marxism is

* Cf. A. MacIntyre, *Universities and Left Review*, Summer 1958.

about more serious matters and has an incomparably wider appeal, Linguistic Philosophy being of its essence an ivory tower pursuit, which can only make sense in an extremely limited environment.

Psycho-analysis, again, is profoundly possessed by a Revelation complex and the custom of explaining away disagreement in terms of the characteristics of the objector. It, too, has its values camouflaged under the notion of health. It, too, makes a specious claim to neutrality, and pliably insinuates the values of the practitioner. It, too, considers itself primarily a study of pathology, though the insights gained are generalised, and it, too, fails to recognise with sufficient clarity that doctrines and values are presupposed by the very drawing of the line between health and disease. As with Marxism and Linguistic Philosophy, the committing of the Naturalist Fallacy is inherent in it when it is treated as a world-outlook.

The similarities and divergences with Existentialism are of a different kind. Despite the profound divergence in the style and tone of the two movements, there is even a positive similarity in their starting points: both started from the realisation that certain questions are very strange and cannot be answered in ordinary ways. There is even a resemblance in the diagnosis of *why* these questions are strange: because we are inescapably involved in the asking and the matter questioned. To ask a conceptual question is, generally, not to ask something that "the world" can answer, at any rate directly, but is rather to ask something about the manner in which *we* handle things. To ask fundamental religious questions—including sceptical queries *about* religion—is to query the manner in which we look at the world. This is one of the key ideas of Wittgenstein's, just as it is of Kierkegaard's account of the religious quest. There is, of course, a difference: for Wittgenstein it was the man the knower, the conceptualiser, the language-user who was inherently too involved in saying things to be able to say what saying things about the world amounted to; whereas, for Kierkegaard, it was man the agent or the chooser who *was* the act or the choice and could not therefore guarantee it by some ratiocination. But this is a difference in the *application* of a similar idea.

There is a further interesting analogy: both sprang from a reaction to pan-logism. Both were born from a rejection of a view that the appearances of this world are a cloak thrown over an underlying structure, which in turn was conceived as a kind of reified version of a current logical theory. It is true that the logical theory in question was quite different in the two cases: in one case, Hegel's dialectic, in the other, modern mathematical logic. A kind of visual concretisation of the former makes some sense with regard to history and society, whilst an interpretation of the latter makes sense for parts of higher mathematics. Neither lends itself to a generalised application as a model outside its home subject, so to speak—if indeed either should be reified at all. But both have been so applied, and in both cases the *reaction* was a doctrine stressing involvement (as opposed to reliance on the alleged underlying structure) and the essential-ness of idiosyncrasy (as opposed to placing stress on the alleged underlying homogeneity). In this way, Kierkegaard and Wittgenstein resemble each other both in the form of their views and in their manner of reaching them.

But from this point onward the two movements cease to be parallel and become almost diametrically opposed mirror-images of each other. Some later Existentialism, just because the question is so strange, makes a positive cult of the act of answering it, and places no taboo on necessarily strange talk about the nature and conditions of such *engagé* and unbacked "answering", or rather, deciding. Linguistic Philosophy, on the other hand, either rules out the odd questions and their answers, or (and here it gets closest to Existentialism) makes a mystique of their ineffability, or (and here it comes to differ from it and becomes most characteristic of itself) comes to claim that answers are not merely impermissible but actually redundant.

It is almost tempting to explain the difference in terms of temperament: on the one side, because there can never be a validated or objective answer, a great fuss is made of this and the matter treated with the greatest of reverence as central to life; on the other, for the same reason, the matter is discounted as pathological and as doomed to wither away when the nature of its oddity is fully understood.

On the side of Continental philosophy, a greater and greater cult of paradox and obscurity, an appetite which feeds on what it consumes and, as with a galloping illness, hardly allows the imagination to conceive its end: who can outdo Heidegger? On the other side, a patient diagnosis of paradox, and an equation of philosophy with the recovery of platitude, and the realisation that an unsatisfiable lament *is* pointless . . . a trend to an era of increasing platitude, dullness and vacuity. On the fundamental issue of values, the two doctrines, disregarding idiosyncrasies of expression and the associated meta-philosophy, are identical: both, in effect, maintain the subjectivity of value as an inescapable feature of the human situation. But one side maintains that, just because it is a necessary fact, it is most deeply tragic or glorious; the other, for the very same reason, maintains that it must therefore be trivial, no cause for worry, or indeed that it cannot be asserted at all. . . .

Thus Existentialism gives odd answers, or quasi-answers of an odd kind, to odd questions: the linguistic philosopher declines to answer the question because it is odd and because the answer would be odd. Both, as it were, find man in the condemned cell, as imagined by Pascal to convey the human situation: one makes a great fuss because the situation is inescapable, the other, because it is inescapable, tries to convince himself that there is no fuss to be made. (He might say: "There is no contrast to this situation, the possibility of death, so how can a contrast-less characteristic be usefully asserted, let alone be a matter for sorrow?") On the one side, a little too much fuss is being made, perhaps; but the nonchalance on the other side is, indisputably, somewhat affected. . . .

The diagnoses of the oddity of the fundamental question remain similar: the involvement, the impossibility of transcendence, the cult of the irreducible idiosyncrasy of the concrete situation in which the question arises.

Both styles of thought make use of these features to account for the fact that they deal with something not covered by science. In both cases, the essential, inescapable idiosyncrasy of the object investigated accounts for how science and its systematic and generalising procedure are avoided; the involvement accounts for the difficulty of any but oblique expression; whilst the impulse to transcendence and its necessary frustration provide the problem.

4. THE NARODNIKS OF NORTH OXFORD

Linguistic Philosophy differs from the other ideologies mentioned by sometimes affecting a certain modesty. It *can* be preached in a dramatic or messianic style, and it is very easy to interpret it as being of the utmost importance (if all past philosophies are wrong, this is no small matter, especially if one understands *why*, and how to avoid mistakes in the future); and although its protagonists are messianic in the sense of being deeply imbued with the conviction of their own rightness, nevertheless it is extremely modest in one important way—it claims not to interfere with anything. It not merely does not teach anyone how to make shoes, but it also claims to abstain from telling anyone how to live, how to find his soul, how to choose his pictures, how to vote, how or where or whether to worship, whether or which authority to obey, and even how to think or talk! Not only does it claim not to do these things, or very seldom (its prescriptions and prohibitions are only directed at other philosophers, and are meant to interfere only with philosophising, and with nothing else), it is extremely proud of this fact, and its practitioners are liable to begin their works with such emphatic disclaimers of evaluative or prescriptive intent that one feels they protest too much.

Linguistic Philosophy, at long last, provided a philosophic form eminently suitable for gentlemen. Nothing is justified. It is merely explained that justification is redundant, that the need for it is pathological. The philosophy is simultaneously esoteric—it is so refined and subtle in its effects that a prolonged habituation to its practices, and hence leisure, is necessary before one sees the point—and yet its message is that everything remains as it is, and no technicality is required. No vulgar new revelation about the world, no guttersnipe demands for reform, no technical specialisms are encouraged.

It is, at the same time, a kind of vindication of the extravert against the introvert. Those who see the world through the haze of their thoughts or their feelings are shown up as somehow philosophically mistaken: those who concentrate on inner feelings, or on the other hand see things as instances of abstract characteristics, are shown up as people who are under the sway of a misunderstanding of language which leads them to over-rate and over-value what is in fact trivial.

Those who see things bluntly and straightforwardly—in effect, conventionally—with no room for strange or unusual doubts, are vindicated. "Nothing is hidden."

The arguments of Linguistic Philosophy are really a kind of inverted mystical exercise—they quite avowedly bring no new truth and change nothing, they simply confirm us in our faith in what we knew anyway: it is, indeed, a mysticism of philistinism, but a mysticism none the less, for it does not argue, it initiates. It seeks devices for making fully acceptable truths which it really holds not merely beyond doubt, but beyond argument. It concentrates on bringing out why argument is unnecessary and irrelevant. Now there may be truths which deserve such reverent treatment: but Linguistic Philosophy equates philosophy with this kind of reverent illumination of the allegedly indubitable, and suggests that common sense or the rules of current use have such a status.

In its preference for and vindication of the simple unspoilt popular view against the reasoned subtleties of the ratiocinator, Linguistic Philosophy is a kind of Populism. The folk whose simple but sound folk-culture is being defended and preserved against corruption by specious, theoretical philosophy is the folk of North Oxford, roughly.

5. SCIENCE, POWER, IDEAS

There are certain features of Linguistic Philosophy which throw a special light on why it was so very acceptable at the very time and place when and where it became fashionable. It provides a powerful rationale for anyone wishing to have nothing or as little as possible to do with any one or more of the following three things:

(1) Science and technicality.
(2) Power and responsibility.
(3) Ideas.

Linguistic Philosophy showed that all these have nothing to do with philosophy (and when it could not show it, it proved it by convenient re-definition); that philosophy has little connection with the deeper intellectual, emotional or moral preoccupations of men. It implicitly and indeed explicitly ridiculed moral and intellectual inquisitiveness. The world is what it is, our duties are what they are, everything is just what it is. To puzzle about it is a sign of confusion, and the unravelling of these confusions is the task of an entertaining specialised discipline whose only final result, however, is to show that the confusions and the utterances made in the course of grappling with them make no difference to anything whatever. Of course, there are people who explore the universe in the factual sense, and indeed there are moral innovators, but the activities of either of these have nothing to do with philosophy.

It is not difficult to understand why the exclusion of science and technicality, of power and responsibility, and of all ideas should be attractive.

Technicality is naturally repulsive to a professional intelligentsia, trained in an untechnical, literary manner. To switch over late in life is painful, and liable to be embarrassingly humiliating. It is seldom, if ever, fertile.

In addition to this powerful motive, the untechnical manner with which Linguistic Philosophy carries on its business fits in well with a certain tradition which abhors "shop" and despises the specialist. For although Linguistic Philosophy is profoundly esoteric in its ideas, tricks, techniques, at the same time its style of discussion is, in a way, non-technical. Anyone accustomed to a certain conversational tradition, one which avoids both ideas and technicality, but indulges in a kind of conspicuous, light-hearted triviality, can take part in a linguo-philosophical discussion without much training: he will easily recognise its rules. He may not know the history or the hidden currents of the activity, but the rules of the game are very much like those of this conversational tradition. Indeed, it hardly matters if he does not know the rationale of Linguistic Philosophy, for, after all, those who practise it try to disdain and forget it. (By the time the stage of pure research has arrived the doctrines about therapy and so on are almost forgotten.)

The abhorrence of responsibility and power—which makes a philosophy proving that the philosopher cannot have them so attractive—is more intriguing.

In the past, philosophers, particularly those employed by educational systems, were often justifiers, rationalisers of contemporary values. Their job was to encourage the young by giving them the conviction that their aspirations, or the best amongst them, were philosophically or cosmically underwritten. The arguments they employed to give this impression may or may not have been good ones.

Now the situation is, at any rate superficially, reversed. There is a set of philosophers who positively glory in proving by arguments (whose logic is not in general so superior to that employed earlier for the opposite purpose) that philosophy has no guidance whatever to offer (although, inconsistently, they also show, or think they do, that there can be no philosophic reasons for revising our concepts, and hence, incidentally, our values). A future social historian may well speculate whether we have here a class of people already convinced of the unimportance of their thought and endeavour, embracing a philosophy which provides them with a seeming justification of their feeling. Their hostility to ideas—which presumes new and general ideas to be "paradoxes", and all "paradoxes" to be confusions—is perhaps intelligible on similar lines, and also in terms of the particular educational institutions in which Linguistic Philosophy flourishes.

The emphasis and manifest enthusiasm with which philosophers of this school stress the impotence, the formality, the general irrelevance of their own work, is something which one must perhaps leave to the social historian to explain. Perhaps the finding of a philosophical theme rationalising the decline in power of an old ruling class may have something to do with it.

A contemporary novelist who does help me to empathise the linguo-philosophic vision of the world is Angus Wilson. The conspicuous thing about Mr. Wilson's novels is that they *are* about intellectuals and yet are *not* about ideas. Ideas are not much present either in direct or in indirect speech. Compare this with the works of Aldous Huxley which, one should have thought, are about the same world at a different point of time: or, further back, with Bernard Shaw. Of course, the idea-saturated conversations in either Huxley or Shaw are in the first instance expressions of the habitual and possibly idiosyncratic ratiocinations of their authors: nevertheless, they must have some resemblance to what did or could take place, and at least the kind of fittingness which could make them into models.

Any similar preoccupation with ideas and argument is largely lacking amongst Mr. Wilson's characters—and that is *not*, I think, an idiosyncrasy of their author's, but, on the contrary, a valid perception on his part. The sociology of this species of intelligentsia-without-ideas is obscure to me, but as far as I can make out, the explanation must be something like this: we have here a sub-group consisting of people who belong to, or emulate, the upper class in manner; who differentiate themselves from the heartier rest of the upper class by a kind of heightened sensibility and preciousness, *and*, at the same time, from the non-U kind of intelligentsia by a lack of interest in ideas, argument, fundamentals or reform. *Both* of these *differentiae* are essential to such a group, and both are conspicuously present. If this diagnosis is correct, it would explain those striking features of the linguo-philosophic fad—the cult of meticulousness, the dislike of ideas, the preciousness, the insistence on practical irrelevance and so on, the conversion of understatement into a philosophy. Linguistic Philosophy is, quite plainly, the suitable academic expression of such an attitude.

6. INTERNAL ORGANISATION

Many of the sociological reflections so far have concerned themselves with what may be called the external sociology of the movement—the reasons for its acceptability and appeal, and so on. One should also deal with its internal sociology, i.e. the customs and relationships which hold between believers and partial adherents of the movement. Two institutions are of great importance for the understanding of the movement:

(1) The esoteric discussion group, and
(2) The tutorial.

The movement has been characterised by being centred on esoteric discussion groups from its very inception. The world has always been given to understand that the truths and mysteries in possession of the movement are too difficult, too oblique, too volatile in their essence to be communicable in ordinary ways. Their communication on the contrary requires a special atmosphere, a special willingness and a special preparation. It is true that the members of the movement have published, but not soon and not much and not willingly; * and it has always been made clear that a perusal of such publications is wholly insufficient for an understanding of a true significance of the ideas contained in them. More is required and that *more* found its home in small circles of the faithful. The authoritarian, capricious, messianic and exclusive characteristics of Wittgen-

* Cf. Professor Hare's article in *Ratio*, 1959. I am greatly indebted to Professor Hare for letting me see this article in advance of publication.

stein's practice are well known.* The features of the circles which have succeeded it and which mutually dispute the succession to leadership are less well known.

The psychological effects of belief reinforced by participation in a group, each member of which sees all others as fully convinced, are fairly obvious, especially when combined with a disregard for and disinterest in the outside world.† The reflection which this inspires is how like the behaviour of groups of believers may be to what is observed in group therapy. The conclaves of linguistic philosophers have much in common with therapeutic groups and with some religious groups, in that the activity consists largely of confession: not indeed of confession of one's sins, memories or emotions, but the confession of one's *concepts*. But this difference may not be psychologically significant: linguistic philosophers would be the first to point out that the sharp line normally drawn between concepts and emotions is invalid. A further possibly important parallel with the therapeutic groups of psychoanalytic inspiration is that there is an assumption that the leader has access to a theory or insights which have healing powers, without, however, this saving truth being directly or succinctly communicable. It must emerge, intangibly, in the course of the confessions. One imagines that the confusion and complexity of one's concepts is as guilt-inspiring, transference-producing and loyalty-safeguarding as the confession of one's misbehaviours and secret desires. Once indulged over a period of time it probably becomes similarly habit-forming: indeed, there is evidence that it does, and that it constitutes the investment of a kind of emotional capital which makes it difficult to break away. There is evidence that powerful transference on leaders of these groups occurs (the inability to suppose him mistaken, etc.).

Some linguistic philosophers believe that the milieu in which Linguistic Philosophy flourishes constitutes a guarantee against dogmatism and uncritical acceptance; and, conversely, they believe that the practices of Linguistic Philosophy are merely an accentuated form of tradition in education, which constitutes a kind of severe and fair natural selection of ideas and is ruled by repeated criticisms. The argument runs something as follows: the very institutions and their ethos ensure maximum criticism.

* Cf. N. Malcolm, *Ludwig Wittgenstein*, London 1958.
† Cf. R. Hare in *Ratio*, 1959.

For one thing, the cornerstone of the educational process is the tutorial, which consists of a critical activity of the tutor, helping the student to examine carefully his own reasonings and presuppositions by cross-examining him on his work, without explicitly teaching him any doctrine of his own. This teaches the pupil to be severely self-critical, without actually prejudging any substantive issues, and leaves him to decide for himself in due course. This theory is extremely naïve. There are many ways of conveying doctrines apart from explicitly stating them: above all, the doctrine may be built into the criteria which determine what the tutor lets pass and what he questions. When the pupil starts the game of "learning philosophy", he does not know the rules of the new game which he is to be taught. It is not very difficult for the tutor to convey by his practice that the game that is now being played, and which is infinitely superior to previous games, is one called common sense. It would of course have been no harder to insinuate the rules of the game which consisted of speculating about the private habits of the Absolute. The very ease with which either game can be taught, and the fact that in either case it seems proper and obvious once learnt, should make one beware.

The existence and stress on tutorial teaching, whilst thus providing no barrier against tacit indoctrination, may moreover help explain why the views, or alleged lack of views, of Linguistic Philosophy are so acceptable. The tutorial system places the teacher in the embarrassing position of having to tell the student something, and a lack of anything to say is more painfully evident than it is in the more distant relationship of the lecture-room. A doctrine which insists that it is not the teacher's job to impart information, but only to aid in the midwifery of ideas already incapsulated in the pupil (in this case, in his knowledge of how to use language), is plainly a doctrine to be welcomed in such circumstances.

The role of ineffability, oblique communication, dark insights, etc., as a camouflage has already been explored. This cluster of ideas is of course tied up with the notion of *therapy* (cure from confusion, not the provision of statable doctrine). The therapy-cum-ineffability view of philosophy is but a new, and negative, version of the Incapsulation theory of knowledge. Unlike the Socratic technique version of it, this one does not elicit buried truths: *its* midwifery elicits buried confusions, simple compulsive models, etc. On the positive side, it only uncovers platitudes, as indeed it itself insists. The usefulness of an incapsulation doctrine for tutorial teaching is obvious, and this is an additional factor in its appeal.

In general, one can say about incapsulation doctrines (cf. the Socratic or psycho-analytic versions) that they are—and cannot but be—selective in what their midwifery elicits,* and that this selectiveness is systematic, and that the theories or practices are in effect insinuations of the criteria—and implicit doctrines thereof—which they use. Incapsulators are insinuators.

Another institutional factor which is naïvely supposed to be a guarantee of the critical spirit is the large number of philosophers who happen to be congregated in Oxford, plus the fact that on the whole they are not ambitious for extra-Oxonian recognition; they content themselves with criticising each other, and in general it is the limit of their mission to do something acceptable to their colleagues. But in fact this absence of an external court of appeal † may make the strength of local pressures almost irresistible.

7. CONSPICUOUS TRIVIALITY

It is a remarkable characteristic of typical discussions carried on by linguistic philosophers that they combine a firm rejection of technicality with an extreme esotericism. The world is what it seems, and it is to be seen in ordinary concepts—and yet to *see* this requires a philosophic illumination! The exclusiveness which after all is acquired by an esotericism is assured not on the whole by a specialised vocabulary, but by a kind of oddity of approach or manner. This type of attitude is characteristic of the dilettante, the unspecialised man of culture, who wishes to distinguish himself both from the uncultured on the one hand and from the despised "professional" specialist on the other. Linguistic Philosophy as a style of thought and speech is reinforced by this tradition and in turn reinforces it. The motives underlying adherence to that tradition and those responsible for

* There are, of course, great differences in the rationale of how things come to be incapsulated—be it in a metaphysical memory, or an Unconscious, or one's speech dispositions.

† This situation is very well described—and claimed to be a salutary one —by Professor Hare, cf. *Ratio* 1959.

the success of Linguistic Philosophy are similar, and indeed the two flourish in the same places.

The minuteness, pedantry, lack of obvious purpose, in brief, the notorious triviality of those discussions, or many of them, can only be explained in Veblenesque terms. Conspicuous Triviality is a kind of Conspicuous Waste (of time, talent and so forth). Not everyone can afford it; in fact the whole existence and survival of Linguistic Philosophy in terms of its own account of its nature and purposes is unintelligible to anyone of a practical orientation.* If indeed this kind of examination of usage makes an end of traditional philosophic problems, if there are good reasons for supposing this to be so, be those reasons formal or pragmatic, ineffable or articulable, why then let us, on seeing those good reasons, give it up and do something more important. There is no need to protract euthanasia quite so long, still less to turn it into an art for art's sake. This objection, or an attitude based on a semi-explicit awareness of it, is the main problem facing those unfortunate linguistic philosophers condemned to teach their creed in Redbrick universities. Pleasing and natural though its practices may be in Oxford, students reaching a university not without sacrifices in some industrial town do not wish to spend their studies acquiring techniques which only cure a conceptual illness from which they barely suffer, with which they have to be artificially infected so as to give the techniques something to work on; still less if they are told that the techniques may be therapeutically ineffective, and must therefore be adopted for their own sake as a kind of pleasurable exercise. There is indeed something particularly comic about those unfortunate linguistic philosophers who are condemned to spreading the illumination in Redbrick universities. In one such place, a philosopher always spent the first

* Cf. Professor C. Broad's comments on it in *Inquiry* (Oslo University Press), Summer 1958, p. 102: " An influential contemporary school, with many very able adherents in England and the U.S.A., would reduce philosophy to the modest task of attempting to cure the occupational diseases of philosophers. In their writings the word 'Philosopher' is commonly used to denote the holder of some opinion . . . which the writer regards as characteristically fatuous. . . . (I will not speculate) how long an impoverished community, such as contemporary England, will continue to pay the salaries of individuals whose only function, on their own showing, is to treat a disease which they catch from each other and impart to their pupils."

term deliberately teaching old-fashioned, "pathological" philosophy, in order to give his colleague the opportunity of then curing the recently infected students in the approved way. One feels that much time could have been saved all round.

8. PHILOSOPHY AS AN INSTITUTION

It is illuminating to think of Linguistic Philosophy in the context of the problem of the institutionalisation of philosophy. Philosophy, roughly speaking, is the discussion of fundamentals, of the central features and problems of the universe, of life, of man, of thought, of society, of the sciences.

Given such a definition of philosophy, it easily becomes manifest why there are difficulties about institutionalising the subject: difficulties which do not arise institutionalising other kinds of activity. To institutionalise a subject means having a steady stream of teachers and doctrine. The regularity of this supply of philosophy is after all required by the high degree of organisation and stability of advanced educational systems. But the kind of talent or vision required for having something of interest to say about fundamental issues, where no recognised techniques are available, is not something that can be regulated: indeed, it cannot be regulated by definition, for if it could we should have a technique. Nor can the occurrence of fundamental conceptual crises, calling for philosophical reorientation, be predicted or regulated.

Strictly speaking, this problem only arises for societies that do not have an established official creed, or which do not take their nominally established creed seriously. Where there is an officially and/or generally recognised body of truth, the problem does not arise; philosophers in such a society have their job clearly defined. It is the exegesis of the known and recognised truth. This was more or less the situation in the universities when most of the teachers of philosophy were ordained.

But a variety of factors made the continuation of this state of affairs impossible: the widening of the functions and recruitment of the universities, the growing importance of science and technology, the decline both of religion and the importance of classical education (themes from which were incorporated in the established creed).

In this situation Linguistic Philosophy was a god-send. The

ideas of Wittgenstein—or most of them—though surely evolved by him with no such motives in mind, could hardly have been better designed to suit the needs of those who have to teach philosophy and yet wish neither to make fools of themselves by mystically communing with the Absolute, nor to be firebrands undermining all bases of morality and society (still less firebrands condemned to combine their arson with a belated mugging up of mathematics).

The professional teacher of philosophy must be engaged in the exegesis of *something*. Linguistic Philosophy provided him with that something on which he could employ his time and talents: common sense and ordinary language. This was neither disagreeably transcendental or archaic, nor on the other hand embarrassingly revolutionary and destructive. It was tangible, and yet pliable and adaptable to personal taste, and it was at the same time eminently accessible without undue and painful mental strain. It enabled him to perform the exegesis—or midwifery—of a kind of secularised established religion, or rather of a secularised established something-or-other conveniently ambiguous between religion and its absence. But then, compromise is the characteristic of successful established doctrine.

9. A SECULARISED ESTABLISHED RELIGION

As indicated, the convolutions of modern philosophy can be explained in part as the consequences of attempting to institutionalise fundamental thought in a society which has no official creed. Of course, Linguistic Philosophy has flourished most in places which until comparatively recently *did* have an official creed, and whose organisation and ethos still reflects this fact.

As Professor G. Ryle remarks,* "In Bradley's youth most Fellows of colleges were in orders, and a big proportion of the undergraduates came from, and were destined to go to, the vicarage or the manse." In such circumstances, the finding of the doctrine whose exegesis should be the heart of philosophic teaching did not constitute a great difficulty. In fact, it was a suitable mixture of religion and classics.

This mixture became gradually more and more unusable with the various changes, social and intellectual, internal and external to the University, which made their impact towards the

* *The Revolution in Philosophy*, 1956, p. 2.

end of the last and throughout the present century. The admission of Nonconformists and unbelievers, scientists and, finally, members of the lower classes; the admission of students doubtful of religion and ignorant of classics, made the old ingredients inadequate.

The first reaction to the situation included the manufacture of philosophies which were secular surrogates for religion, and were sometimes frankly seen to be such. They were not tied to any historical dogma and were thus not vulnerable to the scientific and historical criticisms to which the religions proper were vulnerable. At the same time, they provided some of what religion was meant to provide—a sense of Unity, a foundation for morals, a solace, and so on. Of these surrogates, Absolute Idealism was the most famous and striking. In substance, it maintained that everything was part of one all-embracing, meaningful unity, and it derived many consoling and inspiring particular truths from this view.

Mr. G. J. Warnock, in many ways a typical linguistic philosopher, has suggested * that this type of doctrine declined because people no longer require religion-surrogates.

But this is absurd. The religion—in a literal sense—which preceded Absolute Idealism was an *Established* Religion. In other words, it was an old, living tradition built into the life of a nation, and particularly connected with the ethos of its ruling class. Its age and involvement had mellowed it: it was held without fanaticism, it was not exclusive and jealous, it was not obsessed with doctrine or consistency, it was used to compromise and to being but one amongst many of the beliefs and preoccupations of its adherents.

Absolute Idealism, on the other hand, was a total and all-embracing vision. It failed, not because people do not require a surrogate for religion (which may or may not be the case), but because it was a surrogate for a kind of total, demanding, radical religion which was not locally known, desired or valued.

Linguistic Philosophy, on the other hand, is an excellent secular substitute for an Established religion. It has its vision— in the background. Its practical implications are a careful but pliable conceptual conservatism, a strong distrust of intellectual innovation, a disregard of general consistency (Polymorphism!). It provides something, the exegesis of which can become the

* *English Philosophy since 1900*, p. 145.

content of teaching: the exegesis of common sense or of the contents of the Oxford English Dictionary, which replaces exegesis of a Creed or of the classics; a respect for a linguistic tradition which replaces respect for a Revealed one.

Its deep and effectively armed predisposition against conceptual innovation is invaluable. Let us consider the characteristics of an Establishment religion:

It is not conspicuously given to criticism or conceptual revision.

It is not conspicuously given to insisting on coherent views of things. It is much given to compromises. Too great an inheritance, too many hostages to fortune, make intellectual rigour impossible.

It is quietly confident—it feels in its bones that it is right, that *right-thinking* is defined in terms of agreement with its ideas. It hence conceives its own intellectual task as the "removal of objections,"* not as the attainment of new truths. It conceives of itself as ferreting out the mistakes of reformist innovations (and not of errors well embedded in the tradition). It should do this in a generally intelligible, non-technical way.

Its strength lies in doing this in a supple, non-fanatical way: not *all* traditions need be right, not *all* innovations wrong.

These features are found reproduced in Linguistic Philosophy.

It is also interesting to note how very similar the exegesis of common sense or usage is to the traditional deference of reason to Faith in scholasticism (only the object of reverence has changed): reason explains and defends common sense or usage, and only very seldom, or never, corrects it. . . .

Philosophy was once inherently ungentlemanly. (Aristocrats such as Descartes or Russell who took to philosophy were an embarrassment for their families.) Philosophy consisted of arguing, of justifying and defending, and moreover defending points and issues intimately connected with a man's vision of himself and the world.

To *justify*, to put in doubt, to make dependent a basic position on cleverness—that is, plainly, *un*gentlemanly. Goethe, a not unsympathetic expert on snobbery as on so many other matters, remarked somewhere that the nobility lies in *being*, not knowing

---

* David Hume comments somewhere on the dogmatics of another age, who treat arguments and refutations as *difficulties*, on the assumption, as the term implies, of the rightness of their own views.

or doing. ("Never explain!") Philosophy has always been the ignoble attempt to root or justify or confirm *being* in *knowing*.

Linguistic Philosophy has put an end to all that. It has shown, or so it believes, that no proofs or justifications are required for those fundamental and intimate convictions and ideas that are central to our vision of ourselves and the world. Bradley defined metaphysics as the finding of bad reasons for what we believe by instinct. Linguistic Philosophy has shown that no reasons are required for what we believe through linguistic habit.

By a stroke of genius, it has invented a philosophy fit for gentlemen and, *at the same time*, found a home for professional philosophy, sore pressed for a field by the recession of faith in the transcendent realm and the conquest by science of the immanent world. Professional philosophy was like a tribe on the march in search of new pastures, having lost the old. It has found, or invented, a realm eminently suited to gentlemanly pursuits and to the provision of a home for an untechnical, yet ethereal and esoteric, profession. And this realm is at the same time inaccessible to science because it is idiosyncratic; it is neither committed to transcendentalism nor yet necessarily hostile to established customary forms of it: it is the realm of the diversified, essentially *sui generis* habits of words—too human to admit of any technique, too formal and (allegedly) neutral to be of vulgar practical relevance or to be classed as subversive, too diversified to allow general ideas. The consequence of ordinary language analysis is to give people who lack or dislike ideas and technical tools or an awareness of real problems something else to do. Who can wonder at the success of so attractive a philosophy? It is well deserved.

10. RIVAL STYLES

As yet, there is not a great deal that can be said with accuracy about the internal segmentation of this secularised Established Religion: partly because the situation has not crystallised adequately, partly for lack of documentary evidence. It was a matter of decades before some of the most obvious facts about Wittgenstein, his practices and entourage could be reported and substantiated from printed evidence; and prior to 1953, every exegesis of his ideas was challenged as a misunderstanding, but, although this is still done, the existence of copies of his works and documentation by his devotees now makes it possible to substantiate one's views; moreover, the aura of infallibility and holiness has begun to fade. Concerning the present situation, however, quotable evidence is still scarce.

Nevertheless, certain trends and polarities are discernible. Of these, the most important is the division between what I shall call the Low Church and the High Church. The former venerate the ideas and distrust the ritual. The latter venerate the ritual and distrust the ideas.

The Low Church venerates primarily Wittgenstein's *doctrines* (generally called "insights", in view of their elusiveness), and treat the rituals which he has introduced (study of usage, etc.) as secondary and as something not to be pursued for its own sake.

The High Church is devoted to the ritual, the idolatry of usage, and indeed claims to have pushed further in the direction of details than he has.* On the other hand it views his ideas with distrust or embarrassment, especially the eschatological promises of a *cure*. Though it invokes the doctrines on occasion, on the whole it treats them as an encumbrance—they are a hostage to fortune, they may be implicitly radical, etc. It clearly prefers the ritual as a case of *l'art pour l'art*, and sometimes does not hesitate to say so. ("Pure research": this is a very U activity for obvious Veblenesque reasons.)

The Low Churchmen are earnest and dedicated, and although one or two of them are found in Oxford, most of them teach in provincial Universities. The High Churchmen tend to be concentrated in Oxford. Some of them display a measure of blandness, preciousness and smoothness which would be a credit to the therapeutic power of Wittgensteinian practices, but for the fact that one feels that the dissolution of intellectual cramps could not in their case have been unduly difficult.

There is evidence of hostility between the two camps.† Thus

* Cf. J. O. Urmson's paper at the Royaumont Conference, 1958, published in *La Philosophie Analytique*, Les Editions Minuit, Paris, 1962. I am greatly indebted to Professor Urmson for letting me have a copy.

† The present writer, having previously published in article form some criticisms of Linguistic Philosophy, has had the entertaining experience of having members of *each* of these two groupings assure him, on separate occasions, that his strictures might have been justified had he restricted them to the *other* camp.

Mr. R. F. Holland, for instance, writes with contempt of the school of pure research, describing it as ". . . lexicographical diligence, a collector's interest (methodical or not) in words, an eye for the nattiest line in usages".* The Low Churchmen are liable to see the High as trivialisers and corrupters of the doctrines.

The High Churchmen, however, are liable to see the Low, elusive though Wittgenstein's doctrinal commitment is, as excessively and perilously committed to general ideas. They see themselves as having progressed beyond Wittgenstein in their *caution.*

This progress consists of the following things: stressing the ritual at the expense of the ideas; shedding the ideas as much as possible, especially checkable ones, such as the promise of therapy; † and a systematic indulgence in the device I have called the Whole Circle, and of watering down generally, minimising the possible area open to criticism. Many of the paradoxical denials by Linguistic Philosophy of views which no one had doubted prior to its emergence, are themselves denied in turn, and all this with an air of discovery.

This style tends to avoid any rash claims of Linguistic Philosophy such as the denial of the possibility of improvements to ordinary language: but it tacitly assumes that the discussion will be carried on in the context of taking the ordinary world for granted. This style is parasitic on more full-blooded Linguistic Philosophy, in a manner resembling the way *it* was on Logical Positivism: it both denies it and presupposes its results. It takes the promise (the cure of the temptation to adopt un-ordinary views) for the deed, *and* disowns the arguments which inspired that promise and the promise itself.

Over and above these general stylistic trends, some particular ones are worthy of note. There is Professor John Wisdom's linguistic Hegelianism and pan-relativism, ready to see some illumination and role in anything whatever and ready to play the game at any level of abstraction or repetition. There is the magnificent practice by Professor G. Ryle of the style that may be called the Aphoristic Extravert, or the O. Henry of

* *The Universities Quarterly,* Nov. 1957, p. 81.

† Though Professor Austin, much though he may have disavowed any general claims, uses the language of "tertiary stage", etc., to characterise philosophic theses proper as pathological.

philosophy: a skilful build-up of puzzlement, resolved with a sudden *volte-face* by a neat phrase which shows that, after all, the plain view was right.* There is, again, the tradition of inspired pedantry, of usage-collecting so careful, so resistant to general ideas (and not unenlivened with wit), so consistently common-sensical that it almost has a kind of perverse poetry of its own, and of which one can say that, like logic, it is never wrong, for it says nothing. The idea that there are no ideas is itself a mildly interesting one.

11. EXISTENCE PRECEDES ESSENCE

The completely irrefutable—in a sense—sub-school which bases its position on the rituals and not on the ideas, calls for some further comment.

Its behaviour is on the whole predictable and can be defined as obedience to the following law: If an idea can be found which will justify the perpetuation of verbal ritualism, and that idea is weaker, less exposed to fortune or argument, than the original ideas which led to interest in words, then that new and weaker idea will be adopted.†

This spirit can be found expressed and epitomised in Professor Austin's *A Plea for Excuses* ‡ and in Mr. G. J. Warnock's *English Philosophy since 1900*, both of which contain attempts at justification of the linguistic procedures. Both are minor masterpieces in the art of Hedging One's Bets, although of course in each case it is quite easy to distinguish the statements which express ideas that are in fact cordially believed, practised and followed up, from qualifications which are introduced primarily in order to protect a flank. Without, however, appealing to this distinction (essential though it is to the understanding of their works), the positions outlined call forth some reflections.

The watering-down of the Wittgensteinian rationale of the practice of looking at how we use words proceeds in various

---

* His British Academy lecture, 1958, is a masterpiece of this *genre*.

† The transformation of the ideologies of sects under the impact of external pressures, not least amongst these being the fruits of success and social acceptance, is excellently explored by Dr. B. Wilson in his study of sects in a small English town; the phenomenon discussed appears to be similar in kind. Cf. B. Wilson's, *Sects and Society*, London 1961.

‡ Presidential Address to the Aristotelian Society, 1956.

directions: for instance, there is the matter of *why* ordinary language is supposed to be so inspired, or, again, of *what* is to be expected from an understanding of it.

With regard to the first issue, there is a shift from the Wittgensteinian idea that ordinary language is always and perfectly in order—because to suppose otherwise would be to adhere to the myth of some absolute language which can sit in judgment on the actual employment of words—to the *apparently* weaker and less exposed idea that ordinary language is only very, very likely to be right in the distinctions it draws, given that it has been tested by time and is presumably adapted to the purposes it serves.

This *seems* weaker and less exposed, but in fact is not. Wittgenstein's idea—though, I think, mistaken—was based on the immensely powerful insight that we cannot say how language fits the world, nor improve its *fit*, because to do so would involve our looking at things as they are prior to being described or specified in language. Once this insight is abandoned, once it is conceded that we *can* look at things and decide whether language fits or does not, the whole position crumbles. Its sole persuasive prop has collapsed. Of course, it is still possible to argue in favour of the validity of usage from its *age*. . . . Yes, it *has* survived. But this, by itself, is neither new nor persuasive nor interesting. Moreover, as shown, this argument does not logically *mix* with the Wittgensteinian one.

Consider the matter of what is *expected* from the thorough observation, description of usage. In Wittgenstein, there was the powerful argument that such an observation *must* "dissolve" any philosophic problem, for what else could? And how could it fail?

The latter-day, watered-down version abandons the claims that observing language *must* have therapeutic effects, that there can be no other kind of philosophic problem. At least nominally, it concedes other possibilities. Again, this seems a less exposed, less vulnerable position. In fact, it is much sillier.

The Wittgensteinian argument was powerful, even if mistaken. It was so powerful that it sustained faith in the imminence, or at least in the coming in the distant future, of the "cures" of philosophic problems which were not conspicuous by their immediate arrival (for the tacitly employed model showed that they *had* to be available).

Once, however, the *"must"* of Wittgenstein's (more or less) tacit argument is abandoned, *nothing* remains. We then need specific reasons why detailed examination of the nuances, vagaries and accidents of daily usage are relevant philosophically, or at all. And what specific evidence have we? Actual cures?

The argument is often put in the form that, when we have cleared up the verbal misunderstandings, we shall be better equipped to proceed with the real problems (if any). This assumes, absurdly, that we can tell, without knowing what the real solutions of the real problems will be, what are the preconditions of their solution. . . . Note, incidentally, that the value of clarity is not at issue: people have always realised that they must be as clear and consistent as they can be (with some exceptions—but those exceptions are more numerous among linguistic philosophers, where, as an obverse and reaction to the cult of clarity, one finds a strand of high valuation of mystical aphorism, etc.). What *is* at issue is the very protracted, very meticulous burrowing in the nuances of usage, to the detriment of interest in argument and ideas. And it is absurd to claim, in advance of knowing what the solution of a problem will look like, that it is necessary to begin with *that*.

It should be added that these protestations of modesty, the proclamations of a less ambitious form of Linguistic Philosophy, should not be taken at their face value. For one thing, the insistence on the thoroughness and minuteness of the preliminary study of usage makes it very, very unlikely that the subsequent stage of doing something else will ever be reached. It is possible that those who so assiduously observe usage will one day declare the pre-history of philosophy to be at an end, and inaugurate a new era. This picture, though indisputably entertaining (especially if one imagines some of the particular linguistic philosophers in the role of such a herald), is not convincing. In franker moments, they confess anyway that they still see the alleged propædeutic to be, really, an exorcism. We have, moreover, Professor Austin's programmatic vision of a new science *—there is not much modesty about that. We also have his contemptuous description of the *alternative* to investigating usage: ". . . our common stock of words embodies all the distinctions men have found worth drawing . . . they surely are likely to be . . . more sound . . . than any you or I are likely to

* *Ifs and Cans*, London 1956.

think up in our armchairs of an afternoon—the most favoured alternative method." What we "think up in an armchair of an afternoon"—so much for the history of human ideas!

One of the characteristic defences of Linguistic Philosophy very recently has been that it, or some of it, is really no different from past philosophy—and hence should not be attacked. This is a strange defence for a movement which began by claiming to be a *revolution*, the discovery—at long last—of the right way to philosophise, and the herald of the euthanasia of old philosophy. . . .

This initial promise of the withering away of philosophy, of the "dissolution" of philosophic puzzlement, was of course an odd and a rash one. It was a promise which would mean, if fulfilled, that the linguistic philosopher had worked himself out of a job, and, if not fulfilled, that he was wrong. . . . So, although one still hears views with which linguistic philosophers disagree treated as pathological, as requiring a cure, one tends to hear little about the euthanasia of philosophy. Of course, this promise is too well on record to be simply forgotten, but one is somehow given to understand that they were just kidding. . . .

Mr. Warnock has one or two additional entertaining ideas in defence of Professor Austin's method. In defence of the practice of minute and protracted investigations into the use of words irrespective of whether either the words or the analyses are relevant to some problem, he points out, rightly in a sense, that individual therapy needs to be backed by research if it is not to be "jumbled, improvised, and *ad hoc*".* Indeed! This discovery was long overdue: the very notion of therapy presupposes some tacit ideas both of how things are and how they should be, and this is precisely why the purely therapeutic, neutral, doctrineless and un-general conception of philosophy is absurd.

But the matter is in no way remedied by having *more* of the same kind of minute investigations also undertaken in regions where there is no problem, and hence no call for "therapy". Therapeutic procedure is not made less "jumbled, improvised and *ad hoc*" by the fact that further jumbled, improvised and *ad hoc* enquiries are made in non-problematic regions. It is ingenious, in a way, of Warnock to invoke one defect—pointless

* *English Philosophy since 1900*, p. 159.

investigations—in aid of another, namely criterion-less therapy.
. . . Unfortunately, *this* kind of aid is of no use.*

One should add that it is curious that, with all their stress on
the fact that language is not used out of concrete contexts and
that the purposes which are served by ways of speaking must be
considered, linguistic philosophers of this brand appear to suppose that one can *give an account* of a use of language quite irrespective of any purposes. . . .

Warnock's re-admission of New Visions into philosophy, a
fine example of the Full Circle ploy, has been noted. One
would have thought that this view would not co-exist easily
with the insistence on the minute studies—which by their very
nature preclude the possibility of vision, and indeed were initially justified as *cures* of vision—but in fact the two views appear
to co-habit happily in the book, a case of betting both ways.
Their symbiosis is facilitated by the Interregnum theory, the
view that it is apposite to be a minute thinker in the periods
between great ideas. That may be so in a general sense—if one
has no important ideas, there is little that one can do about it—
but the kind of filling-in described and favoured by Warnock
is not a neutral and universal stand-by for uninspired thought
waiting for the inspiration: it is, on the contrary, with all its
stress on minuteness, etc., as positive and liberating virtues, itself
the feeble fag-end of one particular vision, Wittgenstein's.

There is one point at which Warnock is right—though his
insight, alas, requires a kind of 180 degrees correction—and
that is when he connects the features (virtues, as he thinks) of

---

* In Wittgensteinianism proper, there is an amusing symbiosis, a logical
circularity, between the therapeutic view of philosophy and the polymorphic
view of language: *if* philosophy is essentially therapeutic, then indeed
attention to the individual cases is essential, and generalities are irrelevant
(for therapy is always of the individual) even if true, and hence one must
see language polymorphically. In the reverse direction: *if* the correct view
of language is polymorphic, then indeed philosophy must be therapeutic,
for in an inherently diversified field, where nothing general can be said, we
can cure but we cannot build theories.

This circle is complete, and one can amuse oneself by demonstrations of
either of the two conclusions— from the other. . . .

Latter-day Wittgensteinians use the conclusions and steps in this circular
argument without even sticking consistently to the circle—they keep a
doctrine-less and non-general philosophy, without either guaranteeing
therapy or maintaining the "countless kinds" view of language. . . . Cf.
English Philosophy since 1900, p. 152.

the philosophy he favours with the recent *professionalisation* of philosophy.* The activities and fruits of this profession are indeed such that mostly "the general public neither finds nor could well be expected to find any sort of interest" (Warnock). Quite so. Warnock proceeds to say that "it is only quite recently that the subject-matter, or rather the tasks, of philosophy have come to be clearly distinguished from those of other disciplines." (This, no doubt, is the great *Revolution in Philosophy*.) Given that this field is alleged to cover the general concepts, modes of reasoning, the formal aspects of our way of life, one is rather surprised to hear that philosophy is of no public interest. As now practised, it certainly isn't—but the explanation is slightly different from what Warnock supposes.†

The real situation is not that advances in technique and a revelational revolution have at last turned philosophers into a profession, but that a *pre-existing* profession, lacking something to do, has found a revelation to justify what it wanted to do. The approximate number, distribution, social role, origin and previous training, etc., of academic philosophers would obviously be much the same whether Wittgensteinian ideas had conquered the philosophic world or not. The situation can best be understood in terms of Parkinson's Law, which operates at the level of whole professions as well as individual institutions: *subjects* are found, and expand to occupy the personnel available for teaching them.

Or alternatively, one can understand the situation in terms of Jean-Paul Sartre's principle, *Existence precedes essence*. Irrespective of whether this is true of things in general, it is clearly true of the philosophic profession, which *exists* well before it defines its own essence. In fact, it frequently *re*-defines its own essence without changing its institutional or personal identity. (A cleric who loses his faith abandons his calling, a philosopher who loses *his* re-defines his subject.)

The emergence of Linguistic Philosophy, this strange love-child of Wittgenstein's messianism and Oxonian complacency, is best understood in the light of this. Transcendental surrogates

---

* *English Philosophy since 1900*, p. 171. See also G. Ryle in *The Revolution in Philosophy*, p. 4.

† Warnock quite rightly notes a parallel between the situation in philosophy and in literary criticism, where something similar has occurred. Cf. *English Philosophy since 1900*, p. 172.

were unsatisfactory, going counter to the empiricist spirit of the age. Logical Positivism was unsatisfactory for a number of reasons: the logical activities it programmatically implies are disagreeable; the nihilistic implications which in fact it has, if taken seriously, are embarrassing (the world seen, in effect, as a reiteration or conglomeration of sensation and feeling).

In this situation, the practices and ideas of Wittgenstein were a godsend. He provided interesting, though mistaken, ideas why philosophers should indulge in the exegesis of the Oxford English Dictionary—why they should say nothing philosophical, but merely describe what we normally say.

His reasons for saying nothing were not themselves empty, though they were elusive, cryptic and "ineffable". The second generation of the movement, "Oxford philosophy" proper, consists essentially in saying nothing at *two* levels instead of one, shedding the ideas which Wittgenstein had—though did not clearly avow—which entailed that one could have nothing to say.

My contention that the linguo-philosophic syndrome of views, definitions, practices and values is so to speak independent * of its rationalisations (though of course supported by them) can be supported by noting the divergence and fluctuation in those rationalisations. The therapeutic doctrine or the euthanasia theory, or the view of (good) philosophy as a kind of permanent night-watchman, on guard against false and confused doctrines without producing any of its own, are not in harmony with the "propædeutic" theory, nor with the midwifery (of a new science of Higher Lexicography) idea. A multiplicity of incompatible justifications, eschatologies,† inaugurations,‡ or regencies § are invoked, whilst the thing justified remains, without corresponding differences.

One should add some comments on the harmfulness of the substance. When philosophers simply carried out exegesis of (literally) Established doctrine, this was right and proper. I have neither the competence nor the impertinence to discuss the

---

* On the subject of the continuity of certain attitudes and ideas I am greatly indebted to a brilliant unpublished essay by Pr >fessor W. B. Gallie, though of course he cannot be held responsible for any of my assertions.

† Cf. John Wisdom, *Philosophy and Psycho-Analysis*, Oxford 1953, p. 197.

‡ Cf. J. L. Austin, *Ifs and Cans*, London 1956, p. 131.

§ Cf. G. Ryle, *The Nature of Metaphysics* (ed. Pears), London 1957, p. 156.

merits of Established theology, but the important thing is that
the whole matter was entirely above board. It is wholly legitimate for a religion to have training seminaries, and it is wholly
reasonable for those seminaries to engage in training and exegesis rather than in the subversion of the views they teach.
Those who wish to doubt or argue about fundamentals can do
it elsewhere: they are not obliged to come to the seminary and
argue according to its rules.

The matter is quite different when a secularised version of
that Established doctrine is taught under the pretence that it is
wholly neutral, and the very paradigm of clear and uncom-
mitted thought. The democratisation of the country, the
Scholarship system, have as their consequence that Oxford is
the main centre for training, and so to speak socialising, talent
drawn from all classes and types of opinion, and especially, of
course, non-technical talent.

Through the dominance of Oxford Linguistic Philosophy,
such men are tacitly indoctrinated by a general atmosphere,
which takes it for granted that the best kind of thought, the
best kind of intellectual procedure, is minute, pedantic, dull,
allows its conclusions to be dictated by "common sense", and so
forth, and, conversely, that ideas are generally products of
carelessness and confusion.

This insinuated and presupposed view does most harm, I
suspect, to the non-specialist majority who merely imbibe it *en
passant*, rather than to the "philosophy specialist" who knows
how to discount it. It is the non-specialist who may half-uncon-
sciously accept the linguo-philosophic view of thought and its
role in life. And, given the present recruitment of undergraduates, the harm done may be on a national scale.

A curious kind of dialectic can be discerned as the underlying
pattern of thought of the last hundred years. The first stage,
when the centre of gravity of thought still lies outside the
universities, is characterised by preoccupation with objective
issues, stimulated by new vistas such as those opened up by
Darwinism. The next stage, coinciding with a "professionalisation" of philosophic thought, is marked by an emergence of
formal and epistemological themes: by concentrating on the
Absolute, or on the sense-datum, social and scientific reality is

somehow relegated to the status of mere "content", whose specific features do not really matter for the most ultimate and important kind of truth. This is the first stage of the emasculation of thought.

But the formal and epistemological tradition is not, alas, without its dangers: it cannot be relied upon to be innocuous. For epistemology can be radical. The clarification of the criteria of knowledge soon leads to positions such as Logical Positivism. These are radical not because they include radical substantive material, but because their formal, epistemological criteria are so severe as to undermine much of what orthodoxy requires.

This provokes a further movement of the dialectic: the whole epistemological, formal, critical orientation is rejected, in the name of the priority, inescapable reality of the objective world. ("There is no private language etc., etc. . . ." Wittgenstein "proved" what the more comfortable dons had always been inclined to believe—and, in Moore's case, assert—though they hardly dared hope that it could ever be *demonstrated*, namely, that the world was much as it seemed to them, and that to suppose anything else, or to indulge in deep or general doubts, was but a sign of confusion and of deviation from the healthy state. . . .)

But—this return to objectivity does not mean a return to those interesting substantive issues within it which originally stimulated thought—the discoveries and insights of natural and social science. *Those* are still kept out of bounds, away from philosophy, in virtue of philosophy's formal, linguistic status. . . . Whilst any critical visions which are suggested by reflections on knowledge and meaning are *also* ruled out in virtue of the priority of the objective world. . . .

So we are left with an effectively censored and trivialised objective world, and a necessarily innocuous philosophy. . . . The two successive shifts, skilfully superimposed and blended, now *guarantee* triviality.

CHAPTER X

CONCLUSION

W HAT ARE THE positive conclusions of this book?

To begin with, the need for explicitness. Whatever may be the limits of meaningful discourse, the first principle of semantics must be: *Whatever can be insinuated can be said.* Ineffabilities, and far worse, the camouflaging of presuppositions and values as procedural rules, will not do. If common sense or ordinary language are claimed to be sensible or true, then the claim must be examined.

There is no justification for equating philosophy with self-defeating thought or with its cure, or for assuming that all general ideas (outside sciences) must be wrong. The theory behind these assumptions is false, and the assumption is not warranted by any practical successes of the policy based on it. This being so, the study of conceptual confusion, the importance of minute distinctions, examination of lexicographical evidence may be indulged in when there are genuine grounds for believing it to be relevant, but, in general, truth is not a matter of the ultimate nuance. It may be so *sometimes.* There is no reason for supposing that it is so always or frequently.

Similarly, there is no reason for avoiding generality in our statements. The complexities and untidiness of actual speech seldom contain clues of importance, and generally deserve to be unified under simpler notions. Where this is *not* so, the exceptions have a better chance of standing out clearly if a general claim is made first. The heaven of the linguistic philosopher, the idiographic study of particular expressions, where conceptual issues are said to arise in isolation from substantive ones, and where the analysis is claimed to be wholly neutral, is an utterly unreal realm, as much so as any transcendentalism of past philosophers.

Conceptual investigations are seldom or never separable from either substantive ones or from evaluation. The model on which the contrary assumption was based is false. A philosophy which systematically tries both to insinuate such a model and to deny and camouflage its existence is a dishonest one, even if the dishonesty was not conscious in the minds of the individual philosophers concerned. In fact, "analyses" almost always plainly do have evaluative implications: only the rigid adherence of linguistic philosophers to the tacit model which implied the contrary made them blind to this.

It is true that the contemporary development of specialised sciences often, though not always, disqualifies non-specialists from interfering in substantive issues. (But when this is so they are debarred from "conceptual" issues equally.) What is illegitimate is the building of a philosophy around this disqualification. There are ample fields where the technicalities are not so developed, and where people with a penchant and ability for thinking can be useful.

Nor is it true that there is a residual realm of common sense or ordinary language where technicalities or considerations brought in from specialist fields are irrelevant. On the contrary, most of the interesting general human problems now arise from the impact of the natural and social sciences on our customary ideas, and rightly so. This is not a case of misapplying specialist notions or languages, but, on the contrary, a legitimate and desirable exploration of the implications of intellectual advances in fields other than the ones in which they first occurred. No Maginot Line may be built around common notions for the protection of one's prejudices, by means of the invention of a comfortable philosophy—comfortable for the practitioner and comfortable in its necessarily conformist and conservative conclusions.

Philosophy is indeed partly a matter of making explicit our concepts—*and*, in so doing, evaluating them. This activity is but very seldom so abstract that substantive considerations are irrelevant. This activity proceeds as most thinking does—by the formulation of general ideas and by checking them by argument or in the light of particular cases. It is neither desirable nor even possible to do it at the latter level only (i.e. particular cases *without* ideas): those who think they are doing so are deceiving themselves. Their second-order concepts, like their values, are not absent, but smuggled in.

One overwhelmingly important factor in the emergence of Linguistic Philosophy was the Argument from Impotence. It ran: what else—other than the study of words and our uses of them—*could* philosophy possibly be?

But fundamental thinking aimed at making explicit our picture of the world, our various modes of knowing and forms of activity, at introducing new vistas and at assessing basic alternatives—such thinking is in fact *not* in peril. There is no need to invent a Higher Lexicography in order to provide employment for thinkers.

What is true is that it is not clear whether such thought can be institutionalised, whether, so to speak, its supply can be regulated: but it *is* clear that it cannot be guaranteed *a priori* to be innocuous, in the way in which Linguistic Philosophy *does*. ("Philosophy leaves everything as it is", it is neutral, etc., etc.) What is also true is that it is *not* worth while institutionalising the exegesis of platitude. And *no* philosophy can, as Linguistic Philosophy tries to do, guarantee its own innocuousness in advance.

Even in the modern world, we cannot all of us be technicians all the time. If fundamental thinking disappears it will only be through some social or political pressure. It will not be because of some alleged limits on possible discourse.

It is of course a comparatively minor matter whether such fundamental thinking is called "philosophy", or whether that term is pre-empted for lexicography, be it "pure" or directed at investigating (usually quite hypothetical) delusions springing from an alleged misunderstanding of some word. Logically and historically, it would however seem preferable to retain the use of the word "philosophy" for basic thought, for the discussion of fundamental and genuine conceptual alternatives, and let those who wish to indulge in impressionistic lexicography find a new name of their own, if they can overcome their aversion for neologisms.

Philosophy is explicitness, generality, orientation and assessment. That which one would insinuate, thereof one must speak.

INDEX

INDEX